Contents at a Glance

Table of Contents

Introduction

· · · · · · · · · ·   ·

tive Analytics is the art and science of using data to make better
ned decisions. Predictive analytics helps you uncover hidden
nd relationships in your data that can help you predict with greater
ce what may happen in the future, and provide you with valuable,
able insights for your organization.

About This Book

Our goal was to make this complex subject as practical as possible, in a way
that appeals to everyone from technological experts to non-technical level
business strategists.

The subject is complex because it is not really just one subject. It is the
combination of at least a few multifaceted fields: data mining, statistics and
mathematics.

Data mining requires an understanding of machine learning and information
retrieval. On top of this, mathematics and statistics must be applied to your
business domain; be it marketing, actuary service, fraud, crime, or banking.

Most of the current materials on predictive analytics are pretty difficult to
read if you don't already have a background in some of the aforementioned
subjects. They are filled with complex mathematical equations and modeling
techniques. Or, they are at a high level with specific use cases but with little
guidance regarding implementation. We tried to include both, while trying to
keep a wide spectrum of readers engaged.

The focus of this book will be developing a roadmap for implementing
predictive analytics within your organization. Its intended audience is the
larger community of business managers, business analysts, data scientists,
and information technology professionals.

Maybe you are a business manager and you have heard the buzz about
predictive analytics . Maybe you've been working with data mining and
you want to add predictive analytics to your skill set. Maybe you know R or
Python, but you're totally new to predictive analytics. If this sounds like you,

then this book will be a good fit. Even if you have no experience analyzing data, but want or need to derive greater value from your organization's data, you can also find something of value in this book.

Foolish Assumptions

Without oversimplifying, we have tried to explain technical concepts in non-technical terms, tackling each topic from the ground up.

Even if you are an experienced practitioner, you should find something new, and at the very least, you will gain validation for what you already know, and guidance for establishing best practices.

We also hope to have contributed a few concepts and ideas for the very first time in a major publication like this. For example we explain how you can apply biologically inspired algorithms to predictive analytics.

We assume that the reader will not be a programmer. The code presented in this book is very brief and easy to follow. Readers of all programming levels will benefit from this book, because it is more about learning the process of predictive analytics rather than learning a programming language.

Icons Used in This Book

The following icons in the margins indicate highlighted material that we thought could be of interest to you. Next, we describe the meaning of each icon that is used in this book.

The tips are ideas we would like you to take note of. This is usually practical advice you can apply for that given topic.

This icon is rarely used in this book. We may have used it only once or twice in the entire book. The intent is to save you time by bringing to your attention some common pitfalls that you are better off avoiding.

We have made sincere efforts to steer away from the technical stuff. But when we had no choice we made sure to let you know. So if you don't care too much about the technical stuff you can easily skip this part and you won't miss much. If the technical stuff is your thing, then you may find these sections fascinating.

This is something we would like you to take a special note of. This is a concept or idea we thought it was important for you know and remember. An example of this would be a best practice we think it is noteworthy.

Beyond the Book

A lot of extra content that is not in this book is available at www.dummies.com. Go online to find the following:

✔ **Online articles covering additional topics at**

www.dummies.com/extras/predictiveanalytics

Here you will find articles about advanced topics in predictive analytics, and an overview about learning data mining with R. We have also included top ten qualities for your data science team.

✔ **The Cheat Sheet for this book is at**

www.dummies.com/cheatsheet/predictiveanalytics

Here you'll find the necessary steps needed to build a predictive analytics model and some cases studies of predictive analytics.

✔ **Updates to this book, if we have any, are also available at**

www.dummies.com/extras/predictiveanalytics

✔ **Find a bonus chapter covering major vendors in the predictive analytics industry on the downloads tab at**

www.dummies.com/go/predictiveanalytics

Where to Go from Here

Let's start making some predictions! You can apply predictive analytics to virtually every business domain. Right now there is explosive growth in predictive analytics' market, and this is just the beginning. The arena is wide open, and the possibilities are endless.

Part I
Getting Started with Predictive Analytics

In this part . . .

- ✔ Exploring predictive analytics
- ✔ Identifying uses
- ✔ Classifying data
- ✔ Presenting information
- ✔ Visit www.dummies.com for great Dummies content online.

Chapter 1

Entering the Arena

*P*redictive analytics is a bright light bulb powered by your data.

You can never have too much insight. The more you see, the better the decisions you make — and you never want to be in the dark. You want to see what lies ahead, preferably before others do. It's like playing the game "Let's Make a Deal" where you have to choose the door with the hidden prize. Which door do you choose? Door 1, Door 2, or Door 3? They all look the same, so it's just your best guess — your choice depends on you and your luck. But what if you had an edge — the ability to see through the keyhole? Predictive analytics can give you that edge.

Exploring Predictive Analytics

What would you do in a world where you know how likely you are to end up marrying your college roommate? Where you can predict what profession will best suit you? Where you can predict the best city and country for you to live in?

In short, imagine a world where you can maximize the potential of every moment of your life. Such a life would be productive, efficient, and powerful. You will (in effect) have superpowers — and a lot more spare time. Well, such a world may seem a little boring to people who like to take uncalculated risks, but not to a profit-generating organization. Organizations spend millions of dollars managing risk. And if there is something out there that helps them manage their risk, optimize their operations, and maximize their profits, you should definitely learn about it. That is the world of predictive analytics.

Mining data

Big data is the new reality. In fact, data is only getting bigger, faster, and richer. It's here to stay and you'd better capitalize on it.

Data is one of your organization's most valuable assets. It's full of hidden value, but you have to dig for it. *Data mining* is the discovery of hidden patterns of data through machine learning — and sophisticated algorithms are the mining tools. *Predictive analytics* is the process of refining that data resource, using business knowledge to extract hidden value from those newly discovered patterns.

Data mining + business knowledge = predictive analytics => value

Today's leading organizations are looking at their data, examining it, and processing it to search for ways to better understand their customer base, improve their operations, outperform their competitors, and better position themselves in the marketplace. They are looking into how they can use that information to increase their market share and sharpen their competitive edge. How can they drive better sales and more effectively targeted marketing campaigns? How can they better serve their customers and meet their needs? What can they do to improve the bottom line?

But these tools are useful in realms beyond business. As one major example, government law enforcement agencies are asking questions related to crime detection and prevention. Is this a person of interest? Is this person about to commit a heinous crime? Will this criminal be a repeat offender? Where will the next crime happen?

Other industries, notably those with financial responsibility, could use a trustworthy glimpse into the future. Companies are trying to know ahead of time whether the transaction they're currently processing is fraudulent, whether an insurance claim is legitimate, whether a credit card purchase is valid, whether a credit applicant is worthy of credit . . . the list goes on.

Governments, companies, and individuals are (variously) looking to spot trends in social movements, detect emerging healthcare issues and disease outbreaks, uncover new fashion trends, or find that perfect lifetime partner.

These — and plenty more — business and research questions are topics you can investigate further to find answers to by mining the available data and building predictive analytics models to guide future decisions.

Data + predictive analytics = light.

Highlighting the model

A *model* is a mathematical representation of an object or a process. We build models to simulate real-world phenomena as a further investigative step, in hopes of understanding more clearly what's really going on. For example, to model our customers' behavior, we seek to mimic how our customers have been navigating through our websites:

- What products did they look at before they made a purchase?
- What pages did they view before making that purchase?
- Did they look at the products' descriptions?
- Did they read users' reviews?
- How many reviews did they read?
- Did they read both positive and negative reviews?
- Did they purchase something else in addition to the product they came looking for?

We collect all that data from past occurrences. We look at those historical transactions between our company and our customers — and try to make consistent sense of them. We examine that data and see whether it holds answers to our questions. Collecting that data — with particular attention to the breadth and depth of the data, its quality level, and its predictive value — helps to form the boundaries that will define our model and its outputs.

This process is not to be confused with just reporting on the data; it's also different from just visualizing that data. Although those steps are vital, they're just the beginning of exploring the data and gaining a usable under-standing of it.

We go a lot deeper when we're talking about developing predictive analytics. In the first place, we need to take a threefold approach:

- Thoroughly understand the business problem we're trying to solve.
- Obtain and prepare the data we want our model to work with.
- Run statistical analysis, data-mining, and machine-learning algorithms on the data.

In the process, we have to look at various *attributes* — data points we think are relevant to our analysis. We'll run several *algorithms,* which are sets of mathematical instructions that get machines to do problem-solving.

We keep running through possible combinations of data and investigate what-if scenarios. Eventually we find our answers, build our model, and prepare to deploy it and reap its benefits.

What does a model look like? Well, in programming terms, a predictive analytics model can be as simple as a few `if . . . then` statements that tell the machine, "If this condition exists, then perform this action."

Here are some simple rule-based trading models:

- If it's past 10:00a.m. ET and the market is up, then buy 100 shares of XYZ stock.
- If my stock is up by 10 percent, then take profits.
- If my portfolio is down by 10 percent, then exit my positions.

Here's a simple rule-based recommender system (for more about recommender systems, see Chapter 2):

- If a person buys a book by this author, then recommend other books by the same author.
- If a person buys a book on this topic, then recommend other books on the same and related topic.
- If a person buys a book on this topic, then recommend books that other customers have purchased when they bought this book.

Adding Business Value

In an increasingly competitive environment, organizations always need ways to become more competitive. Predictive analytics found its way into organizations as one such tool. Using technology in the form of machine-learning algorithms, statistics, and data-mining techniques, organizations can uncover hidden patterns and trends in their data that can aid in operations and strategy and help fulfill critical business needs.

Embedding predictive analytics in operational decisions improves return on investment because organizations spend less time dealing with low-impact, low-risk operational decisions. Employees can focus more of their time on high-impact, high-risk decisions. For instance, most standard insurance claims can be automatically paid out. However, if the predictive model comes across a claim that's unusual (an outlier), or if the claim exhibits the same pattern as a fraudulent claim, the system can flag the claim automatically and send it to the appropriate person to take action.

By using predictive analytics to predict a future event or trend, the company can create a strategy to position itself to take advantage of that insight. If your predictive model is telling you (for example) that the trend in fashion is toward black turtlenecks, you can take appropriate actions to design more black-colored turtlenecks or design more accessories to go with the fashionable item.

Endless opportunities

Organizations around the world are striving to improve, compete, and be lean. They're looking to make their planning process more agile. They're investigating how to manage inventories and optimize the allocations of their human resources to best advantage. They're looking to act on opportunities as they arise in real time.

Predictive analytics can make all those goals more reachable. The domains to which predictive analytics can be applied are unlimited; the arena is wide open and everything is fair game. Let the mining start. Let the analysis begin.

Go to your analytics team and have them mine the data you've accumulated or acquired, with an eye toward finding an advantageous niche market for your product; innovate with data. Ask the team to help you gain confidence in your decision-making and risk management.

Albert Einstein once said, "Know where to find information and how to use it; that is the secret of success." If that's the secret to success, then you will succeed by using predictive analytics: The information is in your data and data mining will find it. The rest of the equation relies on your business knowledge of how to interpret that information — and ultimately use it to create success.

Finding value in data equals success. Therefore we can rewrite our predictive analytics equation as

Data mining + business knowledge = predictive analytics => success

Empowering your organization

Predictive analytics empowers your organization by providing three advantages:

- ✓ Vision
- ✓ Decision
- ✓ Precision

Vision

Predictive analytics will lead you to see what is invisible to others — in particular, useful patterns in your data.

Predictive analytics can provide you with powerful hints to lend direction to the decisions you're about to make in your company's quest to retain customers, attract more customers, and maximize profits. Predictive analytics can go through a lot of past customer data, associate it with other pieces of data, and assemble all the pieces in the right order to solve that puzzle in various ways, including

- Categorizing your customers and speculate about their needs.
- Knowing your customers' wish lists.
- Guessing your customers' next actions.
- Categorizing your customers as loyal, seasonal, or wandering.

Knowing this type of information beforehand shapes your strategic planning and helps optimize resource allocation, increase customer satisfaction, and maximize your profits.

Decision

A well-made predictive analytics model provides analytical results free of emotion and bias. The model uses mathematical functions to derive forward insights from numbers and text that describe past facts and current information. The model provides you with consistent and unbiased insights to support your decisions.

Consider the scenario of a typical application for a credit card: The process takes a few minutes; the bank or agency makes a quick, fact-based decision on whether to extend credit, and is confident in their decision. The speed of that transaction is possible thanks to predictive analytics, which predicted the applicant's creditworthiness.

Precision

Imagine having to read a lot of reports, derive insights from the past facts buried in them, go through rows of Excel spreadsheets to compare results, or extract information from a large array of numbers. You'd need a staff to do these time-consuming tasks. With predictive analytics, you can use automated tools to do the job for you — saving time and resources, reduces human error, and improves precision.

For example, you can focus targeted marketing campaigns by examining the data you have about your customers, their demographics, and their purchases. When you know precisely which customers you should market to, you can zero in on those most likely to buy.

Starting a Predictive Analytic Project

For the moment, let's forget about algorithms and higher math; predictions are used in every aspect of our lives. Consider how many times you have said (or heard people say), "I told you that was going to happen."

If you want to predict a future event with any accuracy, however, you'll need to know the past and understand the current situation. Doing so entails several processes:

- Extract the facts that are currently happening.
- Distinguish present facts from those that just happened.
- Derive possible scenarios that could happen.
- Rank the scenarios according to how likely they are to happen.

Predictive analytics can help you with each of these processes, so that you know as much as you can about what has happened and can make better-informed decisions about the future.

Companies typically create predictive analytics solutions by combining three ingredients:

- Business knowledge
- Data-science team and technology
- The data

Though the proportion of the three ingredients will vary from one business to the next, all are required for a successful predictive analytic solution that yields actionable insights.

Business knowledge

Because any predictive analytics project is started to fulfill a business need, business-specific knowledge and a clear business objective are critical to its success. Ideas for a project can come from anyone within the organization, but it's up to the leadership team to set the business goals and get buy-in from the needed departments across the whole organization.

Be sure the decision-makers in your team are prepared to act. When you present a prototype of your project, it needs an in-house champion — someone who's going to push for its adoption.

The leadership team or domain experts must also set clear *metrics* — ways to quantify and measure the outcome of the project. Appropriate metrics keep the departments involved are clear about what they need to do, how much they need to do, and whether what they're doing is helping the company achieve its business goals.

The *business stakeholders* are those who are most familiar with the domain of the business. They'll have ideas about which correlations — relationships between features — of data work and which don't, which variables are important to the model, and whether you should create new variables — as in derived features or attributes — to improve the model.

Business analysts and other domain experts can analyze and interpret the patterns discovered by the machines, making useful meaning out of the data patterns and deriving actionable insights.

This is an *iterative* (building a model and interpreting its findings) process between business and science. In the course of building a predictive model, you have to try successive versions of the model to improve how it works (which is what data experts mean when they say *iterate the model over its lifecycle*). You might go through a lot of revisions and repetitions before you can prove that your model is bringing real value to the business. Even after the predictive models are deployed, the business must monitor the results, validate the accuracy of the models and improve upon the models as more data is being collected.

Data-science team and technology

The technology used in predictive analytics will include at least some (if not all) of these capabilities:

- Data mining
- Statistics
- Machine-learning algorithms
- Software tools to build the model

The business people need not understand the details of all the technology used or the math involved — but they should have a good handle on the process that model represents, and on how it integrates with the overall infrastructure of your organization. Remember, this is a collaborative process; the data scientists and business people must work closely together to build the model.

By the same token, providing a good general grasp of business knowledge to the data scientists gives them a better chance at creating an accurate predictive model, and helps them deploy the model much more quickly. Once the model is deployed, the business can start evaluating the results right away — and the teams can start working on improving the model. Through testing, the teams will learn together what works and what doesn't.

The combination of business knowledge, data exploration, and technology leads to a successful deployment of the predictive model. So the overall approach is to develop the model through successive versions and make sure the team members have enough knowledge of both the business and the data science that everyone is on the same page.

Some analytical tools — specialized software products — are advanced enough that they require people with scientific backgrounds to use them; others are simple enough that any business person within the organization can use them. Selecting the right tool(s) is also a decision that must be taken very carefully. Every company will have different needs and not any one tool can address all those needs. But one thing is certain; every company will have to use some sort of tool to do predictive analytics.

Selecting the right software product for the job depends on such factors as

- The cost of the product
- The complexity of the business problem
- The complexity of data
- The source(s) of the data
- The velocity of the data (the speed by which the data changes)
- The people within the organization who will use the product

The Data

All else being equal, you'd expect a person who has more experience to be better at doing a job, playing a game, or whatever than someone who has less experience. That same thinking can be applied to an organization. If you imagine an organization as a person, you can view the organization's data as its equivalent of experience. By using that experience, you can make more insightful business decisions and operate with greater efficiency. Such is the process of turning data into business value with predictive analytics.

It's increasingly clear that data is a vital asset for driving the decision-making process quick, realistic answers and insights. Predictive analytics empower business decisions by uncovering opportunities such as emerging trends, markets, or customers before the competition.

Data can also present a few challenges in its raw form. It can be distributed across multiple sources, mix your own data with third-party data, and otherwise make the quality of incoming data too messy to use right away. Thus you should expect your data scientists to spend considerable time exploring your data and preparing it for analysis. This process of *data cleansing* and *data preparation* involves spotting missing values, duplicate records, and outliers, generating derived values, and normalization. (For more about these processes, see Chapters 9 and 15.)

Big data has its own challenging properties that include volume, velocity, and variety: In effect, too much of it comes in too fast, from too many places, in too many different forms. Then the main problem becomes separating the relevant data from the noise surrounding it.

In such a case, your team has to evaluate the state of the data and its type, and choose the most suitable algorithm to run on that data. Such decisions are part of an exploration phase in which the data scientists gain intimate knowledge of your data while they're selecting which attributes have the most predictive power.

Surveying the Marketplace

Big data and predictive analytics are bringing equally big changes to academia, the job market, and virtually every competitive company out there. Everybody will feel the impact. The survivors will treat it as an opportunity.

Responding to big data

Numerous universities offer certificates and master's degrees in predictive analytics or big-data analytics; some of these degree programs have emerged within the past year. This reflects the amazing growth and popularity of this field. The occupation of "data scientist" is now being labeled as one of the sexiest jobs in America by popular job journals and websites.

This demand in job growth is expected to grow; the projection is that job positions will outnumber qualified applicants. Some universities are shifting their program offerings to take advantage of this growth and attract more students. Some offer analytics programs in their business schools; while others provide similar offerings in their science and engineering schools. Like the real-world applications that handle big data and predictive analytics, the discipline that makes use of them spans departments — you can find relevant course offerings in business, mathematics, statistics, and computer science. The result is the same: more attractive and relevant degree programs for today's economy, and more students looking for a growing occupational field.

Working with big data

We read stories every day about how a hot new company is springing up using predictive analytics to solve specific problems — from predicting what you will do at every turn throughout the day to scoring how suitable you are as a boyfriend. Pretty wild. No matter how outrageous the concept, someone seems to be doing it. People and companies do it for a straightforward reason: There is a market for it. There is huge demand for social analytics, people analytics, everything-data analytics.

Statisticians and mathematicians — whose primary task once consisted primarily of sitting at desks and crunching numbers for drug and finance companies — are now in the forefront of a data revolution that promises to predict nearly everything about nearly everyone — including you.

So why are we witnessing this sudden shift in analytics? After all, mathematics, statistics and their derivatives, computer science, machine learning, and data mining have been here for decades. In fact, most of the algorithms in use today to develop predictive models were created decades ago. The answer has to be "data" — lots of it.

We gather and generate huge amounts of data every day. Only recently have we been able to mine this data effectively. Processing power and data storage have increased exponentially while getting faster and cheaper. We've figured out how to use computer hardware to store and process large amounts of data.

The field that comprises computers, software development, programming, and making profitable use of the Internet has opened up an environment where everyone can be creatively involved. Most people on earth are now connected via the World Wide Web, social networking, smartphones, tablets, apps, you name it. We spend countless hours on the Internet daily — and generate data every minute while we're at it. With that much online data, it was only natural that companies would start seeing it as a resource to be mined and refined, seeking patterns in our online behavior and exploiting what they find in hopes to capitalizing on this new opportunity. Amazon (see the accompanying sidebar) is a famous example.

In short, this is only the beginning.

Amazing Growth

Throughout this book, we highlight several case studies that illustrate the successful use of predictive analytics. In this section, we'd like to highlight the crème de la crème of predictive analytics: Amazon.

As one of the largest online stores, Amazon is probably one of the best-known businesses associated with predictive analytics. Amazon analyzes endless streams of customer transactions in the quest to discover hidden purchasing patterns, as well as associations among products, customers, and purchases. If you want to see an effective recommender system in action, you'll find it working away on Amazon. Predictive analytics enabled Amazon to recommend products that are the exact product you always wanted, even that elusive "holy grail," the product you didn't realize you wanted. This is the power of analytics and predictive model: seeing patterns in enormous amounts of data.

To create its recommender system, Amazon uses *collaborative filtering* — an algorithm that looks at information on its users and on its products. By looking at the items currently in a user's shopping cart, as well as at items they've purchased, rated, and liked in the past — and then linking them to what other customers have purchased — Amazon cross-sells customers with those one-line recommendations we're all familiar with, such as

Frequently Bought Together

Customers Who Bought This Item Also Bought

Amazon goes even farther in its use of data: Besides generating more money by cross-selling and making marketing recommendations to its customers, Amazon uses the data to build a relationship with its customers — customized results, customized web pages, and personalized customer service. Data fuels every level of the company's interaction with its customers. And customers respond positively to it; Amazon revenues continue to soar every quarter.

Chapter 2

Predictive Analytics in the Wild

· ·

· ·

*P*redictive analytics sounds like a fancy name, but we use much the same process naturally in our daily decision-making. Sometimes it happens so fast that most of us don't even recognize when we're doing it. We call that process "intuition" or "gut instinct": In essence, it's quickly *analyzing* a situation to *predict* an outcome — and then making a decision.

When a new problem calls for decision-making, natural gut instinct works most like predictive analytics when you've already had some experience in solving a similar problem. Everyone relies on individual experience, and so solves the problem or handles the situation with different degrees of success.

You'd expect the person with the most experience to make the best decisions, on average, over the long run. In fact, that is the most likely outcome for simple problems with relatively few influencing factors. For more complex problems, complex external factors influence the final result.

A hypothetical example is getting to work on time on Friday morning: You wake up in the morning 15 minutes later than you normally do. You predict — using data gathered from experience — that traffic is lighter on Friday morning than during the rest of the week. You know some general factors that influence traffic congestion:

✔ How many commuters are going to work at the same time

✔ Whether popular events (such as baseball games) are scheduled in the area you're driving through

✔ Emerging events like car accidents and bad weather

Of course, you may have considered the unusual events (*outliers*) but disregarded them as part of your normal decision-making. Over the long run, you'll make a better decision about local traffic conditions than a person who just moved to the area. The net effect of that better decision mounts up: Congratulations — you've gained an extra hour of sleep every month.

But such competitive advantages don't last forever. As other commuters realize this pattern, they'll begin to take advantage of it as well — and also sleep in for an extra 15 minutes. Your returns from analyzing the Friday traffic eventually start to diminish if you don't continually *optimize* your get-to-work-on-Fridays *model*.

More complex problems lead, of course, to more complex analysis. Many factors contribute to the final decision, besides (and beyond) what the specific, immediate problem is asking for. A good example is predicting whether a stock will go up or down. At the core of the problem is a simple question: Will the stock go up or down? A simple answer is hard to get because the stock market is so fluid and dynamic. The *influencers* that affect a particular stock price are potentially unlimited in number.

Some influencers are logical; some are illogical. Some can't be predicted with any accuracy. Regardless, Nasim Taleb operates a hedge fund that bets on *black swans* — events that are very unlikely to happen, but when they do happen, the rewards can be tremendous. In his book *Black Swan*, he says that he only has to be right once in a decade. For the most of us, that investment strategy probably wouldn't work; the amount of capital required to start would have to be substantially more than most of us make — because it would diminish while waiting for the major event to happen.

After the market closes, news reporters and analysts will try to explain the move with one reason or another. Was it a *macro event* (say, the whole stock market going up or down) or a smaller, company-specific event (say, the company released some bad news or someone tweeted negatively about its products)? Either way, be careful not to read too much into such factors; they can also be used to explain if the exact opposite result happened. Building an accurate model to predict a stock movement is still very challenging.

Predicting the correct direction of a stock with consistency has a rigid outcome: Either you make money or lose money. But the market is not rigid: What holds true one day may not hold true the very next day. Fortunately, most such *predictive modeling* tasks are not quite as complicated as predicting a stock's move upward or downward on a given trading day. Predictive analytics are more commonly used to find insights into nearly everything from marketing to law enforcement:

- ✔ People's buying patterns
- ✔ Pricing of goods and services

✔ Large-scale future events such as weather patterns

✔ Unusual and suspicious activities

These are just a few (highly publicized) examples of predictive analytics. The potential applications are endless.

Online Marketing and Retail

Companies that have successfully used predictive analytics to improve their sales and marketing include Target Corporation, Amazon, and Netflix. Recent reports by Gartner, IBM, Sloan, and Accenture all suggest that many executives use data and predictive analytics to drive sales.

Recommender systems

You've probably already encountered one of the major outgrowths of predictive analytics: *recommender systems*. These systems try to predict your interests (for example, what you want to buy or watch) and give you recommendations. They do this by matching your preferences with items or other like-minded people, using statistics and machine learning algorithms.

If you're an online cruiser, you often see prompts like these on web pages:

✔ People You May Know . . .

✔ People Who Viewed This Item Also Viewed . . .

✔ People Who Viewed This Item Bought . . .

✔ Recommended Based on Your Browsing History . . .

✔ Customers Who Bought This Item Also Bought . . .

These are examples of recommendation systems that were made mainstream by companies like Amazon, Netflix, and LinkedIn.

Obviously, these systems were not created only for the user's convenience — although that reason is definitely one part of the picture. No, recommender systems were created to maximize company profits. They attempt to personalize shopping on the Internet, with an algorithm serving as the salesperson. They were designed to sell, up-sell, cross-sell, keep you engaged, and keep you coming back. The goal is to turn each personalized shopper into a repeat customer. (The accompanying sidebar, "The personal touch," explores one of the successful techniques.)

The personal touch

One of the authors used to work for a speech-recognition company that made order-handling systems for the top Wall Street firms. Every day the company would have to analyze a huge number of trade messages for accuracy and speed. The company came up with a system that was extremely accurate and fast. Using millions of trade messages, they constantly trained and fine-tuned the speech engine to adapt to each user's unique speech profile. The key concept was the use of text analytics and machine learning to predict what the user (in this case, a trader) was going to do (trade) based on what the user was saying:

- ✔ How the grammar was formed

- ✔ Quantifiable attributes such as the size of the trade

- ✔ Whether the trader was buying or selling

The predictive model, created with an ensemble of machine-learning algorithms, would spot patterns in the user's orders — and assign weights to each word that could potentially come next. Then, after the speech engine parsed each word, the system would start predicting which word would come next. The model worked much like an auto-complete feature, using a recommender system.

The company also made noise-cancelling microphones and headsets to compensate for high-noise environments such as trade shows where the products were demonstrated. We would consistently be a convention favorite; our booths would be packed with attendees waiting to participate in our demos. We started selling the products directly at the booth, and we'd have lines of buyers throughout the day.

We had a lot of fun interacting with customers instead of the normal daily routine in front of the computer, programming or analyzing data. We cross-sold accessories and up-sold more expensive microphones and headsets. But the demos and direct selling at the trade shows taught us important lessons: We were so successful not only because we gave great product demos, but also because we were recommending products of ours that would best suit the customers' needs — based on the information they gave us. We were not only presenters but also salespeople; we were the "live-action" recommender system.

Personalize shopping on the Internet

A software recommender system is like an online salesperson who tries to replicate the personal process we experienced at the trade shows. What's different about a recommender system is that it's data-driven. It makes recommendations in volume, with some subtlety (even stealth), with a dash of unconventional wisdom and without feeling of bias. When a customer buys a product — or shows interest in a product (say, by viewing it), the system recommends a product or service that it considers highly relevant to that customer — automatically. The goal is to generate more sales — sales that wouldn't happen if the recommendation(s) weren't given.

Amazon is a very successful example of implementing a recommender system; their success story highlights its importance. When you browse for an item on the Amazon website, you always find some variation on the theme of related items — "Customers who viewed this also viewed" or "Customers who bought items in your recent history also bought."

This highly effective technique is considered one of Amazon's "killer" features — and a big reason for their huge success as the dominant online marketplace. Amazon brilliantly adapted a successful offline technique practiced by salespeople — and perfected it for the online world.

Amazon popularized recommender systems for e-commerce. Their successful example has made recommender systems so popular and important in e-commerce that other companies are following suit.

Implementing a Recommender System

There are three main approaches to creating a recommender system: collaborative filtering, content-based filtering, and a combination of both called the hybrid approach. The collaborative filtering approach uses the collective actions of the user to achieve the goal of predicting the user's future behavior. The content-based approach attempts to match a particular user's preferences to an item without regard to other users' opinions. There are challenges to both the collaborative and content-based filtering approaches, which the hybrid approach attempts to solve.

Collaborative filtering

Collaborative filtering focuses on user and item characteristics based on the actions of the community. It can group users with similar interests or tastes, using classification algorithms such as *k-nearest neighbor* — k-NN for short (see Chapter 6 for more on k-NN). It can compute the similarity between items or users, using similarity measures such as cosine similarity (discussed in the next section).

The general concept is to find groups of people who like the same things: If person A likes X, then person B will also like X. For example: If Tiffany likes watching *Toy Story*, then her neighbor Victoria will also like watching *Toy Story*.

Collaborative filtering algorithms generally require

- ✔ A community of users to generate data
- ✔ Creating a database of interests for items by users
- ✔ Formulas that can compute the similarity between items or users
- ✔ Algorithms that can match users with similar interests

Collaborative filtering uses two approaches: item-based and user-based.

Item-based collaborative filtering

One of Amazon's recommender systems uses *item-based collaborative filtering* — doling out a huge inventory of products from the company database when a user views a single item on the website.

You know you're looking at an item-based collaborative filtering system (or, often, a content-based system) if it shows you recommendations at your very first item view, even if you haven't created a profile.

Looks like magic, but it's not. Although your profile hasn't been created yet (because you aren't logged in or you don't have any previous browser history on that site) the system takes what amounts to a guess: It bases its recommendation on *the item itself* and *what other customers viewed or bought after (or before) they purchased that item*. So you'll see some onscreen message like

Customers who bought this item also bought . . .

Customers who bought items in your recent history also bought . . .

What other items do customers buy after viewing this item?

In essence, the recommendation is based on how similar the currently viewed item is to other items, based on the actions of the community of users.

Table 2-1 shows a sample matrix of customers and the items they purchased. It will be used as an example of item-based collaborative filtering.

Table 2-1		Item-Based Collaborative Filtering			
Customer	**Item 1**	**Item 2**	**Item 3**	**Item 4**	**Item 5**	**Item 6**
A	X	X	X			
B	X	X				
C			X		X	
D			X	X	X	
E		X	X			
F	X	X		X	X	
G	X		X			
H	X					
I						X

Table 2-2 shows a table of item similarity calculated using the cosine similarity formula. The formula for *cosine similarity* is $(A \cdot B) / (||A|| \; ||B||)$, where A and B are items to compare. To read the table and find out how similar a pair of items are, just locate the cell where the two items intersect. The number will be between 0 and 1. A value of 1 means the items are perfectly similar; 0 means they are not similar.

Table 2-2			Item Similarity			
Item 6	0	0	0	0	0	
Item 5	0.26	0.29	0.52	0.82		0
Item 4	0.32	0.35	0.32		0.82	0
Item 3	0.40	0.45		0.32	0.52	0
Item 2	0.67		0.45	0.35	0.29	0
Item 1		0.67	0.40	0.32	0.26	0
	Item 1	Item 2	Item 3	Item 4	Item 5	Item 6

The system can provide a list of recommendations that are above a certain similarity value or can recommend the top *n* number of items. In this scenario, we can say that any value greater than or equal to 0.40 is similar; the system will recommend those items.

For example, the similarity between item 1 and item 2 is 0.67. The similarity between item 2 and item 1 is the same. Thus the table is a mirror image across the diagonal from lower-left to upper-right. You can also see that item 6 is not similar to any other items because it has a value of 0.

This implementation of an item-based recommendation system is simplified to illustrate how it works. For simplicity, we only use one criterion to determine item similarity: whether the user purchased the item. More complex systems could go into greater detail by

- Using profiles created by users that represent their tastes

- Factoring in how much a user likes (or highly rates) an item

- Weighing how many items the user purchased that are similar to the potential recommended item(s)

- Making assumptions about whether a user likes an item on the basis of whether the user has simply viewed the item, even though no purchase was made

Here are two common ways you could use this recommender system:

- **Offline** via an e-mail marketing campaign or if the user is on the website while logged in.

  The system could send marketing ads or make these recommendations on the website:

  - **Item 3 to Customer B**

    Recommended because Customer B purchased Items 1 and 2, and both items are similar to Item 3.

  - **Item 4, then Item 2, to Customer C**

    Recommended because Customer C purchased Items 3 and 5. Item 5 is similar to Item 4 (similarity value: 0.82). Item 2 is similar to Item 3 (similarity value: 0.45).

  - **Item 2 to Customer D**

    Recommended because Customer D purchased Items 3, 4, and 5. Item 3 is similar to Item 2.

- **Item 1 to Customer E**

  Recommended because Customer E purchased Items 2 and 3, both of which are similar to Item 1.

- **Item 3 to Customer F**

  Recommended because Customer F purchased Items 1, 2, 4, and 5. Items 1, 2, and 5 are similar to Item 3.

- **Item 2 to Customer G**

  Recommended because Customer G purchased Items 1 and 3. They are both similar to Item 2.

- **Item 2, then Item 3, to Customer H**

  Recommended because Customer H purchased Item 1. Item 1 is similar to Items 2 and 3.

- **Undetermined item to Customer A**

  Ideally, you should have a lot more items and users. And there should be some items that a customer has purchased that are similar to other items that he or she has not yet purchased.

- **Undetermined item to Customer I**

  In this case, the data is insufficient to serve as the basis of a recommendation. This is an example of the cold-start problem (more about this problem later in this chapter).

✔ **Online** via a page view while the user is not logged in.

Order matters — the recommendations must start from highest similarity.

The system would recommend similar items if the user is viewing one of its items:

- If Item 1 is being viewed, the system recommends Items 2 and 3.

- If Item 2 is being viewed, the system recommends Items 1 and 3.

- If Item 3 is being viewed, the system recommends Items 5, 2, and 1.

- If Item 4 is being viewed, the system recommends Items 5.

- If Item 5 is being viewed, the system recommends Items 4 and 3.

- If Item 6 is being viewed, there is insufficient data to make a recommendation. This is an example of the cold-start problem (as described later in this chapter).

Whether the user is logged in will affect the recommendation that the system makes. After all, you want to avoid recommending an item that the customer has already purchased. If the user is logged in, the system will use the profile that the user created (or it created for the user). Within that profile, the system will have a record of previous purchases; it removes already-purchased items from the recommendation list.

In the example, Customer H only purchased a single item (Item 1). However, the item she purchased was similar to other items that show up in data from other customer purchases.

A customer viewing Item 6 is an example of the cold-start problem: Item 6 hasn't been purchased by enough people yet, perhaps because it's new or not very popular. Either way, the system doesn't have enough to go on. Collaborative filtering takes a little training with data before it can be effective.

Initially, of course, these data tables will be sparse until enough data points come in. As more data points are included in the collaborative filtering algorithm, the recommender system becomes more accurate.

User-based collaborative filtering

With a user-based approach to collaborative filtering, the system can calculate similarity between pairs of users by using the cosine similarity formula, a technique much like the item-based approach. Usually such calculations take longer to do, and may need to be computed more often, than those used in the item-based approach. That's because

- You'd have a lot more users than items (ideally anyway).
- You'd expect items to change less frequently than users.
- With more users and less change in the items offered, you can use many more attributes than just purchase history when calculating user similarity.

A user-based system can also use machine-learning algorithms to group all users who have shown that they have the same tastes. The system builds neighborhoods of users who have similar profiles, purchase patterns, or rating patterns. If a person in a neighborhood buys and likes an item, the recommender system can recommend that item to everyone else in the neighborhood.

As with item-based collaborative filtering, the user-based approach requires sufficient data on each user to be effective. Before the system can make recommendations, it must create a user profile — so it also requires that the user create an account and be logged in (or store session information in the browser via cookies) while viewing a website. Initially the system can ask the user explicitly to create a profile, flesh out the profile by asking questions, and then optimize its suggestions after the user's purchase data has accumulated.

Netflix is an example of quickly building a profile for each customer. Here's the general procedure:

1. Netflix invites its customers to set up queues of the movies they'd like to watch.

2. The chosen movies are analyzed to learn about the customer's tastes in movies.

3. The predictive model recommends more movies for the customer to watch, based on the movies already in the queue.

Netflix has discovered that the more movies you have in your queue, the more likely you are to stay a customer.

Table 2-3 — a sample matrix of customers and their purchased items — is an example of user-based collaborative filtering. For simplicity, we will use a rule that a user neighborhood is created from users who bought at least two things in common.

Table 2-3		User-Based Collaborative Filtering				
Customer	*Item 1*	*Item 2*	*Item 3*	*Item 4*	*Item 5*	*Item 6*
A - N1	X	X	X			
B - N1	X	X				
C - N2			X		X	
D - N2			X	X	X	
E - N1		X	X			
F - N1	X	X		X	X	
G - N1	X		X			
H - N3	X					
I - N3						X

There are three user neighborhoods formed: N1, N2, and N3. Every user in neighborhoods N1 and N2 has purchased at least 2 items in common with someone else in the same neighborhood. N3 are users that have not yet met the criteria and will not receive recommendations until they purchase other items to meet the criteria.

Here's an example of how you could use this recommender system:

Offline via an e-mail marketing campaign or if the user is on the website while logged in. The system could send marketing ads or make recommendations on the website as follows:

- ✔ **Item 3 to Customer B**
- ✔ **Item 4 to Customer C**
- ✔ **Item 1 to Customer E**
- ✔ **Item 3 to Customer F**
- ✔ **Item 2 to Customer G**
- ✔ **Undetermined item to Customers A and D**

 Ideally you should have a lot more items than six. And there should always be some items in a customer's neighborhood that the customer hasn't purchased yet.

- ✔ **Undetermined item to Customers H and I**

    In this case, there is insufficient data to serve as the basis of a recommendation.

Initially, this system can recommend all items that other members of the group already have that each individual member doesn't have. In this simple example, the recommendations are similar to those produced by the item-based collaborative filter approach. You should expect the recommendations to diverge between approaches as more users, items, and data points come in.

 One very important difference is that since each customer belongs to a group, any future purchases that a member makes will be recommended to the other members of the group until the filter is retrained. So customer A and D will start getting recommendations very quickly since they already belong to a neighborhood and surely the other neighbors will buy something soon.

For example: if Customer B buys Item 6, then the recommender system will recommend item 6 to everyone in N1 (Customer A, B, E, F and G).

Customer F can potentially belong to either neighborhood N1 or N2 depending how the collaborative filtering algorithm is implemented. We have chosen to group Customer F with neighborhood N1 because the user is most similar to Customer B (which belongs to N1) using cosine similarity measure. Either way, Item 3 will be recommended under this scenario.

Customers H and I provide examples of the *cold-start problem:* The customer just hasn't generated enough data to be grouped into a user neighborhood. In the absence of a user profile, a new customer with very little or no purchase history — or who only buys obscure items — will always pose the cold-start problem to the system, regardless of which collaborative filtering approach is in use.

Customer I illustrates an aspect of the cold-start problem that's unique to the user-based approach. The item-based approach would start finding other items similar to the item that the customer bought; then, if other users start purchasing Item 6, the system can start making recommendations. No further purchases need be made by the user; the item-based approach can start recommending. In a user-based system, however, Customer I has to make additional purchases in order to belong to a neighborhood of users; the system can't make any recommendations yet.

Okay, there's an assumption at work in these simple examples — namely, that the customer not only purchased the item but liked it enough to make similar purchases. What if the customer didn't like the item? The system needs, at very least, to produce better precision in its recommendations. You can add a criterion to the recommender system to group people who gave similar ratings to the items they purchased. If the system finds customers who like and dislike the same items, then the assumption of high precision is valid. In other words, there is a high probability that the customers share the same tastes.

User-based versus item-based collaborative filtering

In general, item-based collaborative filtering for large-scale e-commerce systems is faster and more scalable. Finding similar users, however — especially users with lots of features — takes longer than finding similar items.

Building user neighborhoods may be too time-consuming for large datasets, and may not be appropriate for large e-commerce sites that depend on real-time recommendations.

The user-based system also suffers more acutely than the item-based system from two other challenges: the cold-start problem (mentioned earlier) and *sparsity* — essentially the fact that even the most prolific customers can't be expected to purchase even a fraction of a percent of the whole product catalog. So building user neighborhoods based on limited purchase histories may not produce very accurate recommendations.

The user-based approach also comes with a key restriction: Each user has to be logged in (or have a profile in his or her browser history) for user-based filtering to work. Before the system can make a recommendation, it has to know something about the prospective customer.

Content-based filtering

Content-based recommender systems mostly match *features* (tagged keywords) among similar items and the user's profile to make recommendations. When a user purchases an item that has tagged features, items with features that match those of the original item will be recommended. The more features match, the higher the probability the user will like the recommendation. This degree of probability is called *precision*.

Content-based filtering uses various techniques to match the attributes of a particular item with a user's profile. These techniques include machine-learning algorithms to determine a user's profile without having to ask. This technique is called *implicit data gathering*. A more direct approach is to use *explicit data gathering:* Use a questionnaire to ask the users what features they like in an item. An example of that would be asking what genre of movie or which actresses they like when they first sign up for a movie subscription.

Tagging to describe items

In general, the company doing the selling (or the manufacturer) usually tags its items with keywords. In the Amazon website, however, it's fairly typical never to see the tags for any items purchased or viewed — and not even to be asked to tag an item. Customers can review the items they've purchased, but that's not the same as tagging.

Tagging items can pose a scale challenge for a store like Amazon that has so many items. Additionally, some attributes can be subjective and may be incorrectly tagged, depending on who tags it. One solution that solves the scaling issue is to allow customers or the general public to tag the items. (Photos are a good example of user-based tagging.) To keep tags manageable and accurate, an acceptable set of tags may be provided by the website. Only when an appropriate number of users agree (that is, use the same tag to describe an item), will the agreed-upon tag be used to describe the item.

User-based tagging, however, turns up other problems for a content-based filtering system (and collaborative filtering):

- ✔ **Credibility:** Not all customers tell the truth (especially online), and users who have only a small rating history can skew the data. In addition, some vendors may give (or encourage others to give) positive ratings to their own products while giving negative ratings to their competitors' products.

- ✔ **Sparsity:** Not all items will be rated or will have enough ratings to produce useful data.

- ✔ **Inconsistency:** Not all users use the same keywords to tag an item, even though the meaning may be the same. Additionally, some attributes can be subjective. For example, one viewer of a movie may consider it short while another says it's too long.

Attributes need clear definitions. An attribute with too few boundaries is hard to evaluate; imposing too many rules on an attribute may be asking users to do too much work, which will discourage them from tagging items.

Attributes with vague or undefined boundaries can result from offering the user free-form input fields on e-commerce shopping forms. If you restrict the user to selecting tag values from a set range of possible inputs, the resulting data is easier to analyze; you won't have to cleanse "dirty data" of irrelevant content. Of course, many existing systems were built without analytics in mind, so cleansing the data is a large part of data preparation. You can save some of that cleansing time by building predictive analytic solutions into your system. One way to do so is to carefully consider and define the allowable inputs when you're (re)building your e-commerce site.

Tagging most items in a product catalog can help solve the cold-start problem that plagues collaborative filtering. For a while, however, the precision of the system's recommendations will be low until it creates or obtains a user profile.

Table 2-4, a sample matrix of customers and their purchased items, shows an example of content-based filtering.

Table 2-4	Content-Based Filtering				
Items	*Feature 1*	*Feature 2*	*Feature 3*	*Feature 4*	*Feature 5*
Item 1	X	X			
Item 2		X	X		
Item 3	X		X	X	
Item 4		X		X	X
Item 5	X		X		X

Here, if a user likes Feature 2 — and that's recorded in her profile — the system will recommend all items that have Feature 2 in them: Item 1, Item 2, and Item 4.

This approach works even if the user has never purchased or reviewed an item. The system will just look in the product database for any item that has been tagged with Feature 2. If (for example) a user who's looking for movies with Audrey Hepburn — and that preference shows up in the user's profile — the system will recommend all the movies that feature Audrey Hepburn to this user.

This example, however, quickly exposes a limitation of the content-based filtering technique: The user probably already knows about all the movies that Audrey Hepburn has been in, or can easily find out — so, from that user's point of view, the system hasn't recommended anything new or of value. In this case, the system should recommend something relevant that the user wouldn't have thought of. In the absence of telepathy, what's needed is greater precision.

Improving precision with constant feedback

One way to improve the precision of the system's recommendations is to ask customers for feedback whenever possible. Collecting customer feedback can be done in many different ways, through multiple channels. Some companies ask the customer to rate an item or service after purchase. Other systems provide social-media-style links so customers can "like" or "dislike" a product. Constant interaction between customers and companies may make the customer feel more fully engaged.

For instance, Netflix asks its customers to rate movies they've watched so that the company can use that data to train their systems (models) to make more precise movie recommendations. Amazon sends you an e-mail asking you to rate items you've purchased after you've had enough time to evaluate the product and the buying experience.

Such data points constantly improve the recommendation models — and they're possible because Amazon and Netflix make a point of convincing customers that their feedback benefits all customers. Such continuous interaction with customers to collect feedback not only increases the precision of the system's recommendations, it can also make customers happier, reduce churn (subscription cancellation), and generate repeat business. This is a type of cycle that results in more product sales that generate more revenue for the company.

Measuring the effectiveness of system recommendations

The success of a system's recommendations depends on how well it meets two criteria: *precision* (think of it as a set of perfect matches — usually a small set) and *recall* (think of it as a set of possible matches — usually a larger set). Here's a closer look:

- ✔ **Precision** measures how accurate the system's recommendation was. Precision is difficult to measure because it can be subjective and hard to quantify. For instance, when a user first visits the Amazon site, can Amazon know for sure whether its recommendations are on target? Some recommendations may connect with the customer's interests but the customer may still not buy. The highest confidence that a recommendation is precise comes from clear evidence: The customer buys the item. Alternatively, the system can explicitly ask the user to rate its recommendations.

- ✔ **Recall** measures the set of possible good recommendations your system comes up with. Think of recall as an inventory of possible recommendations, but not all of them are perfect recommendations. There is generally an inverse relationship to precision and recall. That is, as recall goes up, precision goes down, and vice versa. You can't expect to have a large inventory of items that a customer *will* buy. You may expect to have a large inventory of items that a customer *might* consider buying. But a large inventory is only half the battle; see the cautionary sidebar, "Precision versus recall."

The ideal system would have both high precision and high recall. But realistically, the best outcome is to strike a delicate balance between the two. Emphasizing precision or recall really depends on the problem you're trying to solve.

One major problem with content-based recommender systems is that it's easy to give them too narrow a focus. They make recommendations based on past purchases, likes, and dislikes. They may fall short for customers who are looking to try new things and experiences. Those customers want to hear about something totally different from what they've already bought or seen. People can be unpredictable that way.

Precision versus recall

The relationship between precision and recall is best described through an example: A recommendation system generally recommends a list of several items (the top *n*), not just one or two. Let's assume that the recommendation list only contains two precise recommendations. So the system can recommend those two items and it will have perfect precision. However, what if you need to show recommendations for an e-mail campaign that has 10 slots? You must include 8 other possible recommendations that are not perfectly precise. Those additional 8 recommendations bring down the precision. In contrast, recall has gone up because the system determined that there were 20 possible recommendations, of which the system initially only showed the top two. Recall has gone up from 2/20 to 10/20.

Having a large inventory of recommendations seems an advantage, but what if they keep failing to stimulate a sale? Well, one problem

is the customers' reaction if they perceive the system's recommendations as poor: They lose interest and go elsewhere. Thus offering everything and anything just to fish for possible sales can cause more damage than good: Repeated off-target recommendations can irritate customers; future attempts to market to those customers may end up in the spam folder.

Take, for example, a job-listing site that sends a customer even one advertisement for a job that is completely inappropriate for the customer — say, advertising an opening in heavy construction to a person whose experience and expertise are in running a florist's shop. The customer will probably consider the recommendation poor, even crazy. If the company doesn't boost the precision of its recommendation algorithm, there goes the job seeker to a competing job-listing site.

Hybrid recommender systems

The best implementation may be a *hybrid* approach to creating a recommender system. By combining content-based and collaborative filtering into a single approach, the system can try to overcome each one's shortcomings.

A major problem with the content-based approach is its accuracy and narrow focus. The recommendations may not be very interesting or unique. Many of the recommendations may have already been known to the user, so the system isn't providing anything new from the user's perspective. However, the implementation is much simpler than that of collaborative filtering. The content-based approach requires only that a profile be created for the items (keyword tagging). The user's profile can be implicitly or explicitly created. This system can start working right away.

A major problem with collaborative filtering is that it suffers from the cold-start problem. Many users who are just starting out won't receive accurate recommendations — or any recommendations at all — until enough data is gathered from the community of users. The data collection will require time to complete — and that collection depends on how active the website is. It may also require users to create accounts in their systems (in order to create a profile) before they can start receiving recommendations.

A hybrid recommender system can try to solve both these problems. It can start by using the content-based approach to avoid the cold-start problem. Once enough data is collected from the community of users, the system can then use the collaborative filtering approach to produce more interesting and personalized recommendations.

Target Marketing

Predictive analytics make your marketing campaigns more customer-oriented. The idea is to customize your advertisements to target a segment of your total customer base — not the whole. If you send only the ads that are relevant to a segment of customers, you increase the likelihood that those particular visitors will perform the action that you hope for — buying. If you can determine which segment of your customer base will respond best to your message, you save money on the cost of convincing a customer to make the purchase (acquisition costs) and improve overall efficiency.

For example, when you pay an online ad network — for example, Google AdWords — to display your ads, typically you pay for each click that sends traffic to your website through a sponsored ad that appears in response to a search. Getting the visitor ultimately to do what you hope she'll do while she's on your website — become a paying customer — should be part of your marketing strategy. This type of marketing cost structure is called *pay per click*. You pay the network (in this case, Google) for each click, whether or not the visitor converts into a sale.

Because you are paying for each click with no guarantee of converting each visit into a sale, you'll want to create some sort of filter to ensure that those likeliest to become customers receive your advertisement. No point displaying your ad to just anyone — a shotgun strategy is far from optimal, and your acquisition costs would be through the roof. Your ad's target audience should be those visitors who have the highest chance of conversion.

This is where predictive analytics can come to your aid for target marketing. By creating an effective predictive model that ranks the customers in your database according to who is most likely to buy, subscribe, or meet some other organizational goal, you have the potential to increase the return on your marketing investment. Specifically, predictive analytics for marketing can

- ✔ Increase profitability

- ✔ Increase your conversion ratio

- ✔ Increase customer satisfaction by reducing unwanted contact

- ✔ Increase operational efficiencies

- ✔ Learn what works (or doesn't) in each marketing campaign

Targeting using predictive modeling

Traditional marketing targets a group of customers without applying such modern techniques as predictive modeling using data-mining, and machine-learning algorithms to the dataset. Predictive modeling, in the area of direct marketing is called *response modeling using predictive analytics* (or simply *response modeling* from here on). Sometimes analysts create filters to apply to the dataset, thereby creating a select group to target. But that select group may not be optimally configured. Response modeling, on the other hand, seeks to discover patterns in the data that are present but not immediately apparent; the result is an optimized group to target.

Table 2-5 uses a small sample to compare the profit generated by direct mailings — traditional marketing versus response modeling.

Table 2-5	Comparing Direct Mailing Results (Small Sample)	
	Traditional Marketing	Response Modeling
Number of customers targeted	1000	100
Cost per customer targeted (assume $2)	$2	$2
Number of responses	20	10
Response rate	2 percent	10 percent
Total revenue (assume $100 per response)	$2,000	$1,000
Total cost of campaign	$2,000	$200
Total profit	$0	$800

In Table 2-5, response modeling has targeted 10 percent of the traditional number of customers (100 instead of 1000) to an optimized subset. The response rate should be higher with response modeling — 10 percent instead of the 2 percent that is typical for traditional marketing. The net result is a profit of $800 under response modeling; traditional marketing breaks even. Also, as per-customer targeting costs increase, response modeling's value gets even better — without even taking into account the implicit benefits of not targeting unqualified customers.

If you make constant contact with a customer without providing any benefit, you run the risk of being ignored in the future.

Table 2-6 is an example that shows the profit comparison between direct mailings using traditional marketing and response modeling with a larger sample size.

Table 2-6	Comparing Direct Mailing Results (Larger Sample)	
	Traditional Marketing	Response Modeling
Number of customers targeted	10000	1000
Cost per customer targeted	$2	$2
Number of responses	200	100
Response rate	2 percent	10 percent

	Traditional Marketing	Response Modeling
Total revenue (assume $100 per response)	$20,000	$10,000
Total cost of campaign	$20,000	$2000
Total profit	$0	$8,000

In Table 2-6, response modeling has (again) targeted only 10 percent of the 10,000 prospective customers traditionally targeted. In an optimized subset of 1,000, the response rate should be higher. We assumed a response rate of 2 percent for a traditional direct-mailing marketing campaign; with response modeling, the response rate is 10 percent because the customers are likelier to buy in the first place.

Response modeling creates a profit of $8,000 under this scenario; traditional marketing breaks even. As in the previous scenario, any revenue earned using traditional marketing is consumed by marketing costs. Thus, as the accuracy of customers targeted, increases, the value of response modeling also increases.

Uplift modeling

So how do you know that the customer you targeted wouldn't have purchased anyway? To clarify this question, you can restate it in a couple different ways:

- ✔ How do you know the customer wouldn't have purchased even if she didn't get the marketing contact from you?
- ✔ How do you know that what you sent to the customer influenced her to make the purchase?

Some modelers claim that the problems with response modeling are as follows:

- ✔ You're taking a subset of your customers whom you've predicted will have some interest in the product or service already.
- ✔ You're wasting marketing dollars on customers who don't need the extra influence to convert.
- ✔ You may be decreasing your net margins because the discounts you're using to entice the customer to buy may be unnecessary.

✔ You may be reducing your customer satisfaction because some customers don't want to be (constantly) contacted.

✔ You're incorrectly taking credit for the response in your evaluation of the model.

Uplift modeling, also called *true lift modeling* and *net modeling* among other terms, aims to answer those criticisms by predicting which customers will *only* convert if contacted.

Uplift modeling works by separating customers into four groups:

✔ **Persuadables:** Customers who can be persuaded to purchase — but will only buy if contacted.

✔ **Sure Things:** Customers who will buy, regardless of contact.

✔ **Lost Causes:** Customers who will not buy, regardless of contact.

✔ **Do Not Disturbs:** Customers whom you should not contact. Contacting them may cause a negative response like provoking them to cancel a subscription, return a product, or ask for a price adjustment.

Uplift modeling works by generating predictive scores that aim at ranking individuals, from those who can be influenced, to those who can't be disturbed. It looks at these four possible groupings of customers:

✔ It generally requires a larger sample size than for response modeling, since it has segmented the sample into four groups and only uses the group of Persuadables. It then has to be further split up for measuring the effectiveness of the model. This group will potentially be much smaller than the target size for response modeling. With a smaller target size and complexity, however, the operating effort and cost may not justify the use over response modeling.

✔ It's difficult to segment the customers perfectly into those four distinct groups, just as it's hard to measure the accuracy of the segmentation.

✔ It's difficult to measure the success of such a model because it's attempting to measure change in a customer's behavior, not the concrete action of whether the customer purchased after receiving contact.

To measure a single customer's behavior accurately, you would (in effect) have to clone her and split the identical clones into groups. The first (treated group) would receive the advertisement; the second (control group) would not. Setting aside such sci-fi scenarios, you have to make some concessions to reality and employ some alternative (more difficult) methods to get a useful estimate of the model's success.

Even with these difficulties, some modelers argue that uplift modeling provides true marketing impact. They consider it more efficient than response modeling because it doesn't include the Sure Things in the targeting (which artificially inflates response rates). For that reason, they feel uplift modeling is the choice for target marketing using predictive analytics.

Uplift modeling is still a relatively new technique in target marketing. More companies are starting to use it and have found success using it in their customer retention, marketing campaigns, and even presidential campaigns.

Some pundits are crediting uplift modeling for President Obama's 2012 presidential campaign win. The campaign's data analyst used uplift modeling to heavily target voters who were most likely to be influenced by contact. They used personalized messages via several channels of contact: social media, television, direct mail, and telephone. They concentrated their efforts to persuade the group of Persuadables. They invested heavily in this strategy; apparently it paid off.

Predictive Analytics Fight Fraud and Crime

In addition to enhancing marketing campaigns, predictive analytics can serve as a weapon against fraud and crime. Many industries are plagued with fraud, — which is costly to combat on a large scale. Accordingly, these industries have developed algorithms to detect unusual activity, behaviors, and patterns among employees as a first line of defense against fraud.

Outlier detection algorithms are in use as tools of fraud detection. The thinking is that fraud is unusual, and won't happen as commonly as normal transactions. Thus the algorithm looks for events that fall outside regular patterns to detect fraud. Here are some examples:

- Credit card companies have historically used predictive analytics to review credit applications and determine creditworthiness based on the widely popular FICO score.

- Insurance industries use predictive analytics not only to price insurance products, but also to scan through insurance claims for auto, property, health, and life.

- States and government apply predictive analytics to detect fraudulent tax returns, spot money laundering, verify unemployment claims, and check workers' compensation claims.

✔ Law enforcement agencies use predictive analytics to combat crime and fraud. Even though these organizations have highly qualified detectives and analysts who investigate white-collar crime, the sheer quantity of such crimes and their level of sophistication make fraudsters hard to detect. Fortunately, predictive analytics can reduce the time wasted pursuing false leads.

Content and Text Analytics

There's no shortage of information out there these days — but your success demands that you find and gather only the useful stuff. Valuable content is scattered across a massive number of files throughout your company. Harvesting that content and making sense of it can provide valuable insight — but doing that is challenging. The approach that meets the challenge is *content analytics* — analyzing content found in various types of documents and from a variety of sources. For example, the correct analysis of content from Word documents, system files, presentations, e-mails, and websites can illuminate a question from various angles.

Most content from such data sources is unstructured, at least as far as your business purposes are concerned. Content analytics can help you organize it into a structure that makes it easier to access, query, analyze, or feed directly into a traditional predictive analytic model.

Some common uses for content analytics and text analytics include

✔ **Summarizing documents:** Reducing a document to its most import features or concepts can give the reader quick overview, saving time.

✔ **Analyzing sentiments:** Determining the mood or opinion of a person as evident in the content — say, regarding a product after it's launched or the campaigns or policies of a political figure — can help clarify what the response should be.

✔ **Scoring essays:** Automatic scoring of essays for exams can help universities filter applications.

✔ **Categorizing news:** Categorizing news articles according to content can enable a recommender system to link recommended news articles to users.

✔ **Retrieving information:** Finding and gathering content of interest from various data sources.

Chapter 3

Exploring Your Data Types and Associated Techniques

In This Chapter

▶ Understanding your data, its types, and its categories

▶ Capturing the driving forces

▶ Connecting predictive analytics to statistics, data mining, and machine learning

I n this information age, data is being accumulated at such a rapid pace that it can be overwhelming. That data is usually stored in a database, or scattered across documents, e-mails, and text or audiovisual files.

Knowing your data types — whether attitudinal or behavioral, structured or unstructured, static or streamed — will position you to have a deeper and broader understanding of your data. Learning how to categorize your data can bring you the rest of the way to that deeper understanding — which in turn can facilitate your predictive analytics efforts.

The handiest way to define those efforts is in terms of the tools they use: *Predictive analytics* is an approach to business data that uses the techniques, tools, and algorithms of three disciplines — data mining, statistics, and machine learning — to develop a predictive model. When carefully built, that model can help decision-makers spot trends and patterns that represent enhanced business opportunities. Understanding the connection between predictive analytics and the three disciplines that provide its primary tools will strengthen your analysis.

There are two major ways to implement predictive analytics:

✔ **Data-driven:** This approach is based solely on your data.

✔ **User-driven:** This approach explores ideas you have — say, for example, about your customers and their behavior — and examines whether your data supports those ideas.

Recognizing Your Data Types

If your company is like most others, you've gathered a large amount of data through the years — simply as a result of operating a business. Some of this data can be found in your databases; some may be scattered across hard drives on your company's computers or in its online content.

Your raw data may consist of presentations, individual text files, images, audio and video files, and e-mails — for openers.

The sheer amount of this data can be overwhelming. If you categorize it, however, you create the core of any predictive analytics effort. The more you learn about your data, the better able you are to analyze and use it. You can start by getting a good working knowledge of your data types — in particular, structured versus unstructured data, and streamed versus static data. The upcoming sections give you a closer look at these data types.

Structured and unstructured data

Data contained in databases, documents, e-mails, and other data files can be categorized either as structured or unstructured data.

Structured data is well organized, follows a consistent order, is relatively easy to search and query, and can be readily accessed and understood by a person or a computer program.

A classic example of structured data is an Excel spreadsheet with labeled columns. Such structured data is consistent; column headers — usually brief, accurate descriptions of the content in each column — tell you exactly what kind of content to expect. In a column labeled *e-mail address,* for example, you can count on finding a list of (no surprise here) e-mail addresses. Such overt consistency makes structured data amenable to automated data management.

Structured data is usually stored in well-defined schemas such as databases. It's usually tabular, with columns and rows that clearly define its attributes.

Unstructured data, on the other hand, tends to be free-form, non-tabular, dispersed, and not easily retrievable; such data requires deliberate intervention to make sense of it. Miscellaneous e-mails, documents, web pages, and files (whether text, audio, and/or video) in scattered locations are examples of unstructured data.

It's hard to categorize the content of unstructured data. It tends to be mostly text, it's usually created in a hodgepodge of free-form styles, and finding any attributes you can use to describe or group it is no small task.

The content of unstructured data is hard to work with or make sense of programmatically. Computer programs cannot analyze or generate reports on such data, simply because it lacks structure, has no underlying dominant characteristic, and individual items of data have no common ground.

In general, there's a higher percentage of unstructured data than structured data in the world. Unstructured data requires more work to make it useful, so it gets more attention — thus tends to consume more time. No wonder the promise of a processing capability that can swiftly make sense of huge bodies of unstructured data is a major selling point for predictive analytics.

 Don't underestimate the importance of structured data and the power it brings to your analysis. It's far more efficient to analyze structured data than to analyze unstructured data. Unstructured data can also be costly to preprocess for analysis as you're building a predictive analytics project. The selection of relevant data, its cleansing, and subsequent transformations can be lengthy and tedious. The resultant newly organized data from those necessary preprocessing steps can then be used in a predictive analytics model. The wholesale transformation of unstructured data however, may have to wait until you have your predictive analytics model up and running.

Data mining and text analytics are two approaches to structuring text documents, linking their contents, grouping and summarizing their data, and uncovering patterns in that data. Both disciplines provide a rich framework of algorithms and techniques to mine the text scattered across a sea of documents.

It's also worth noting that search engine platforms provide readily available tools for indexing data and making it searchable.

Table 3-1 compares structured and unstructured data.

Table 3-1	Characteristics of Structured and Structured Data	
Characteristics	*Structured*	*Unstructured*
Association	Organized	Scattered and dispersed
Appearance	Formally defined	Free-form
Accessibility	Easy to access and query	Hard to access and query
Availability	Percentagewise lower	Percentagewise higher
Analysis	Efficient to analyze	Additional preprocessing is needed

Unstructured data does not completely lack structure — you just have to ferret it out. Even the text inside digital files still has some structure associated with it, often showing up in the metadata — for example, document titles, dates the files were last modified, and their authors' names. The same thing applies for e-mails: The contents may be unstructured, but structured data is associated with them — for example, the date and time they were sent, the names of their senders and recipients, whether they contain attachments.

The idea here is that you can still find some order you can use while you're going through all that "unstructured data". Of course, you may have to do some digging. The content of a thread of 25 e-mails shooting back and forth between two recipients may wander away from the subject line of the first original e-mail, even if the subject line stays the same. Additionally, the very first subject line in that e-mail thread may not accurately reflect even the content of that very first e-mail. (For example, the subject line may say something as unhelpful as "Hi, there!")

The separation line between the two data types isn't always clear. In general, you can always find some attributes of unstructured data that can be considered structured data. Whether that structure is reflective of the content of that data — or useful in data analysis — is unclear at best. For that matter, structured data can hold unstructured data within it. In a web form, for example, users may be asked to give feedback on a product by choosing an answer from multiple choices — but also presented with a comment box where they can provide additional feedback. The answers from multiple choices are structured; the comment field is unstructured because of its free-form nature. Such cases are best understood as a mix of structured and unstructured data. Most data is a composite of both.

Technically speaking, there will always be some exceptions in defining data categories; the lines between the two can be blurry. But the idea is to make a useful distinction between structured and unstructured data — and that is almost always possible.

For a successful predictive analytics project, both your structured and unstructured data must be combined in a logical format that can be analyzed.

Static and streamed data

Data can also be identified as streamed, static, or a mix of the two. *Streamed data* changes continuously; examples include the constant stream of Facebook updates, tweets on Twitter, and the constantly changing stock prices while the market is still open.

Streamed data is continuously changing; *static data* is self-contained and enclosed. The problems associated with static data include gaps, outliers, or incorrect data, all of which may require some cleansing, preparation, and preprocessing before you can use static data for an analysis.

As with streamed data, other problems may arise. Volume can be a problem; the sheer amount of non-stop data constantly arriving can be overwhelming. And the faster the data is streaming in, the harder it is for the analysis to catch up.

The two main models for analyzing streamed data are as follows:

- ✔ **Examine only the newest data points and make a decision about the state of the model and its next move.** This approach is incremental — essentially building up a picture of the data as it arrives.

- ✔ **Evaluate the entire dataset, or a subset of it, to make a decision each time new data points arrive.** This approach is inclusive of more data points in the analysis — what constitutes the "entire" dataset changes every time new data is added.

Depending on the nature of your business and the anticipated impact of the decision, one model is preferable over the other.

Some business domains, such as the analysis of environmental, market, or intelligence data, prize new data that arrives in real time. All this data must be analyzed as it's being streamed — and interpreted not only correctly but right away. Based on the newly available information, the model redraws the whole internal representation of the outside world. Doing so provides you with the most up-to-date basis for a decision you may need to make and act upon quickly.

For example, a predictive analytics model may process a stock price as a data feed, even while the data is rapidly changing, analyze the data in the context of immediate market conditions existing in real time, and then decide whether to trade a particular stock.

Clearly, analyzing streamed data differs from analyzing static data. Analyzing a mix of both data types can be even more challenging.

Identifying Data Categories

As a result of doing business, companies have gathered masses of data about their business and customers, often referred to as *business intelligence*. To help you develop categories for your data, what follows is a general rundown of the types of data that are considered business intelligence:

Behavioral data derives from transactions, and can be collected automatically:

- ✔ Items bought
- ✔ Methods of payment
- ✔ Whether the purchased items were on sale

✔ The purchasers' access information:

  • Address

  • Phone number

  • E-mail address

  All of us have provided such data when making a purchase online (or even when buying at a store or over the phone).

Other types of data can be collected from customers with their co-operation:

✔ Data provided by customers when they fill out surveys

✔ Customers' collected answers to polls via questionnaires

✔ Information collected from customers who make direct contact with companies

  • In a physical store

  • Over the phone

  • Through the company website

In addition, the type of data that a business collects from its operations can provide information about its customers. Common examples include the amount of time that customers spend on company websites, as well as customers' browsing histories. All that data combined can be analyzed to answer some important questions:

✔ How can your business improve the customer experience?

✔ How can you retain existing customers and attract new ones?

✔ What would your customer base like to buy next?

✔ What purchases can you recommend to particular customers?

The first step toward answering these questions (and many others) is to collect and use all customer-related operations data for a comprehensive analysis. The data types that make up such data can intersect and could be described and/or grouped differently for the purposes of analysis.

Some companies collect these types of data by giving customers personalized experiences. For example, when a business provides its customers with the tools they need to build personalized websites, it not only empowers customers (and enriches their experience of dealing with the company), it also allows the company to learn from a direct expression of its customers' wants and needs: the websites they create.

Attitudinal data

Any information that can shed light on how customers think or feel is considered *attitudinal data*.

When companies put out surveys that ask their customers for feedback and their thoughts about their line of businesses and products, the collected data is an example of attitudinal data.

Attitudinal data has a direct impact on the type of marketing campaign a company can launch. It helps shape and target the message of that campaign. Attitudinal data can help make both the message and the products more relevant to the customers' needs and wants — allowing the business to serve existing customers better and attract prospective ones.

The limitation of attitudinal data is a certain imperfection: Not everyone objectively answers survey questions, and not everyone provides all the relevant details that shaped their thinking at the time of the survey.

Behavioral data

Behavioral data derives from what customers do when they interact with the business; it consists mainly of data from sales transactions. Behavioral data tends to be more reliable than attitudinal data because it represents what actually happened.

Businesses know, for example, what products are selling, who is buying them, and how customers are paying for them.

Behavioral data is a by-product of normal operations, so is available to a company at no extra cost. Attitudinal data, on the other hand, requires conducting surveys or commissioning market research to get insights into the minds of the customers.

Attitudinal data is analyzed to understand *why* customers behave the way they do, and details their views of your company. Behavioral data tells you *what* is happening and records customers' real actions. Attitudinal data provides insight into motivations; behavioral data provides the who-did-what — the overall context that led to customers' particular reactions. Your analysis should include groups for both types of data; they are complementary.

Combining both attitudinal and behavioral data can make your predictive analytics models more accurate by helping you define the segments of your customer base, offer a more personalized customer experience, and identify the drivers behind the business.

Table 3-2 compares attitudinal and behavioral data.

Table 3-2	Comparing Attitudinal and Behavioral Data	
Characteristics	*Attitudinal*	*Behavioral*
Data Source	Customers' thoughts	Customers' actions
Data Means	Collected from surveys	Collected from transactions
Data Type	Subjective	Objective
Data Cost	May cost extra	No extra cost

Demographic data

Demographic data comprises information including age, race, marital status, education level, employment status, household income, and location. You can get demographic data from the U.S. Census Bureau, other government agencies, or through commercial entities.

The more data you have about your customers, the better the insight you'll have into identifying specific demographic and market trends as well as how they may affect your business. Measuring the pulse of the demographic trends will enable you to adjust to the changes and better market to, attract, and serve those segments.

Different segments of the population are interested in different products.

Small businesses catering to specific locations should pay attention to the demographic changes in those locations. All of us have witnessed populations changing over time in certain neighborhoods. Businesses must be aware of such changes; they may affect business significantly.

Demographic data, when combined with behavioral and attitudinal data, allows marketers to paint an accurate picture of their current and potential customers, allowing them to increase satisfaction, retention, and acquisition.

Generating Predictive Analytics

There are two ways to go about generating or implementing predictive analytics: purely on the basis of your data (with no prior knowledge of what you're after) or with a proposed business goal that the data may or may not support. You don't have to choose one or the other; the two approaches can be complementary. Each has its advantages and disadvantages.

Whether you're coming up with hypotheses to test, analyzing the results that come out of your data analysis (and making sense of them), or starting to examine your data with no prior assumptions of what you may find, the goal of your analysis is always the same: to decide whether to act on what you find. You have an active role in implementing the process needed for either approach to predictive analytics. Both approaches to predictive analytics have their limitations; keep risk management in mind as you cross-examine their results. Which approach do you find to be both promising of good results and relatively safe?

Combining both types of analysis empowers your business and enables you to expand your understanding, insight, and awareness of your business and your customers. It makes your decision process smarter and subsequently more profitable.

Data-driven analytics

If you're basing your analysis purely on existing data, you can use internal data — accumulated by your company over the years — or external data (often purchased from a source outside your company) that is relevant to your line of business.

To make sense of that data, you can employ data-mining tools to overcome both its complexity and size; reveal some patterns you were not aware of; uncover some associations and links within your data; and use your findings to generate new categorizations, new insights and new understanding. Data-driven analysis can even reveal a gem or two that can radically improve your business — all of which gives this approach an element of surprise that feeds on curiosity and builds anticipation.

Data-driven analysis is best suited for large datasets because it's hard for human beings to wrap their minds around huge amounts of data. Data-mining tools and visualization techniques help us get a closer look and cut the overwhelming mass of data down to size. Keep these general principles in mind:

- ✔ The more complete your data is, the better the outcome of data-driven analytics. If you have extensive data that has key information to the variables you're measuring, and spans an extended period of time, you're guaranteed to discover something new about your business.

- ✔ Data-driven analytics is neutral because no prior knowledge about the data is necessary and you're not after a specific goal in particular, but analyzing the data for the sake of it.

- ✔ The nature of this analysis is broad and it does not concern itself with a specific search or validation of a preconceived idea. This approach to analytics can be viewed as sort of random and broad data mining.

- ✔ If you conduct such data analysis, and if you learn something about your business from the analysis, you'll still need to decide whether the results you're getting are worth implementing or acting upon.

- ✔ Relying solely on data-driven analytics adds some risk to the resulting business decisions. You can, however, limit that risk by incorporating some of the realism that characterizes user-driven analytics (described in the next section). When real-world data proves (or at least supports) the correctness of your original ideas, then the appropriate decision is practically already made. When an informed hunch is validated by the data, the whole analysis shows itself as driven by strategic ideas that were worth pursuing and verifying.

User-driven analytics

The *user-driven* approach to predictive analytics starts with you (or your managers) conceiving of ideas and then taking refuge in your data to see whether those ideas have merit, would stand testing, and are supported by the data.

The test data can be a very small subset of your total business data; it's something you define and choose as you deem relevant for testing your ideas.

The process of picking the right datasets and designing accurate testing methods — in fact, the whole process from inception to adoption — has to be guided by careful consideration and meticulous planning.

User-driven analytics requires not only strategic thinking but also enough in-depth knowledge of the business domain to back up the strategizing. Vision and intuition can be very helpful here; you're looking for how the data lends specific support to ideas you deemed important and strategic. This approach to predictive analytics is defined (and limited) by the scope of the ideas you're probing. Decision-making becomes easier when the data supports your ideas.

Relying only on user-driven analytics can cost you in terms of insight; you may miss the hidden connections that may lurk in your data. Your ideas may miss the subtle changes that have been occurring in your business over time — which can only come to light if you apply data-driven analytics to complete the picture.

In short, your ideas should also include an awareness of the unknowns that surround your business, and probe them by looking for interconnected variables in the many aspects of your business. This is hard to achieve but data-driven analysis can help. For example, you may analyze the importance of the cost of raw material you need to create your product, the demand for the product, and how the costs affect your price. But you may miss hidden and other correlated factors that have influence on the pricing — such as the state of the economy as a whole, the turnover rate of employees at your company, and subtle changes in how your product is being consumed.

The process of probing your ideas may not be as straightforward as analyzing whole datasets. It can also be affected by your bias to prove the correctness of your initial assumptions.

Table 3-3 compares data-driven and user-driven data.

Table 3-3	Data-Driven and User-Driven Analytics	
Characteristics	*Data-Driven*	*User-Driven*
Business Knowledge Needed	No prior knowledge	In-depth domain knowledge
Analysis and Tools Used	Broad use of data-mining tools	Specific design for analysis and testing
Big Data	Suited for large-scale data	Applied on smaller datasets
Analysis Scope	Open scope	Limited scope
Analysis Conclusion	Needs verification of results	Easier adoption of analysis results
Data Pattern	Uncovers patterns and associations	May miss hidden patterns and associations

Connecting to Related Disciplines

Predictive analytics makes heavy use of three related disciplines: data mining, statistics, and machine learning. All four disciplines intersect to such a large degree that their names are often used interchangeably. Just to keep the record straight, there are some distinctions: predictive analytics combines many of the techniques, tools, and algorithms that data mining, statistics, and machine learning have in common. Its goal, however, is to use those tools to understand the data, analyze it, learn from it, and create a mathematical model that can make useful business predictions. That futuristic orientation combines aspects of the three disciplines in the various steps and or stages required to develop the model.

It's the predictive capability that sets apart this specialized use of statistics, data mining, and machine learning. The upcoming sections examine the contributions of each discipline.

Statistics

Statistics are numbers that result from measuring empirical data over time. As a discipline, statistics concerns itself with gathering and analyzing data — often to tell a story in numbers.

Statistics can infer relationships within data; thus it plays an active role in presenting data and helping us understand it. Using only a sample of the data, statistics can give us a basis for inferring hypotheses about the data as a whole. Thus the discipline is both *descriptive* and *inferential*.

Inferential statistics is concerned with making inferences or predictions about the characteristics of a whole population from a sample dataset. Sample data for analysis is chosen at random, in a way that represents (but does not include) the whole population. If the sample dataset is well chosen, analyzing it allows the investigator to project the findings of the analysis onto the whole population with a realistic degree of accuracy.

Statistics relies, of course, on mathematics to analyze the data by verifying a hypothesis or theory, determining its accuracy, and drawing a conclusion.

Unlike data mining, statistics doesn't involve data cleansing or preprocessing. But descriptive statistics and data mining do have data grouping in common; both aim to describe data and define the processes used to categorize it.

A common denominator among all these disciplines is the underlying mathematics. The math is at the heart of statistics, and all algorithms and programming used in data mining, machine learning, and predictive analytics. Another common denominator is data analysis, a quest for better-informed, smarter decisions about future outcomes.

Data mining

Data mining is concerned mainly with analyzing data through describing, summarizing, classifying, and clustering the data so as to find useful patterns, links, or associations within it.

Data mining is often used interchangeably with *machine learning* but there are some distinctions between the two terms. For example: data miners are familiar with the use of machine learning to perform some tasks involving large amounts of data. However, they can also create a sophisticated and optimized query on a database without the use of machine learning — which would still be considered data mining.

For more about the specific use of data mining in predictive analytics, see Chapters 6 and 7.

Machine learning

Machine learning is another discipline that focuses on analyzing the data and making sense of it — but does so by teaching a computer program to do the work. The more data is analyzed, the more the system can learn about it, what to expect from it, and what to do with it. Data analysis becomes a source of continuous feedback to the system, which promptly analyzes data, attempts to understand and make sense of it, and gets better at those tasks.

When a new special case, usually an exception or a new behavior, is processed for the first time, the knowledge base of the system is incremented to include the new case. The more special cases are handled, the better equipped the system is to make decisions that produce the most useful outcome. This is the nature of the learning that the machine is programmed to do.

Machine learning is the equivalent of teaching a system the rules of a game, and then getting the system to practice the game by playing at elementary and intermediate levels. After that preparation, the system can play at advanced levels in real time.

Machine learning is perfectly suited for

- Complex data
- Data in various forms
- Data collected from diverse sources
- Data in large amounts

Data mining can uncover previously unknown connections and associations in the data. Machine learning can categorize the new and upcoming unknowns, learn from them based on its previous processing of the data, and get better at incorporating them into the known data. Both techniques lead to greater insight and understanding of the data.

Chapter 4

Complexities of Data

· ·

In This Chapter

▶ Meeting the challenges of big data

▶ Making your data semantically retrievable

▶ Distinguishing between business intelligence and data analytics

▶ Using visualizations to guide the cleaning of data

· ·

*Y*our Google search log, tweets, Facebook status updates, and bank statements tell a story about your life. Your geographical locations logged by your cellphone carrier, your most frequent places visited, and your online purchases can define your habits, your preferences, and your personality.

This avalanche of data, being generated at every moment, is referred to as *big data,* and it's the main driver of many predictive analytics models. Capturing all different types of data together in one place and applying analytics to it is a highly complex task. However, you might be surprised that only about 1 percent of that data is used for analysis that results in real, valuable results. This 1 percent of big data is actually *smart data* — the nucleus that makes sense out of big data. Only this 1 percent will make it into the elevator pitch that justifies your analytical results.

The secret recipe for a truly successful predictive analytics project starts with filtering out the dirt, noise, invalid data and misleading data. When you've done that task, then ultimately you can extract smart data from big data. Analyzing smart data leads to extracting the value of predictive analytics.

So how do we go from big data to smart data to tangible value? At what rate must data be captured, considering how fast it's being generated? Can visualization of raw data give you a clue as to what to correct, exclude, or include? Relax. This chapter addresses all those questions.

Finding Value in Your Data

Any successful journey takes serious preparation. Predictive analytics models are essentially a deep dive into large amounts of data. If the data is not well prepared, the predictive analytics model will emerge from the dive with no fish. The key to finding value in predictive analytics is to prepare the data — thoroughly and meticulously — that your model will use to make predictions.

Processing data beforehand can be a stumbling block in the predictive analytics process. Gaining experience in building predictive models — and, in particular, preparing data — teaches the importance of patience. Selecting, processing, cleaning, and preparing the data is laborious. It's the most time-consuming task in the predictive analytics lifecycle. However, proper and systematic preparing of the data will significantly increase the chance that your data analytics will bear fruit.

Although it takes both time and effort to build that first predictive model, once you take the first step — building the first model that finds value in your data — then future models will be less resource-intensive and time-consuming, even with completely new datasets. Even if you don't use the same data for the next model, your data analysts will have gained valuable experience with the first model.

Delving into your data

Using a fruit analogy, you not only have to remove the bad peel or the cover, but dig into it to get to the nucleus; as you get closer to the nucleus, you get to the best part of the fruit. The same rule applies to big data, as shown in Figure 4-1.

Big Data

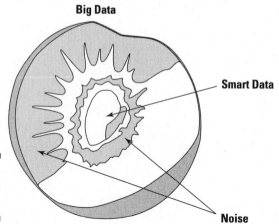

Smart Data

Figure 4-1:
Big data and
smart data.

Noise

Data validity

Data is not always valid when you first encounter it. Most data is either *incomplete* (missing some attributes or values) or *noisy* (containing outliers or errors). In the biomedical bioinformatics fields, for example, outliers can lead the analytics to generate incorrect or misleading results. Outliers in cancer data, for example, can be a major factor that skews the accuracy of medical treatments: Gene-expression samples may appear as false cancer positives because they were analyzed against a sample that contained errors.

Inconsistent data is data that contains discrepancies in data attributes. For example, a data record may have two attributes that don't match: say, a zip code (such as 20037) and a corresponding state (Delaware). Invalid data can lead to wrong predictive modeling, which leads to misleading analytical results that will cause bad executive decisions. For instance, sending coupons for diapers to people who have no children is a fairly obvious mistake. But it can happen easily if the marketing department of a diaper company ends up with invalid results from their predictive analytics model. Gmail might not always suggest the right people if you're trying to fill in the prospective customers you might have forgotten to include in a group e-mail list. Facebook, to give another example, may suggest friends who might not be the type you're looking for.

In such cases, it's possible that there's too large a margin of error in the models or algorithms. In most cases, the flaws and anomalies are in the data initially selected to power the predictive model — but the algorithms that power the predictive model might have large chunks of invalid data.

Data variety

The absence of uniformity in data is another big challenge known as *data variety*. From the endless stream of unstructured text data (generated through e-mails, presentations, project reports, texts, tweets) to structured bank statements, geolocation data, and customer demographics, companies are starving for this variety of data.

Aggregating this data and preparing it for analytics is a complex task. How can you integrate data generated from different systems such as Twitter, Opentable. com, Google search, and a third party that tracks customer data? Well, the answer is that there is no common solution. Every situation is different, and the data scientist usually has to do a lot of maneuvering to integrate the data and prepare it for analytics. Even so, a simple approach to standardization can support data integration from different sources: You agree with your data providers to a standard data format that your system can handle — a framework that can make all your data sources generate data that's readable by both humans and machines. Think of it as a new language that all big-data sources will speak every time they're in the big-data world.

Constantly Changing Data

This section presents two main challenges of big data: velocity and volume. These are (respectively) the rate at which data is being generated, received, and analyzed, and the growing mass of data.

Data velocity

Velocity is the speed of an object moving in a specific direction. *Data velocity* refers to another challenge of big data: the rate at which data is being generated, captured, or delivered. The challenge is figuring out how to keep up.

Think of the data being generated by a cellphone provider. It includes all customers' cellphone numbers, call durations, and GPS locations (for openers). This data is growing all the time, making the task of capturing smart data from big data even more challenging.

So how do you overcome this challenge? There isn't one simple solution available yet. However, your team can (in fact, must) decide

✔ How often you can capture data

✔ What you can afford in terms of both resources and finances

If (for example) you own a supercomputer and you have the funds, then you should capture as much data as you can — but you might also need to take into consideration how often that data is changing.

High volume of data

A common mistake that people make when they talk about big data is to define it as merely a large amount of data. Big data is not just about large volumes of data; it's more about a wide *variety* of data (yes, in huge amounts) generated at high speed and frequency. In Figure 4-2, big data spans three dimensions in spiral exponential fashion; it looks like a tsunami.

Big data is "big" not only because of its large volume; it's also — and mainly — about those other three dimensions: volume, velocity and variety.

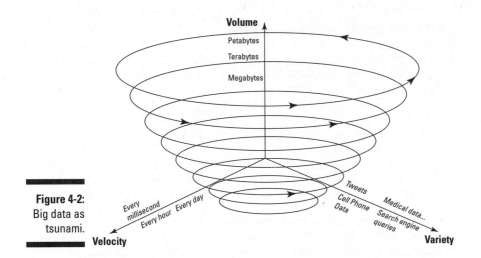

Figure 4-2:
Big data as
tsunami.

Complexities in Searching Your Data

This section presents the two main concepts of searching your data in preparation for using it in predictive analytics:

✔ Getting ready to go beyond the basic keyword search

✔ Making your data semantically searchable

Keyword-based search

Imagine if you were tasked with searching large amounts of data. One way to approach the problem is to issue a search query that consists (obviously) of words. The search tool looks for matching words in the database, the data warehouse, or goes rummaging through any text in which your data resides. Assume you're issuing the following search query: *the President of the United States visits Africa*. The search results will consist of text that contains exactly one or a combination of the words *President, United States, visits, Africa*. You might get the exact information you're looking for, but not always.

How about the documents that do not contain any of the words previously mentioned, but some combination of the following: *Obama's trip to Kenya*.

None of the words you initially searched for are in there — but the search results are *semantically* (meaningfully) useful. How can you prepare your data to be semantically retrievable? How can you go beyond the traditional keyword search? Your answers are in the next section.

Semantic-based search

An illustration of how semantic-based search works is a project that Anasse Bari led at the World Bank Group, an international organization whose primary mission is to fight poverty around the world. The project aimed to investigate existing large scale enterprise search and analytics in the market and build a prototype for a cutting-edge framework that would organize the World Bank data — most of which was an unstructured collection of documents, publications, project reports, briefs, and case studies. This massive valuable knowledge is a resource used toward the Bank's main mission of reducing world poverty. But the fact that it's unstructured makes it challenging to access, capture, share, understand, search, data-mine, and visualize.

The World Bank is an immense organization, with many divisions around the globe. One of the main divisions was striving to have a framework and was ready to allocate resources to assist the Bari team was the Human Development Network within the World Bank.

The vice president of the Human Development Network outlined one problem that sprang from ambiguity: His division used several terms and concepts that had the same overall meaning but different nuances. For instance, terms such as *climatology, climate change, gas ozone depletion,* and *greenhouse emissions* were all semantically related but not identical in meaning. He wanted a search capability smart enough to extract documents that contained related concepts when someone searched any of these terms.

The prototype framework for that capability that the Bari team selected was the Unstructured Information Management Architecture (UIMA), a software-based solution. Originally designed by IBM Research, UIMA is available in IBM software such as IBM Content Analytics, one of the tools that powered IBM Watson, the famous computer that won the Jeopardy game. The Bari team joined forces with a very talented team from IBM Content Management and Enterprise Search, and later with an IBM Watson team, to collaborate on this project.

An *Unstructured Information Management (UIM)* solution is a software system that analyzes large volumes of unstructured information (text, audio, video, images, and so on) to discover, organize and deliver relevant knowledge to the client or the application end-user.

The *ontology* of a domain is an array of concepts and related terms particular to a domain. A UIMA-based solution uses ontologies to provide semantic tagging, which allows enriched searching independent of data format (text, speech, PowerPoint presentation, e-mail, video, and so on). UIMA appends another layer to the captured data, and then adds *metadata* to identify data that can be structured and semantically searched.

Semantic search is based on the contextual meaning of search terms as they appear in the searchable data space that UIMA builds. Semantic search is more accurate than the usual keyword-based search because a user query returns search results of not only documents that contain the search terms, but also of documents that are semantically relevant to the query.

For instance, if you're searching for *biodiversity in Africa,* a typical (keyword-based) search will return documents that have the exact words *biodiversity* and *Africa*. A UIMA-based semantic search will return not only the documents that have those two words, but also anything that is semantically relevant to "biodiversity in Africa" — for example, documents that contain such combinations of words as "plant resources in Africa," "animal resources in Morocco," or "genetic resources in Zimbabwe."

Through semantic tagging and use of ontologies, information becomes semantically retrievable, independent of the language or the medium in which the information was created (Word, PowerPoint, e-mail, video, and so on). This solution provides a single hub where data can be captured, organized, exchanged, and rendered semantically retrievable.

Dictionaries of synonyms and related terms are open-source (freely available) — or you can develop your own dictionaries specific to your domain or your data. You can build a spreadsheet with the root word and its corresponding related words, synonyms, and broader terms. The spreadsheet can be uploaded into a search tool such as IBM Content Analytics (ICA) to power the enterprise search and content analytics.

Differentiating Business Intelligence from Big-Data Analytics

Be sure to make a clear distinction between business intelligence and big data. Here are the basics of the distinction:

- ✔ **Business intelligence (BI)** is about building a model that answers specific business questions. You start with a question or a set of questions, gather data and data sources, and then build a computer program that uses those resources to provide answers to the business questions you've targeted. Business intelligence is about providing the infrastructure for searching your data and building reports. Business intelligence uses *controlled data* — predefined, structured data, stored mainly in data-warehousing environments. BI uses *online analytical processing (OLAP)* techniques to provide some analytical capabilities — enough to construct dashboards you can use to query data, as well as create and view reports, to answer predefined questions. BI does not provide data mining or new insights.

✔ **Big-data analytics** is a more generalized data-exploration task: You don't necessarily know exactly what you're looking for, but you're open to all discoveries. Analytics can dive into the collected and prepared data to unveil insights that could have gone undiscovered otherwise. Analytics rely on newer technologies that allow deeper knowledge discovery in large bodies of data of any type (structured, unstructured, or semi-structured); technologies designed for such work include Hadoop and MapReduce.

Predictive Analytics emerged to complement, rather than compete with, business intelligence. You can co-ordinate your pursuit of analytics with business intelligence: by using BI to preprocess the data you're preparing for use in your predictive analytics model. You can point BI systems to different data sources — and use the visualizations that BI produces from raw data — to give you an overview of your data even before you start designing your analytics model. This approach leads to the visualization of large amounts of raw data, as discussed in the next section.

Visualization of Raw Data

A picture is worth a thousand words — especially when you're trying to get a good handle on your data. At the pre-processing step, while you're preparing your data, it's a common practice to visualize what you have in hand before continuing to the next step.

You start by using a spreadsheet such as Microsoft Excel to create a data matrix — which consists of candidate data _features_ (also referred to as _attributes_). Several business intelligence software packages (such as Tableau) can give you a preliminary overview of the data to which you're about to apply analytics.

Identifying data attributes

In programming terms, data is a collection of objects and their corresponding attributes. A _data object_ is also called a _record, item, observation, instance,_ or _entity_. A data object can be described by a collection of attributes that describe it. A data _attribute_ is also known as _feature, field,_ or _characteristic._ Attributes can be nominal, ordinal, or interval:

✔ **Nominal attributes** are numbers (for example, zip codes) or nouns (for example, gender).

✔ **Ordinal attributes,** in most cases, represent ratings or rankings (for example, degree of interest in buying Product A, ranked from 1 to 10 to represent least interest to most interest).

✔ **Interval attributes** represent data range, such as calendar dates.

One motivation behind visualizing raw data is to select that subset of attributes that will potentially be included in the analytics. Again, this is one of the tasks that will lead you to the nucleus — the smart data to which you'll apply analytics. To get there, you have to reduce the attributes in your data and focus your analysis of the most important ones.

Your data scientist might be applying predictive models to a database or data warehouse that stores terabytes (or more) of data. Don't be surprised if it takes a very long time to run models over the whole database. You'll need to select and extract a good representative sample of your large body of data — one that produces nearly the same analytical results as the whole body. Selecting a sampling of your data is a step toward *data reduction*. Another helpful step, called *dimension reduction,* starts when you select the data attributes that are most important — and here visualization can be of help.

Visualization can give you an idea of the dispersion of the attributes in your data. For instance, taking a spreadsheet of numerical data and with a few clicks in Excel, you can identify the maximum, minimum, variance, and median. You can picture spikes in your data that might lead you to quickly find those outliers that are easy to capture. The next sections illustrate examples of visualizations that you can apply to raw data to detect outliers, missing values, and (in some cases) early insights.

Exploring data visualization

When you request a cleaning service to come to your house and the company you hire has never been to your house, naturally you'd expect the company to ask you about (you guessed it) your house. They might also ask about structural features such as the number of rooms and baths, the current overall state of the house, and when they can visit the house to see it before they start cleaning — or even give you an estimate of the cost. Well, getting your data in order is similar to getting your house in order.

Suppose you've captured a large amount of data. You'd like to see it before you even start building your predictive analytics model. Visualizing your data will help you in the very first steps of data preparation by

✔ Guiding you to where to start cleaning your data

✔ Providing clues to which values you need to fill

✔ Pointing you to easy outliers and eliminating them

✔ Correcting inconsistent data

✔ Eliminating redundant data records

Tabular visualizations

Tables are the simplest, most basic pictorial representation of data. Tables (also known as *spreadsheets*) consist of rows and columns — which correspond, respectively, to the objects and their attributes mentioned earlier as making up your data. For instance, consider online social network data. A data object could represent a user. Attributes of a user (data object) can be headings of columns: Gender, Zip Code, or Date of Birth.

The cells in a table represent values as shown in Figure 4-3. Visualization in tables can help you easily spot missing attribute values of data objects.

Data Source#1: Online Social Network Data

Social Network User ID	Date of Birth	Gender	Zip Code	Friends Count	Relationship Status
556694901	6/3/1985	M	21036	859	In relationship
556694902	8/1/1977	F	94024	332	Married
556694903	9/5/1978	F	21794	754	In relationship
556694904	3/9/1986	M	21737	20	Single
556694905	2/7/1984	F	33109	169	Single
556694906	4/7/1983	F	21131	-63	Married
556694907	9/1/1982	M	21042	12	Married
556694908	1/3/1981	F	92067	185	In relationship
556694909	4/5/1980	M	92662	123	Single
556694910	5/3/2029	F	93108	174	Married
556694911	6/9/1994	F	94027	1236	In relationship
556694912	8/1/1978	F	90402	963	Single
556694913	9/8/1980	F	92661	414	Married
556694914	2/3/1982	F	94024	795	Single
556694915	6/6/1981	F	94957	1186	In relationship
556694916	8/8/1994	M	94028	367	Complicated
556694917	2/7/1989	R	33109	45	Complicated
556694918	5/2/1996	M	11962	1247	In relationship
...	...	...	.....	...	...

Figure 4-3: Example of Online Social Network Data in Tabular Format.

Tables can also provide the flexibility of adding new attributes that are combinations of other attributes. For instance, in social network data, you can add another column called Age, which can be easily calculated — as a derived attribute — from the existing Date of Birth attribute. In Figure 4-4, the tabular social network data shows a new column, Age, created from another existing column (Date of Birth).

Data Source#1: Online Social Network Data

Social Network User ID	Date of Birth	Gender	Zip Code	Friends Count	Relationship Status	Age
556694901	6/3/1985	M	21036	859	In relationship	28
556694902	8/1/1977	F	94024	332	Married	36
556694903	9/5/1978	F	21794	754	In relationship	35
556694904	3/9/1986	M	21737	20	Single	27
556694905	2/7/1984	F	33109	169	Single	29
556694906	4/7/1983	F	21131	-63	Married	30
556694907	9/1/1982	M	21042	12	Married	31
556694908	1/3/1981	F	92067	185	In relationship	32
556694909	4/5/1980	M	92662	123	Single	33
556694910	5/3/2029	F	93108	174	Married	-16
556694911	6/9/1994	F	94027	1236	In relationship	19
556694912	8/1/1978	F	90402	963	Single	35
556694913	9/8/1980	F	92661	414	Married	33
556694914	2/3/1982	F	94024	795	Single	31
556694915	6/6/1981	F	94957	1186	In relationship	31
556694916	8/8/1994	M	94028	367	Complicated	19
556694917	2/7/1989	R	33109	45	Complicated	24
556694918	5/2/1996	M	11962	1247	In relationship	17
...	...	...	.....	...	...	...

Figure 4-4: Example of Derived Attributes.

Bar charts

Bar charts can be used to spot spikes or anomalies in your data. You can use it for each attribute to quickly picture minimum and maximum values. Bar charts can be also used to start a discussion of how to normalize your data. *Normalization* is the adjustment of some — or all — attribute values on a scale that makes the data more usable. In Figure 4-5, for example, you can easily see that there's an error in the data: The Age bar on one record is negative. That anomaly is more easily depicted by a bar chart than by a table of data.

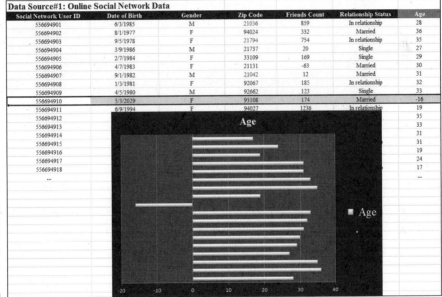

Data Source#1: Online Social Network Data

Social Network User ID	Date of Birth	Gender	Zip Code	Friends Count	Relationship Status	Age
556694901	6/3/1985	M	21036	859	In relationship	28
556694902	8/1/1977	F	94024	332	Married	36
556694903	9/5/1978	F	21794	754	In relationship	35
556694904	3/9/1986	M	21737	20	Single	27
556694905	2/7/1984	F	33109	169	Single	29
556694906	4/7/1983	F	21131	-63	Married	30
556694907	9/1/1982	M	21042	12	Married	31
556694908	1/3/1981	F	92067	185	In relationship	32
556694909	4/5/1980	M	92662	123	Single	33
556694910	5/3/2029	F	93108	174	Married	-16
556694911	6/9/1994	F	94027	1236	In relationship	19
556694912						35
556694913						33
556694914						31
556694915						31
556694916						19
556694917						24
556694918						17
...						...

Figure 4-5: Online social network data on a bar chart.

Pie charts

Pie charts are used mainly to show percentages. They can easily illustrate the distribution of several items, and highlight the most dominant. In Figure 4-6, raw data of social network is represented according to the Age attribute. Notice that the chart shows not only a clear distribution of males versus females, but also a probable error: R as a value for gender type, possibly created when the data was collected.

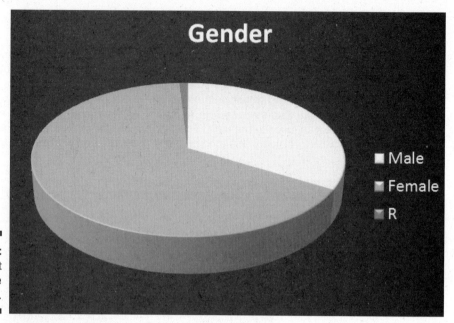

Figure 4-6:
Pie chart
of the Age
attribute.

Graph charts

Graph theory provides a set of powerful algorithms that can analyze data structured and represented as a graph. In computer science, a *graph* is data structure, a way to organize data that represents relations between pairs of data objects. A graph consists of two main parts:

- Vertices, also known as *nodes*
- Edges, which connect pairs of nodes

Edges can be directed (drawn as arrows) and can have weights, as shown in Figure 4-7. You can decide to place an edge (arrow) in between two nodes (circles) — in this case, the members of the social network who are connected to other members as friends:

The arrow's direction indicates who "friends" whom first, or who initiates interactions most of the time.

The weight assigned to a particular edge (the numerical value of the edge, as shown in Figure 4-7) can represent the level of social interaction that two social network members have. This example uses a scale of 10: The closer the value is to 10, the more the network members interact with one another.

Here a *social interaction* is the process in which at least two members of a social network act and or respond to each other. The interaction can be offline and go beyond just the online interactions that are happening on the network. For instance, offline interactions can include meetings, conference calls, "live" social gatherings, group travel, social events, mobile communications, and text messaging. All such interactions can be represented as numbers, each with a *score* (a weighted sum of all types of interactions).

The weight on the graph can also represent the *influence rate*. How influential is one member on another? Several algorithms can calculate influence rate between two social network members, based on their online posts, common friends, and other criteria.

In Figure 4-7, social network members are represented with black circles; each relationship represented by an edge shows a level of interaction, which is in turn represented as number on the edge. From an initial view, you can spot two disconnected groups — a quick insight that crops up even before you apply analytics.

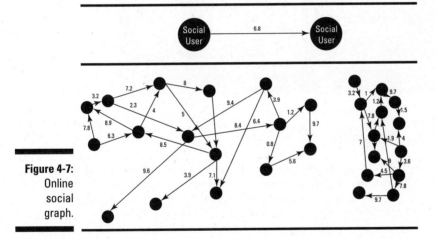

Figure 4-7: Online social graph.

You might want to focus on either or both of these two groups; you may want to include one of them in the data you're preparing as a resource for when you build your predictive model. Applying your analytics to one of the groups may enable you to dive into the data and extract patterns that are not obvious.

Word clouds as representations

Consider a list of words or concepts arranged as a *word cloud* — a graphic representation of all words on the list, showing the size of each word as proportional to a metric that you specify. For instance, if you have a spreadsheet of words and occurrences and you'd like to identify the most important words, try a word cloud.

Word clouds work because most organizations' data is text; a common example is Twitter's use of trending terms. Every term in Figure 4-8 (for example) has a weight that affects its size as an indicator of its relative importance. One way to define that weight could be by the number of times a word appears in your data collection. The more frequently a word appears, the "heavier" its weight — and the larger it appears in the cloud.

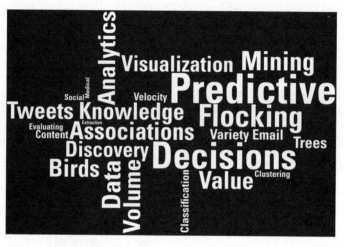

Figure 4-8:
Word importance represented as weight and size in a word cloud.

Line graphs

Line graphs — a traditional way of representing data — enable you to visualize multiple series or multiple attributes (columns) in the same graph. (Figure 4-9, for example, represents two data series: Friends Count and Age.) One advantage of line graphs is flexibility: You can combine different series in one line graph for several purposes. One such graph could depict a correlation between attributes.

Flocking birds representation

"Birds of a feather flock together" is a traditional saying that provides instant insight as a way of visualizing data: Individuals of similar tastes, interests, dreams, goals, habits, and behaviors tend to congregate in groups.

Natural flocking behavior in general is a self-organizing system in which objects (in particular, living things) tend to behave according to (a) the environment they belong to and (b) their responses to other existing objects. The flocking behavior of natural societies such as those of bees, flies, birds, fish, and ants — or, for that matter, people — is also known as *swarm intelligence*.

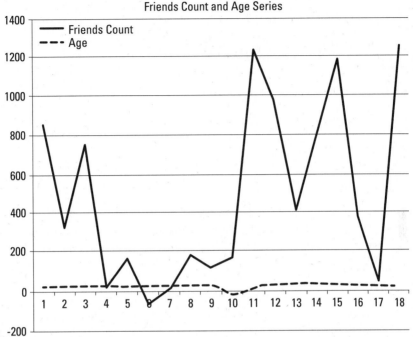

Figure 4-9:
Online
social data
on a line
graph.

Birds follow natural rules when they behave as a flock. *Flock-mates* are birds located with a certain distance from each other; those birds are considered similar. Each bird moves according to the three main rules that organize flocking behavior.

- ✔ **Separation:** Flock-mates must not collide with each other.
- ✔ **Alignment:** Flock-mates move in the same average direction as their neighbors.
- ✔ **Cohesion:** Flock-mates move according to the average position or location of their flock-mates.

Modeling those three rules can enable an analytical system to simulate flocking behaviors. That's because biologically inspired algorithms, in particular those derived from bird-flocking behavior, offer a simple way to model social network data. Using the self-organized natural behavior of flocking birds, you can convert a straightforward spreadsheet into a visualization such as Figure 4-10. The key is to define the notion of similarity as part of your data — and construct a mathematical function that supports that similarity. Start with a couple of questions:

- ✔ What makes two data objects in your data similar?
- ✔ Which attributes can best drive the similarity between two data records?

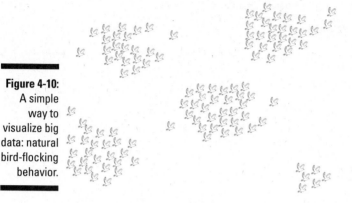

Figure 4-10:
A simple
way to
visualize big
data: natural
bird-flocking
behavior.

For instance, in social network data, the data records represent individual users; the attributes that describe them can include Age, Zip Code, Relationship Status, List of Friends, Number of Friends, Habits, Events Attended, Books Read, and other groups of particular interests (Sports, Movies, and so on).

You can define the similarity for your group according to nearly any attribute. For example, you can call two members of a social network *similar* if they read the same books, have a large number of common friends, and have attended the same events. Those two similar members will flock together if they're represented by birds flocking in a virtual space.

In the healthcare and biomedical fields, the data object could be patient data. And you could base the attributes on the patient's personal information, treatments, and information related to diagnosis. Then, by plotting the data as a visualization based on the flocking of birds, you might be able to visualize and discern insights before you even apply data analytics. Some interesting patterns in your data would become apparent, including some characteristic groupings — and even data anomalies.

Flocking behavior is iterative because behavior, while consistent, is not static. At each iteration (or round), birds move. Using flocking birds as a visualization technique is an especially relevant way to represent streamed data. With streaming data, at each point the visualization of data objects can change according to the new incoming data. In Figure 4-10, a flocking bird in a virtual space, represents a data object (such as an individual user) in the dataset in question (such as the social network). Similar birds in the virtual space that represent similar data objects in real life will flock together and appear next to each other in the visualization, as shown in Figure 4-10.

Part II

Incorporating Algorithms in Your Models

Data Source#1: Online Social Network Data					
Social Network User ID	**Date of Birth**	**Gender**	**Zip Code**	**Friends Count**	**Relationship Status**
556694901	6/3/1985	M	21036	859	In relationship
556694902	8/1/1977	F	94024	332	Married
556694903	9/5/1978	F	21794	754	In relationship
556694904	3/9/1986	M	21737	20	Single
556694905	2/7/1984	F	33109	169	Single
556694906	4/7/1983	F	21131	-63	Married
556694907	9/1/1982	M	21042	12	Married
556694908	1/3/1981	F	92067	185	In relationship
556694909	4/5/1980	M	92662	123	Single
556694910	5/3/2029	F	93108	174	Married
556694911	6/9/1994	F	94027	1236	In relationship
556694912	8/1/1978	F	90402	963	Single
556694913	9/8/1980	F	92661	414	Married
556694914	2/3/1982	F	94024	795	Single
556694915	6/6/1981	F	94957	1186	In relationship
556694916	8/8/1994	M	94028	367	Complicated
556694917	2/7/1989	R	33109	45	Complicated
556694918	5/2/1996	M	11962	1247	In relationship
...	...	...	....	...	...

Visit www.dummies.com/extras/predictiveanalytics for great Dummies content online.

In this part . . .

- Modeling systems
- Evaluating case studies
- Finding similarities in data
- Creating predictions
- Visit `www.dummies.com/extras/` `predictiveanalytics` for great Dummies content online.

Chapter 5

Applying Models

· ·

· ·

*B*ig data is like an engine that drives our lives. It includes everything about us. Predictive analytics can use big data to foresee our future moves and make predictions about our likely actions — especially if we're someone's prospective customers. Hypothetically, a predictive analytics model can know when you're asleep and can predict the time you'll wake up.

Companies are capturing and storing information at every opportunity. They store every purchase you make, every online search you do, every website you visit, and your preferences. Everything is closely monitored and analyzed. This has become the new norm in our lives. Your doctor, your employer, your next-door grocer will be all analyzing data about you soon, if they aren't already.

The rule for using all this data is clear: Whichever company can accurately find patterns in your data, analyze them, and use them effectively, will profit from it.

So what are some of the business implications of using predictive analytics on big data? And how can businesses or organizations make profit or make their own success stories from your data? For that matter, how can you do the same? To clarify that picture, this chapter introduces different types of models and highlights some recent case studies from different domains, including healthcare, social media, marketing, and politics.

Modeling Data

Most predictive analytics tools come equipped with common algorithms, the underlying mathematical formulas, to help you build your model. A completed model can be applied in a few minutes. In fact, a business analyst with no specific background in statistics, data mining, or machine learning can run powerful algorithms on the data relatively quickly, using available predictive analytics tools.

Suppose a business analyst at a retail company would like to know which customer segments to upsell to. She can load each customer's data, purchase history, preferences, demographics, and any other type of relevant data; run a few models to determine the likely segments of interest, and put the results to use right away in a sales campaign.

Those of us who do this type of work for a living (such as data scientists) tend to seek the ultimate results — to build the all-powerful model to wow the business stakeholders and to showcase the wealth of our knowledge.

In pursuit of this goal, the model-building may take a little longer than in the retailer example. Instead of aiming for a quick victory, we want to optimize performance by building a model with the highest accuracy possible.

A lot of tweaking and experimentation is needed. We may start with a large number of variables or features that are available in our dataset, and funnel our way through until we get to the very few variables that have the most predictive power. This process requires running as many simulations as possible while changing the values of the parameters and plotting the results.

Another common technique is to build an ensemble model (see Chapter 7), evaluate the results of the models that make it up, and present the user with the highest-scoring model among them. Or (at the very minimum) we can run multiple and separate techniques on the data, compare results, and eventually pick the one model that consistently scores higher for most of our simulations and what-if scenarios.

Building a model is part science and part art. The science refers to well-established statistical techniques, machine learning, and data-mining algorithms. Tweaking is the art.

Models and simulation

A model is nothing but a mathematical representation of a segment of the world we are interested in. A model can mimic behavioral aspects of our customers. It can represent the different customer segments. A well-made, well-tuned model can *forecast* — predict with high accuracy — the next outcome of a given event.

From this definition, you can already deduce that it's possible to build a model to mimic and represent virtually about anything you want to analyze. As you might imagine, this process can quickly and easily become very complex and difficult.

To start with the potential complexity, imagine you're working with dataset that has many associated variables with a wide range of values. Going through all the possible values and permutations across the entire dataset can be time-consuming.

The standard approach is to run *what-if scenarios* — hypothetical situations that your simulations investigate. The general outline of running a what-if scenario looks like this:

1. Build the model.

2. Start changing the values of parameters and examining the new results, or use a *tool* — a specialized software program that automates that whole process for you.

3. Look at the report that the model generates.

4. Evaluate the result and pick the most important predictors; if you've run multiple models, pick the right model.

The process looks simpler on the page than it is in practice. Certain tasks lend themselves easily to canned solutions. Others can be very hard to solve — two notoriously hard examples are predicting extended weather conditions or stock-market performance. The farther into the future you try to predict, the faster the accuracy of the predictions diminishes. It may be possible to say (for example) that it will snow within the next 12 hours, but it's hard to come up with an accurate prediction that it will snow in three weeks from now.

Similar uncertainty crops up when predicting a hurricane's path; it's difficult to know with certainty the exact path the farther out into the future one gets. That's why new data is immediately made available for these models, and the forecast is continuously updated.

Simulating the stock market is also extremely difficult, for a simple reason: The market can be affected by virtually everything.

Complex problems require clever solutions, constant tweaking, and continuous refreshment of the deployed models.

✔ **Clever solutions:** One way to smarten up the model is to include variables not usually associated with the field you're investigating. To analyze the stock market, for example, you might include data about parking activities at malls, or analyze data about daily local newspapers from around the country.

Another clever solution involves divorce lawyers acquiring data from credit card companies. Apparently those companies know couples are headed for divorce, about two years before the actual divorce dates. And they know that with an accuracy of 98 percent — mainly based on the spending habits of the couples.

✔ **Tweaking** is a process of many parts: Going through what-if scenarios, running multiple algorithms, and including or excluding certain variables as you step through the analysis. You get the most from this process if you always re-evaluate and try to understand your data in light of the business problem at hand, ask the hard questions, explore the data, and experiment with the different approaches.

✔ **Continuous refreshing of the model:** Updating your model periodically, in light of new information, is recommended to counteract the model's tendency to decay over time.

When new data becomes available, preserve your competitive edge by updating the model; to keep this process relevant, closely track and monitor your model's performance in real time.

When all companies are doing the same thing, exploring the same gaps, and competing in the same space, you have to stay ahead of the curve. One way to do so is to vary your tactics, spice up your campaigns, and hone your ability to detect the changing trends, positioning your business and to take full advantage of them.

In short, building a predictive model is an ongoing process, not a set-it-and-forget-it solution. Getting a business to think that way represents a cultural shift for most organizations, but that's what current market conditions demand.

One other form of complexity is the multiple directions your model-building can go. You can build a model about anything and everything — where do you start? The next section helps clear up the potential confusion by categorizing the different types of models.

Categorizing models

You have various ways to categorize the models used for predictive analytics. In general, you can sort them out by

- The business problems they solve and the primary business functions they serve (such as sales, advertising, human resources, or risk management).

- The mathematical implementation used in the model (such as statistics, data mining, and machine learning).

Every model will have some combination of these aspects; more often than not, one or the other will dominate. The intended function of the model can take one of various directions — predictive, classification, clustering, decision-oriented, or associative — as outlined in the following sections.

Predictive models

Predictive models analyze data and predict the next outcome. This is the big contribution of predictive analytics, as distinct from business intelligence. Business intelligence monitors what's going on in an organization now. Predictive models analyze historical data to make an informed decision about the likelihood of future outcomes.

Given certain conditions (recent number and frequency of customers complaints, the date of renewal of service approaching, and the availability of cheaper options by the competition) how likely is this customer to churn?

The output of the predictive model can also be a binary, yes/no or 0/1 answer: whether a transaction is fraudulent, for example. A predictive model can generate multiple results, sometimes combining yes/no results with a probability that a certain event will happen. A customer's creditworthiness, for example, could be rated as yes or no, and a probability assigned that describes how likely that customer is to pay off a loan on time.

Clustering and classification models

When a model uses clustering and classification, it identifies different groupings within existing data. You can still build a predictive model on top of the output of your clustering model using the clustering to classify new data points. If, for example, you run a clustering algorithm on your customers' data and thereby separate them into well-defined groups, you can then use classification to learn about a new customer and clearly identify his group. Then you can tailor your response (for example, a targeted marketing campaign) and your handling of the new customer.

Classification uses a combination of characteristics and features to indicate whether an item of data belongs to a particular class.

Many applications or business problems can be formulated as classification problems. At the very basic level, for example, you can classify outcomes as desired and undesired. For instance, you can classify an insurance claim as legitimate or fraudulent.

Decision models

Given a complex scenario, what is the best decision to make — and if you were to take that action, what would the outcome be? Decision-oriented models (simply called *decision models*) address such questions by building strategic plans so as to identify the best course of action, given certain events. Decision models can be risk mitigations strategies, helping to identify your best response to unlikely events.

Decision models probe various scenarios and select the best of all courses. To make an informed decision, you need deep understanding of the complex relationships in the data and the context you're operating in. A decision model serves as a tool to help you develop that understanding.

Association models

Associative models (called *association models*) are built on the underlying associations and relationships present in the data. If (for example) a customer is subscribed to a particular service, it's most likely that she will order another specific service. If a customer is looking to buy Product A (a sports car), and that product is associated with Product B (say, sunglasses branded by the carmaker), he is more likely to buy Product B.

Some of these associations can easily be identified; others may not be so obvious. Stumbling over an interesting association, previously unknown, can lead to dramatic benefits.

Another way of finding an association is to determine whether a given event increases the probability that another event will take place. If, for example, a company that leads a certain industrial sector just reported stellar earnings, what is the probability that a basket of stocks in that same sector to go up in value?

Describing and summarizing data

At the start of a predictive analytics project, the data scientist and the business analyst are not fully familiar with the data yet, and don't know what analysis will work best. Substantial time must be spent exploring that data with the sole goal of gaining familiarity. Visualization tools can help with this.

Describing your data can provide a precise summary of the characteristics and underlying structure that make the data relevant and useful. For example, identifying different groupings within the data is an essential step toward building a model that accurately represents your data — which makes a useful analytical result more likely.

Making better business decisions

Business leaders use predictive analytics, first and foremost, to empower business decision-making. The value of data to an organization is, essentially, how well it drives decision-making toward the organization's success.

Data-driven decisions give your business and managerial processes a solid footing, enhance your customers' satisfaction, and increase your return on investment. In a world marketplace full of ever-changing variables — governed by complex rules and immensely interdependent global systems — organizations can navigate more successfully by using predictive analytics to replace guesswork with actions based on real data.

Predictive analytics can transform your business by generating useful new insights that can serve as the basis of sound strategies and effective decision-making based on facts.

Healthcare Analytics Case Studies

The healthcare domain offers examples of predictive analytics in action. This section offers two case studies. In one, search queries predict a flu outbreak in a given region. In the other, cancer data predicts the survival rate of breast cancer patients.

Google search queries as epidemic predictors

People use Google to search for nearly everything, nearly all the time — their next destination, the name of the person they just met, topics they want to learn about, and even the symptoms of some disease they might think they have. That's where online searches become medically relevant.

Google researchers found that certain search terms are good indicators that an outbreak of a disease — in particular, influenza — is in progress.

This insight appeared in a recent research paper by Jeremy Ginsberg and several others, published in the journal *Nature*. The title sums up the unlikely-sounding premise: "Detecting Influenza Epidemics Using Search Engine Query Data". The results, however, are real: Google has been using search terms to predict the current flu activity, almost in real time, around the world.

Ginsberg and his colleagues discovered a strong correlation between the number of individuals who search for flu-related terms and the number of individuals who actually *have* the flu. Although an Internet search for information about a disease may seem an obvious action to take if you're feeling ill, consider why it seems obvious: An underlying pattern of behavior exists. The pattern shows up in the data.

Google insights derived from search terms reveal patterns that emerge from similar search queries and real-life phenomena. As stated on Google's site, "[there are] more allergy-related searches during allergy season, and more sunburn-related searches during the summer".

Google sees the patterns, and utilizes those search queries to extract trends. The result is the building of reliable models that can predict real-life events such as outbreaks in certain regions of the world, in real time.

The clinical data traditionally used for disease surveillance includes number of visits to hospitals, patients' symptoms, and patients' treatments. Such data elements can be used to detect or predict the spread of an epidemic. The Centers for Disease Control and Prevention (CDC) uses traditional surveillance systems with a one-to-two-week "reporting lag," according to Google. The government data that Google used — readily available from the CDC website (http://www.cdc.gov/flu/weekly) — consists of how many patients' visits were flu-related across the nine regions of the United States.

Based on a training dataset that encompassed five years of search queries and publicly available government data on influenza, Google built a model for the international surveillance of influenza.

Cancer survivability predictors

The medical uses of predictive analytics include the use of algorithms to predict the survivability rate among breast cancer patients. According to American Cancer Society Surveillance Research, breast cancer was the leading type of cancer in 2013. An estimated 232,340 new cases of breast cancer were expected to be diagnosed among American women in 2013, with 39,620 deaths expected from breast cancer in the same year.

Professor Abdelghani Bellaachia and his team at George Washington University made a powerful connection between predictive analytics and human benefit in a research paper published by the Society of Industrial and Applied Mathematics (SIAM): "Predicting Breast Cancer Survivability Using Data Mining Techniques."

In the course of developing the results described in this paper, the team used publicly available historical data about breast cancer survivability to build the model. That data can be downloaded from National Cancer Institute's Surveillance Epidemiology and End Results website, SEER for short (`http://seer.cancer.gov`).

SEER's database encapsulated historical data about different types of cancer. The collected data on breast cancer included several attributes such as survival time, vital status, and cause of death.

The predictive analytics model adopted for this case study was classification-based. Three algorithms were used — Naïve Bayes, Neural Network, and Decision Trees. (See Chapter 7 for more on these algorithms.) Researchers compared their accuracy and ultimately selected the best for use in their model.

Since this was a classification-based prediction, the model had to be trained by using clusters or classes of data. The pre-classification step requires organizing the data into *clusters* (classes): `survived` and `not survived`. Thus the dataset represents two groups of patients. Each row or record corresponds to a breast cancer patient; each can be labeled as `survived` or `not survived`.

The training set contains the records of patient data used to build the model; the rest of the records (test data) were used to test the model.

In the case study, a model was selected for breast cancer survivability after comparing all three algorithms' outputs. For this specific application in this specific study, the Decision Trees model performed better by accurately classifying the test data and labeling the target group.

Social and Marketing Analytics Case Studies

On a whole different note, social and marketing analytics provide further evidence of startling-but-useful connections between online activity and useful predictions. The next sections examine three examples: the use of Twitter to predict the stock market; the use of shopping data over time to predict pregnancy status of the customer; and using Twitter to predict earthquakes and election outcomes. Relax. It only looks like magic.

Tweets as predictors for the stock market

Twitter can be a surprisingly valuable source of data when you're building a predictive model for the stock market. A paper by Johan Bollen and his colleagues, "Twitter Mood Predicts the Stock Market," summarizes an analysis of about ten million tweets (by about three million users), which were collected and used to predict the performance of the stock market, up to six days in advance.

The study aggregated tweets by date, and limited its scope to only those (three million) tweets that explicitly contained sentiment-related expressions such as "I feel, I am feeling, I'm feeling, I don't feel" were considered in the analysis. The researchers used two tools in this classic example of opinion mining:

- **Opinion Finder** is a sentiment-analysis tool developed by researchers at the University of Pittsburgh, Cornell University, and the University of Utah. The tool mines text and provides a value that reflects whether the mood discovered in the text is negative or positive.

- **GPOMS (Google Profile of Mood States)** is a sentiment analysis tool provided by Google. The tool can analyze a text and generate six mood values that could be associated with that text: calm, happy, alert, sure, vital, and kind.

The research followed this general sequence of steps:

1. By aggregating the collected tweets by date and tracking the seven values of the discovered moods, the study generated a *time series* — a sequence of data points taken in order over time. The purpose was to discover and represent public mood over time.

2. For comparison, the researchers downloaded the time series for the Dow Jones Industrial Average (DIJA) closing values (posted on Yahoo! Finance) for the period of time during which they collected the tweets.

3. The study correlated the two time series, using *Granger causality analysis* — a statistical analysis that evaluates whether a time series can be used to forecast another time series — to investigate the hypothesis that public mood values can be used as indicators to predict future DJIA value over the same time period.

4. The study used a Fuzzy Neural Network model (see Chapter 7) to test the hypothesis that including public mood values enhances the prediction accuracy of DJIA.

Although the research did not provide a complete predictive model, this preliminary correlation of public mood to stock-market performance identifies a quest worth pursuing.

Target store predicts pregnant women

In an unintentionally invasive instance, the Target store chain used predictive analytics on big data to predict which of its customers were likely to be pregnant. (Charles Duhigg, a reporter at *The New York Times,* initially covered this story.) Target collected data on some specific items that couples were buying, such as vitamins, unscented lotions, books on pregnancy, and maternity clothing.

Using that data, Target developed predictive models for pregnancy among its customers. The models scored the likelihood of a given customer to be pregnant.

Keep in mind that predictive analytics models don't rely on only one factor (such as purchasing patterns) to predict the likelihood of an event. Target probably did not rely on only one factor to make its predictions. Rather, the model looked at factors that included purchase patterns of pregnancy-related products, age, relationship status, and websites visited. Most important, the resulting predictions were based on events that happened over a period of time, not on isolated events. For instance, a couple buys vitamins at some point in time, a pregnancy-guide magazine at another point in time, hand towels at yet another time, and maternity clothes at a still different time. Further, the same couple could have visited websites related to pre-pregnancy, or could have visited websites to look for baby names or lessons for couples on how to cope with the first days of pregnancy. (This information could have been saved from search queries done by the couple.) Once Target identified potential customers as probably pregnant, it could then send specialized coupons for products such as lotion and diapers to those customers.

Details of the exact model that Target used to predict customer pregnancy are not available. One way to build such a model, however, is to use classification-based prediction. (Note that this is not the only possible way, and may not be the approach used at Target.) The general procedure would look like this:

1. Collect data about past, current, or potential customers, and their activities over time in cyberspace.

   You can use one of the predictive analytics tools mentioned in this book to connect to data sources such as social networks, micro-blogs, blogs, and healthcare websites. Or you can buy third-party research to provide you with data. Note that big data may have all kinds of emerging properties.

2. Collect transactional data from customers who actually purchase the products you're interested in, some of which are pregnancy-related.

3. Select training data that will be used to build your classification-based model, and set aside some of the past data to use in testing your model.

4. Test the model until it's validated and you're happy with the accuracy of its performance on historical data.

5. Deploy your model. As new incoming data for a given customer arrives, your model will classify that customer as either potentially pregnant or not.

Twitter-based predictors of earthquakes

Another astonishing use of predictive analytics is to detect earthquakes. Yes, earthquakes. Researchers Sakaki, Okazaki, and Matsuo from the University of Tokyo — situated in a region known for seismic activity — used postings on the Twitter microblog social network to detect an earthquake in real time. A summary of their 2010 research ("Earthquake Shakes Twitter Users: Real-Time Event Detection by Social Sensors") was published in the proceedings of the 2013 International Conference on World Wide Web.

The researchers' approach was to utilize Twitter users as sensor that can signal an event through tweets. Because Twitter users tend to tweet several times daily, the researchers could capture, analyze and categorize tweets in real time. They sought to predict the occurrence of earthquakes of Intensity three or more by monitoring those tweets. One result of the research was an earthquake-based Twitter monitoring system that sends e-mails to registered users to notify them of an earthquake in progress. Apparently the registered users of this system received notification much faster than from the announcements broadcasted by the Japan Meteorological Agency. The Twitter-based system was based on a simple idea:

1. The earthquake-detection application starts collecting tweets about an event that's happening in real time.

2. The collected tweets would be used to trace the exact location of the earthquake.

One problem: Tweets containing the word *earthquake* may or may not be about an actual earthquake. The data collected was originally focused on tweets consisting of words directly related to an earthquake event — for example, such phrases as "Earthquake!" or "Now it's shaking!" The problem was that the meanings of such words might depend on context. *Shaking* crops up in phrases such as "someone is shaking hands with my boss" — and even *earthquake* might mean a topic rather than an event (as in, "I am attending an earthquake conference"). For that matter, the verb tense of the tweet might refer to a past event (as in a phrase such as, "the earthquake yesterday was scary").

To cut through these ambiguities, the researchers developed a classification-based predictive model based on the Support Vector Machine (see Chapter 7).

- A tweet would be classified as positive or negative on the basis of a simple principle: A positive tweet is about an actual earthquake; a negative tweet is not.

- Each tweet was represented by using three groups of features.

  The number of words in the tweet and the position of the query word within the tweet.

  The keywords in the tweet.

The words that precede and follow a query word such as *earthquake* in the tweet.

✔ The model makes these assumptions:

That a tweet classified as positive contains the tweeter's geographical location.

That a tweeter who sends a positive tweet can be interpreted as a virtual sensor.

That such a tweeter is actively tweeting about actual events that are taking place.

Twitter-based predictors of political campaign outcomes

In a relatively short time, political activity has saturated online social media — and vice versa — even at the higher levels of government. At the United States House of Representatives, for example, it's common to see congressional staffers in the House gallery, busily typing tweets into their BlackBerries while attending a session. Every senator and congressman or congresswoman has a Twitter page — and they (or their staffers) have to keep it active, so they tweet about everything happening inside the House.

Even so, some things never change: A successful political campaign still focuses on making its candidate popular enough to get elected. A winning candidate is the one who can make a lot of people aware of him or her — and (most importantly) get people talking positively about him or her. That's where politics and social media grab hold of each other.

An Indiana University study has shown a statistically significant relationship between Twitter data and U.S. election results. DiGrazia et al. published a paper titled "More Tweets, More Votes: Social Media as a Quantitative Indicator of Political Behavior". (An electronic copy is available at: `http://ssrn.com/abstract=2235423`.) The study found a correlation between the number of times a candidate for the House of Representatives was mentioned on Twitter in the months before an election and that candidate's performance in that election. The conclusion: The more a candidate is mentioned on Twitter, the better.

According to a *Washington Post* article, the sentiments expressed in tweets as reactions to the political events of the 2012 elections matched the balance of public opinion (as indicated by a random-sample survey) about 25 percent of the time.

As Nick Kolakowski relates in an article published online at Slashdot (`http://slashdot.org/`), a team at the Oxford Internet Institute, led by Mark Graham, investigated the relationship between Twitter and election results. They collected thirty million Tweets in October 2012, and counted how many tweets mentioned the two presidential candidates. They found that Obama was mentioned in 132,771 tweets; Romney was mentioned in 120,637 tweets. The Institute translated the count into projected percentages of the popular vote — 52.4 percent for Obama versus 47.6 percent for Romney. At least in terms of popular votes, those figures predicted Obama's victory.

However, a certain ambiguity tended to cloud the picture: The user who tweeted *about* a candidate might not vote *for* that candidate. One way to unveil the intention of such a Twitter user would be to apply sentiment analysis to the text of the tweet. In fact, Graham admitted that they should have analyzed the sentiments of the tweets. Clearly, sentiment analysis plays a major role in building a predictive analytics model for such situations.

So, if you're building a model that seeks to predict victory or defeat for the next prominent political candidate, here's a general approach:

1. Start by collecting a comprehensive training dataset that consists of data about past political campaigns, and present data about all current candidates.

   Data should be gathered from microblogs such as Twitter or Tumblr, and also from news articles, YouTube videos (include the number of views and viewer comments), and other sources.

2. Count the mentions of the candidates from your sources.

3. Use sentiment analysis to count the number of positive, negative, and neutral mentions for each candidate.

4. As you iterate through the development of your model, make sure your analysis includes other criteria that affect elections and voting.

   Such factors include scandals, candidates' interviews, debates, people's views as determined by opinion mining, candidates' visits to other countries, sentiment analysis on the candidates' spouses, and so on.

5. *Geocode* — record the geographical coordinates of — your criteria so you can predict by locations.

   One or more of the features you identify will have predicting power; those are the features that indicate whether a candidate won a past election. Such results are relevant to your model's predictions.

When your training data has been gathered and cleaned, then a suitable model can be based on classification. At this point, you can use Support Vector Machines, decision trees, or an ensemble model (see Chapter 7 for more on these algorithms) that would base predictions on a set of current criteria *and* past data for each of the political candidates. The idea is to score the results; the higher score should tell you whether the candidate in question will win.

Chapter 6

Identifying Similarities in Data

*T*here is so much data around us that it can feel overwhelming. Large amounts of information are constantly being generated, organized, analyzed, and stored. *Data clustering* is the process that can help you make sense of this flood of data by discovering hidden groupings of similar data items. Data clustering provides a description of your data that says, in essence, *your data contains x number of groups of similar data objects.*

Clustering — in the form of grouping similar things — is part of our daily activities. You use clustering any time you group similar items together. For example, when you store groceries in your fridge, you group the vegetables by themselves in the crisper, put frozen foods in their own section (the freezer), and so on. When you organize currency in your wallet, you arrange the bills by denomination — larger with larger, smaller with smaller. Clustering algorithms achieve this kind of order on a large scale for businesses or organizations — where datasets can comprise thousands or millions of data records associated with thousands of customers, suppliers, business partners, products, services, and so on.

In short, data clustering is an intelligent separation of data into groups of similar data items. The algorithms that do this task have been applied in fields such as biology, marketing, information retrieval, and the analysis of online social networks.

This chapter guides you through the mechanics of data clustering and outlines its importance in predictive analytics.

Explaining Data Clustering

A *dataset* (or data collection) is a set of items. For instance, a set of documents is a dataset where the data items are documents. A set of social network users' information (name, age, list of friends, photos, and so on) is a dataset where the data items are profiles of social network users.

Data clustering is the task of dividing a dataset into subsets of similar items. Items can also be referred to as instances, observation, entities or data objects. In most cases, a dataset is represented in table format — *a data matrix*. A data matrix is a table of numbers, documents, or expressions, represented in rows and columns as follows:

- ✔ Each row corresponds to a given item in the dataset.

  Rows are sometimes referred to as *items, objects, instances, or observations.*

- ✔ Each column represents a particular characteristic of an item.

  Columns are referred to as *features or attributes.*

Applying data clustering to a dataset generates groups of similar data items. These groups are called *clusters* — collections of similar data items.

Similar items have a strong, measurable relationship among them — fresh vegetables, for example, are more similar to each other than they are to frozen foods — and clustering techniques use that relationship to group the items.

The strength of a relationship between two or more items can be quantified as a *similarity measure:* A mathematical function that computes the correlation between two data items. The results of that computation, called *similarity values,* essentially compare a particular data item to all other items in the dataset. Those other items will be either more similar or less similar in comparison to that specific item.

Computed similarities play a major role in assigning items to groups (*clusters*). Each group has an item that best represents it; this item is referred to as a *cluster representative.*

Consider a dataset that consists of several types of fruits in a basket, as shown in Figure 6-1. The basket has fruits of different types such as apples, bananas, lemons, and pears. In this case, fruits are the data items. The data clustering process extracts groups of similar fruits out of this dataset (basket of different fruits).

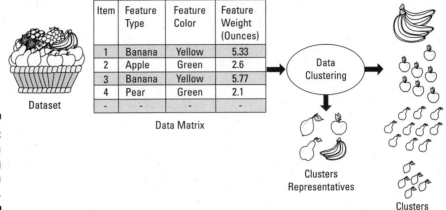

Figure 6-1:
Data
clustering
applied to a
fruit dataset.

The first step in a data clustering process is to translate this dataset into a data matrix: One way to model this dataset is to have the rows represent the items in the dataset (fruits); and the columns represent characteristics, or features, that describe the items.

For instance, a fruit feature can be the fruit type (such as a banana or apple), weight, color, or price. In this example dataset, the items have three features: fruit type, color, and weight.

In most cases, applying a data clustering technique to the fruit dataset as described above allows you to

✔ **Retrieve groups (clusters) of similar items.** You can tell that your fruit is of N number of groups. After that, if you pick a random fruit, you will be able to make a statement about that item as being part of one of the N groups.

✔ **Retrieve cluster representatives of each group.** In this example, a cluster representative would be picking one fruit type from the basket and putting it aside. The characteristics of this fruit are such that that fruit best represents the cluster it belongs to.

When you're done clustering, your dataset is organized and divided into natural groupings.

Motivation

Data clustering reveals structure in the data by extracting natural groupings from a dataset. Therefore discovering clusters is an essential step toward formulating ideas and hypotheses about the structure of your data and deriving insights to better understand it.

Data clustering can also be a way to model data: It represents a larger body of data by clusters or cluster representatives.

In addition, your analysis may seek simply to partition the data into groups of similar items — as when *market segmentation* partitions target-market data into groups such as

- ✔ Consumers who share the same interests (such as Mediterranean cooking)
- ✔ Consumers who have common needs (for example, those with specific food allergies)

Identifying clusters of similar customers can help you develop a marketing strategy that addresses the needs of specific clusters.

Moreover, data clustering can also help you identify, learn, or predict the nature of new data items — especially how new data can be linked with making predictions. For example, in *pattern recognition,* analyzing patterns in the data (such as buying patterns in particular regions or age groups) can help you develop predictive analytics — in this case, predicting the nature of future data items that can fit well with established patterns.

The fruit basket example uses data clustering to distinguish between different data items. Suppose your business assembles custom fruit baskets, and a new, unknown fruit is introduced to the market. You want to learn or predict which cluster the new item will belong to if you add it to the fruit basket. Because you've already applied data clustering to the fruit dataset, you have four clusters — which makes it easier to predict which cluster (specific type of fruit) is appropriate for the new item. All you have to do is compare the unknown fruit to the other four clusters' representatives and identify which cluster is the best match. Although this process may seem obvious for a person working with a small dataset, it's not so obvious at a larger scale — when you have to cluster millions of items without examining each one. The complexity becomes exponential when the dataset is large, diverse, and relatively incoherent — which is why clustering algorithms exist: Computers do that type of work best.

A similar, common, and practical example is the application of data clustering to e-mail messages, dividing a dataset of e-mails into spam and non-spam clusters. An ideal spam-detection tool would need to first divide a dataset (all past e-mails) into two types (groups): spam and non-spam. Then the tool predicts whether unknown incoming e-mail is spam or non-spam. This second step, often referred to as data classification, is covered in detail in Chapter 7.

The goal would be to minimize the number of spam e-mails that end up in your inbox and also minimize the number of legitimate e-mails that end up in your spam folder. (As you've no doubt noticed, this kind of clustering and classification isn't quite perfected yet.)

Data clustering is used in several fields:

- ✔ **Computer imaging:** Data clustering is part of *image segmentation* — the process of dividing a digital image into multiple segments in order to analyze the image more easily. Applying data clustering to an image generates segments (clusters) of contours that represent objects — aiding the detection of threatening health conditions in medical diagnosis and in the screening of airport baggage for suspicious materials.

- ✔ **Information retrieval:** Here the aim is to search and retrieve information from a collection of data, for instance a set of documents. Dividing a collection of documents into groups of similar documents is an essential task in information retrieval. Data clustering of documents by topic improves information search.

- ✔ **Medicine:** Applying data clustering to a matrix of gene expression (often known as *microarray gene expression data*) from different cancer-diagnosed patients can generate clusters of positively and negatively diagnosed cancer patients, which can help predict the nature of new cases.

- ✔ **Marketing:** Using data clustering to group customers according to similar purchase behavior improves the efficiency of targeted marketing.

- ✔ **Law enforcement:** In social network analysis, the same data-clustering techniques that can help detect communities of common interests can also help identify online groups involved in suspicious activity.

Converting Raw Data into a Matrix

Before you can extract groups of similar data items from your dataset, you might need to represent your data in a tabular format known as a *data matrix*. This is a preprocessing step that comes before data clustering.

Creating a matrix of terms in documents

Suppose the dataset that you're about to analyze is contained in a set of Microsoft Word documents. The first thing you need to do is to convert the set of documents into a data matrix. Several commercial and open-source tools can handle that task, producing a matrix (often known as a *document-term matrix*), in which each row corresponds to a document in the dataset. Examples of these tools include RapidMiner, and R text-mining packages such as tm.

The next section explains how documents can be converted into a data matrix.

A *document* is, in essence, a set of words. A *term* is a set of one or multiple words.

Every term that a document contains is mentioned either once or several times in the same document. The number of times a term is mentioned in a document can be represented by *term frequency* (TF), a numerical value.

We construct the matrix of terms in the document as follows:

- ✔ The terms that appear in all documents are listed across the top row.
- ✔ Document titles are listed down the leftmost column
- ✔ The numbers that appear inside the matrix cells correspond to each term's frequency.

For instance, in Table 6-1, Document A is represented as set of numbers (5,16,0,19,0,0.) where 5 corresponds to the number of times the term *predictive analytics* is repeated, 16 corresponds to the number to times *computer science* is repeated, and so on. This is the simplest way to convert a set of documents into a matrix.

Table 6-1	Converting a Collection of Documents into a Matrix					
	Predictive Analytics	*Computer Science*	*Learning*	*Clustering*	*2013*	*Anthropology*
Document A	5	16	0	19	0	0
Document B	8	6	2	3	0	0
Document C	0	5	2	3	3	9
Document D	1	9	13	4	6	7
Document E	2	16	16	0	2	13
Document F	13	0	19	16	4	2

Term selection

One challenge in clustering text documents is determining how to select the best terms to represent all documents in the collection. How important a term is in a collection of documents can be calculated in different ways. If, for example, you count the number of times a term is repeated in a document and compare that total with how often it recurs in the whole collection, you get a sense of the term's importance relative to other terms.

Basing the relative importance of a term on its frequency in a collection is often known as *weighting*. The weight you assign can be based on two principles:

- ✔ Terms that appear several times in a document are favored over terms that appear only once.

- ✔ Terms that are used in relatively few documents are favored over terms that are mentioned in all documents.

If (for example) the term *century* is mentioned in all documents in your dataset, then you might not consider assigning it enough weight to have a column of its own in the matrix.

Similarly, if you're dealing with a dataset of users of an online social network, you can easily convert that dataset into a matrix. User IDs or names will occupy the rows; the columns will list features that best describe those users. (An example of a data matrix of social network users appears later in this chapter.)

Identifying K-Groups in Your Data

An *algorithm* is a step-by-step mathematical formula used for solving a problem. One of the most popular and simple algorithm used in data clustering, *K-means,* is named after the algorithm's input and output:

> **K** is an input to the algorithm; it stands for the number of groupings that the algorithm must extract from a dataset, expressed algebraically as *k*.

> **means** are outputs of the algorithm; they refer to the set of representatives that represent *k* clusters. A *cluster representative* is the statistical mean of all the data items in the same cluster. The next section explains in detail how to derive a cluster representative (that is, a mean).

K-means clustering algorithm

A K-means algorithm divides a given dataset into *k* clusters. The algorithm performs the following operations:

1. Pick *k* random items from the dataset and label them as cluster representatives.

2. Associate each remaining item in the dataset with the nearest cluster representative, using a Euclidean distance calculated by a similarity function (explained later in this chapter).

3. Recalculate the new clusters' representatives.

4. Repeat Steps 2 and 3 until the clusters do not change.

A representative of a cluster is the mathematical *mean* (average) of all items that belong to the same cluster. This representative is also called a *cluster centroid.* For instance, consider three items from the fruits dataset where

Type 1 corresponds to bananas.

Type 2 corresponds to apples.

Color 2 corresponds to yellow.

Color 3 corresponds to green.

Table 6-2 shows 3 items of the fruits dataset. We will assume that these items are assigned to the same cluster.

Table 6-2	Three Items from the Fruit Dataset		
Item	*Feature#1 Type*	*Feature#2 Color*	*Feature#3 Weight (Ounces)*
1	1	2	5.33
2	2	3	9.33
3	1	2	2.1

Table 6-3 shows the calculations of a cluster representative of three items that belong to the same cluster. The cluster representative is a vector of three attributes. Its attributes are the average of the attributes of the items in the cluster in question.

Table 6-3	Calculating the Representative of Three Items		
Item	*Feature#1 Type*	*Feature#2 Color*	*Feature#3 Weight (Ounces)*
1	1	2	5.33
2	2	3	9.33
3	1	2	2.1
Cluster Representative (Centroid Vector)	(1+2+1)/3=1.33	(2+3+2)/3=2.33	(5.33 + 9.33 + 2.1)/3= 5.59

The dataset shown in Table 6-4 consists of seven customers' ratings of two products, A and B. The ranking represents the number of points (between 0 and 20) that each customer has given to a product — the more points given, the higher the product is ranked. Using a K-means algorithm and assuming that k is equal to 2, the dataset will be partitioned into two groups. The rest of the procedure looks like this:

1. **Pick two random items from the dataset and label them as cluster representatives (as shown in Table 6-5).**

   Table 6-6 shows the initial step of selecting random centroids from which the K-means clustering process begins. The initial centroids are selected randomly from the data that you are about to analyze. In this case, you're looking for two clusters, so two data items are randomly selected: Customers 1 and 5. At first, the clustering process builds two clusters around those two initial (randomly selected) cluster representatives. Then the cluster representatives are recalculated; the calculation is based on the items in each cluster.

Table 6-4   Dataset of Customer Ratings for Products A and B

Customer ID	Customer Ratings of Product A	Customer Ratings of Product B
1	2	2
2	3	4
3	6	8
4	7	10
5	10	14
6	9	10
7	7	9

2. **Inspect every other item (customer) and assign it to the cluster representative to which it is most similar.**

   Use the *Euclidean distance* to calculate how similar an item is to a group of items:

   Similarity of Item I to Cluster X = $\sqrt{(f_1 - x_1)^2 + (f_2 - x_2)^2 + \cdots + (f_n - x_n)^2}$

   The values $f_1, f_2, \ldots, f_n$ are the numerical values of the features that describe the item in question. The values $x_1, x_2, \ldots, x_n$ are the features (mean values) of the cluster representative (centroid), assuming that each item has n features.

For instance, consider the item called Customer 2 (3, 4): The customer's rating for Product A was 3 and the rating for Product B was 4. The cluster representative feature, as shown in Table 6-6, is (2, 2). The similarity of Customer 2 to Cluster 1 is calculated as follows:

Similarity of Item 2 to Cluster 1 = $\sqrt{(3-2)^2+(4-2)^2}=2.24$

Here's what the same process looks like with Cluster 2:

Similarity of Item 2 to Cluster 2 = $\sqrt{(3-10)^2+(4-14)^2}=12.21$

Comparing these results, you assign Item 2 (that is, Customer 2) to Cluster 1 because the numbers say Item 2 is more similar to Cluster 1.

3. **Apply the same similarity analysis to every other item in the dataset.**

   Every time a new member joins a cluster, you must recalculate the cluster representative, following the example shown in Table 6-3.

   The use of K-means is an iterative process. At each iteration, the algorithm steps shown here are repeated until the clusters show no further changes. Tables 6-6 and 6-7 show these iterations and assignments of items to clusters. At the end of Iteration 1, Cluster 1 contains Items 1, 2, and 3; Cluster 2 contains Items 4, 5, 6 and 7. The new cluster representatives are (3.67, 4.67) for Cluster 1 and (8.25, 10.75) for Cluster 2.

   Table 6-6 depicts the results of the first iteration of K-mean algorithm. Notice that k equals 2, so you're looking for two clusters, which divides a set of customers into two meaningful groups. Every customer is analyzed separately and is assigned to one of the clusters on the basis of the customer's similarity to each of the current cluster representatives. Note that cluster representatives are updated each time a new member joins a cluster.

4. **Iterate the dataset again, going through every element; compute the similarity between each element and its current cluster representative.**

   Notice that Customer 3 has moved from Cluster 1 to Cluster 2. This is because Customer 3's distance to the cluster representative of Cluster 2 is closer than to the cluster representative of Cluster 1.

Table 6-5   Selecting Random Initial Cluster Representatives

	Cluster Representative (Centroid Vector)
Cluster 1	Customer ID#1 (2, 2)
Cluster 2	Customer ID#5 (10,14)

| Table 6-6 | First Iteration of Applying a K-Means Algorithm to the Dataset of Customer Ratings | | | |

Iteration#1	Customer Cluster 1		Customer Cluster 2	
Customer to be examined	Customer IDs belonging to Cluster 1	Cluster Representative	Customer IDs belonging to Cluster 1	Cluster Representative
1		(2, 2)	5	(10, 14)
2	1, 2	(2.5, 3)	5	(10, 14)
3	1, 2, 3	(3.67, 4.67)	5	(10, 14)
4	1, 2, 3	(3.67, 4.67)	4, 5	(8.51, 12)
6	1, 2, 3	(3.67, 4.67)	4, 5, 6	(8.67, 11.33)
7	1, 2, 3	(3.67, 4.67)	4, 5, 6, 7	(8.25, 10.75)

Table 6-7 shows a second iteration of K-means algorithm on customer data. Each customer is being re-analyzed. Customer 2 is being assigned to Cluster 1 because Customer 2 is closer to the representative of Cluster 1 than Cluster 2. The same scenario applies to Customer 3. Notice that a cluster representative is being recalculated (as in Table 6-3) each time a new member is assigned to a cluster.

| Table 6-7 | Second Iteration of Applying a K-Means Algorithm to the Dataset of Customer Ratings | | | |

Iteration#2	Customer Cluster 1		Customer Cluster 2	
Customer to be examined	Customer IDs belonging to Cluster 1	Cluster Representative	Customer IDs belonging to Cluster 2	Cluster Representative
1	1, 2, 3	(3.67, 4.67)	4, 5, 6, 7	(8.25, 10.75)
2	1, 2, 3	(3.67, 4.67)	4, 5, 6, 7	(8.25, 10.75)
3	1, 2	(2.5, 3)	3, 4, 5, 6, 7	(7.8, 10.2)
4	1, 2	(2.5, 3)	3, 4, 5, 6, 7	(7.8, 10.2)
5	1, 2	(2.5, 3)	3, 4, 5, 6, 7	(7.8, 10.2)
6	1, 2	(2.5, 3)	3, 4, 5, 6, 7	(7.8, 10.2)
7	1, 2	(2.5, 3)	3, 4, 5, 6, 7	(7.8, 10.2)

Clustering by nearest neighbors

Nearest Neighbors is a simple algorithm widely used to cluster data by assigning an item to a cluster by determining what other items are most similar to it. A typical use of the Nearest Neighbors algorithm follows these general steps:

1. Derive a similarity matrix from the items in the dataset.

   This matrix, referred to as the *distance matrix,* will hold the similarity values for each and every item in the data set. (These values are elaborated in detail in the next example.)

2. With the matrix in place, compare each item in the dataset to every other item and compute the similarity value (as shown in the previous section).

   Initially, every item is assigned to a cluster of one item.

3. Using the distance matrix, examine every item to see whether the distance to its neighbors is less than a value that you have defined.

   This value is called the *threshold.*

4. The algorithm puts each element in a separate cluster, analyzes the items, and decides which items are similar, and adds similar items to the same cluster.

5. The algorithm stops when all items have been examined.

Consider, for example, a dataset of eight geographical locations where individuals live. The purpose is to divide these individuals into groups based on their geographical locations, as determined by the Global Positioning System (see Table 6-8).

Table 6-8 shows a simple dataset of individuals' geographic data. For purposes of simplicity, global positional longitude and latitude are depicted as whole numbers. Assume that all the data collected about these eight individuals was collected at a specific point in time.

Table 6-8	GPS Dataset	
Individual ID	*GPS - Geographical Longitude*	*GPS - Geographical Latitude*
1	2	10
2	2	5
3	8	4
4	5	8

Individual ID	GPS - Geographical Longitude	GPS - Geographical Latitude
5	7	5
6	6	4
7	1	2
8	4	9

As with K-means, the first pre-step is to calculate the similarity values for every pair of individuals. One way to calculate a similarity between two items is to determine the Euclidean distance (as described in the previous section). The similarity value between two points is calculated as shown earlier in Table 6-9.

Similarity between Item A and Item B = $\sqrt{\left(f_{a,1}-f_{b,1}\right)^2+\left(f_{a,2}-f_{b,2}\right)^2+\cdots+\left(f_{a,n}-f_{b,n}\right)^2}$

Here $f_{a,1}$ is the first feature of Item A, $f_{a,2}$ is the second feature of Item A, and corresponding values labeled b represent the features of Item B. The variable n is the number of features. In this example, n is 2. For instance, the similarity between Item 1 and Item 2 is calculated as follows:

Similarity between Item 1 and Item 2 = $\sqrt{(2-2)^2+\left(10-5\right)^2}=5$

On the basis of this measurement of similarity between items, you can use the Nearest Neighbor algorithm to extract clusters from the dataset of geographical locations.

The first step is to place the individual whose ID is 1, longitude is 2, and latitude is 10 in cluster C1. Then go through all remaining individuals computing how similar each one is to the individual in C1. If the similarity between Individual 1 and another Individual x is less than 4.5 (the threshold value beyond which an item is too dissimilar — the user of the algorithm can set or choose this value), then Individual x will join C1; otherwise you create a new cluster to accommodate Individual x.

Table 6-9 shows the similarities and numerical relationships between Individuals 1 through 8. The similarity of these data elements is calculated as a Euclidean distance (explained earlier in this chapter); for instance, the similarity between Individual 1 and Individual 5 is 7.07. Individuals with similarity values closer to 0 have greater similarity. Half the matrix is not filled because the matrix is *symmetric* (that is, the similarity between Individuals 1 and 4 is the same as the similarity between Individuals 4 and 1).

Table 6-9 Determining the Degree Of Similarity (Euclidean Distance) Between Individuals

	Individual#1	Individual#2	Individual#3	Individual#4	Individual#5	Individual#6	Individual#7	Individual#8
Individual#1	0	5	8.49	3.61	7.07	7.21	8.06	2.24
Individual#2		0	6.08	4.24	5	4.12	3.16	4.47
Individual#3			0	5	1.41	2	7.28	6.40
Individual#4				0	3.61	4.12	7.21	1.41
Individual#5					0	1.41	6.71	5
Individual#6						0	5.39	5.39
Individual#7							0	7.62
Individual#8								0

You have now assigned Individual 1 to the first cluster (C1). The similarity between Individual 1 and Individual 2 is equal to 5, which is greater than the threshold value 4.5. A new cluster is generated — and Individual 2 belongs to it. At this stage, you have two clusters of one item each: C1 = {Individual 1} and C2 = {Individual 2}.

Moving the focus to Individual 3, you find that the similarity between Individual 3 and Individual 2 & 1 is larger than the threshold value 4.5. Thus you assign Individual 3 to a new cluster containing one item: C3 = {Individual 3}.

Moving to Individual 4, you calculate how similar Individual 4 is to Individuals 1, 2, and 3. The nearest (most similar) to Individual 4 happens to be Individual 1. The similarity between 4 and 1 is approximately 3.61, which is less than the threshold value 4.5. Individual 4 joins Individual 1 in Cluster C1. The clusters constructed so far are: C1 = {Individual 1, Individual 4}, C2 = {Individual 2} and C3 = {Individual 3}.

Next is to examine Individual 5 and calculate how similar it is to Individuals 1, 2, 3, and 4. The item nearest in distance (most similar) to Individual 5 is Individual 3. The similarity is $\sqrt{2}$, which is less than the threshold value of 4.5. Thus Individual 5 joins C3. The clusters constructed so far are: C1 = {Individual 1, Individual 4}, C2 = {Individual 2} and C3 = {Individual 3, Individual 5}.

When you examine Individual 6 and calculate how similar it is to Individuals 1, 2, 3, 4, and 5, you discover that Individual 5 is nearest (most similar) to Individual 6. Thus Individual 6 joins C3. The clusters constructed so far are: C1 = {Individual 1, Individual 4}, C2 = {Individual 2} and C3 = {Individual 3, Individual 5, Individual 6}.

When you examine Individual 7 and calculate how similar it is to Individuals 1, 2, 3, 4, 5, 6, and 7, you find that the nearest (most similar) item to Individual 7 is Individual 2. Thus Individual 7 joins C2. The clusters constructed so far are: C1 = {Individual 1, Individual 4}, C2 = {Individual 2, Individual 7} and C3 = {Individual 3, Individual 5, Individual 6}.

When you examine Individual 8, and calculate its similarity to Individuals 1, 2, 3, 4, and 5, you find that the nearest (most similar) item to Individual 8 is Individual 4. Thus Individual 8 joins C1.

The clusters constructed so far, containing items most similar to each other, are

C1 = {Individual 1, Individual 4, Individual 8}

C2 = {Individual 2, Individual 7}

C3 = {Individual 3, Individual 5, Individual 6}

Finding Associations Among Data Items

The use of predictive analytics as a data-mining tool also seeks to discover hidden relationships among items in your data. These hidden relationships are called *mining association rules*.

Consider a large dataset of customer transactions, where a *customer transaction* consists of the product(s) purchased by a customer at a given time. In a scenario like this one, the purpose of predictive analytics *as a tool* is to identify associations between products in the dataset. An association between two products is a *relation*, which can help the analyst discern a pattern and derive a rule from the raw data of customer transactions. An instance of such a rule could be grocery-buying patterns: If a customer purchases butter and bread, he or she is also likely to buy milk. The rule discovered in this case can be written as

{butter, bread} → {milk}.

In data-mining terms, {butter, bread} is called a *basket*. A real-world basket contains items, of course, and so does this basket: butter and bread. The discovered rule just described is that if a basket contains the items butter and bread, then it is also very likely to contain milk.

Finding such *association rules* in a dataset of customer transactions helps a company (in this case, a grocery store) maximize revenue by deciding which products should be on sale, how to position products in the store's aisles, and how and when to offer promotional pricing.

Analyzing the data generated by past transactions in order to maximize profit is a common practice. Sales data collected regularly (daily, weekly, monthly) from point-of-sale systems such as online stores, supermarkets, bookstores, and restaurants is referred to as *basket data* — which is, in this case, essentially large-scale data about sales transactions. Association rules are generated with a score known as *confidence* — which refers to how likely they are to hold true. For instance, if a generated rule shows that 98% of the people who purchased butter and bread also purchased milk, that percentage value (98%) is the *confidence value*.

Other terms associated with a rule are *antecedent* (the "if" part of an "if-then" statement) and the *consequent* (the "then" part of the "if-then"). In the previous example, the antecedent is butter and bread; milk is the consequent.

In practice, your company will use predictive analytics to retrieve association rules from a customer database. The analyst issues queries whose purpose is to find rules that are either related to the antecedent (what was bought) or rules that can lead to the consequent (what can be expected to be bought).

In another example, consider a coffee shop manager who wants to maximize profit using association rules as a data-mining tool. The store manager would request items like these:

- ✔ Generate all rules that have *croissant* in the antecedent and *café latte* in the consequent.

    Such rules would help the manager develop recommendations for which products to sell together with croissants; if café latte is prominent as a consequent, it's highly likely that the recommendation will be to sell café latte with croissants.

- ✔ Generate all rules that have *chocolate chip cookie* as an antecedent.

    These rules may help outline and design a plan for increasing sales of chocolate chip cookies.

- ✔ Generate all rules that have *espresso* as an antecedent.

    These rules would determine the products whose sales may be affected if the store runs out of espresso.

Applying Biologically Inspired Clustering Techniques

Nature is a collection of beautiful, simple, and efficient systems. Even a natural process as simple as an apple falling from a tree inspired Newton to identify the law of gravity. But nature is also the best place to look for patterns that suggest solutions to complex problems — natural collective behaviors such as schooling fish, flocking birds, and marching ants have led experts in predictive analytics to design biologically inspired data-clustering algorithms.

Designing a biologically inspired solution involves these steps.

1. Observe and analyze a phenomenon in nature.

2. Mimic or model the behavior and design a representation for it that a computer can comprehend.

3. Use the representation to solve a real-world problem.

In data clustering, two widely-used algorithms purely inspired by nature are based on the flocking of birds and the collective behavior of ant colonies. Both algorithms can model and cluster your data in a simple and natural way.

Birds flocking

Imagine birds' flocking behavior as a model for your company's data. Each data item corresponds to a single bird in the flock; an appropriate visual application can show the flock in action in an imaginary visual space. Your dataset corresponds to the flock. The natural flocking behavior corresponds to data patterns that might otherwise go undiscovered. The aim is to detect swarms (data clusters) among the flocking birds (data elements).

Flocking behavior has been used in real-life applications such as robotics-based rescue operations and computer animation. For example, the producer of the movie *Batman Returns* generated mathematical flocking behavior to simulate bat swarms and penguin flocks.

The use of flocking behavior as a predictive analytics technique — analyzing a company's data as flocks of similar data elements — is based on the dynamics behind flocking behavior as it appears in nature.

Flocking behavior of birds, fish, flies, bees, and ants is a self-organizing system; the individuals tend to move in accordance with both their environment and neighboring individuals.

In a flock of birds, each bird applies three main rules while flocking:

- ✔ **Separation** keeps a bird apart from its nearest flock mates.
- ✔ **Alignment** allows a bird to move along the same average heading as that of its flock mates.
- ✔ **Cohesion** keeps the bird within the local flock.

Each bird in a flock moves according to these rules. A bird's *flock mates* are birds found within a certain distance of the bird, and a certain distance from each other. To avoid collision between birds, a minimum distance must be kept; it can also be mathematically defined. Such are the rules that orchestrate flocking behavior; using them to analyze data is a natural next step.

Consider a dataset of online social network users. Data clustering can identify social communities that share the same interests. Identifying social communities in a social network is valuable tool that can transform how organizations think, act, operate, and manage their marketing strategies.

Suppose that Zach is an active social network user whose profile has over a thousand friends. If you know who Zach's top ten closest online friends are, who among them he interacts with the most, *and* (from other data analytics sources) that Zach has just bought a book named *Predictive Analytics For Dummies,* you can then target his closest friends (those who are most similar to Zach) and suggest the same book to them, rather than trying to suggest it to all 1,000 of his friends.

In addition, detection of online social clusters can be extremely valuable for intelligence agencies, especially if (say) Zach and some of his closest friends — but not all of his friends — are involved in suspicious activities.

How do you obtain a dataset of social network users? Well, some of the data and tools are already available: Major social networks and micro-blog websites such as Facebook and Twitter provide an application programming interface (API) that allows you to develop programs that can obtain public data posted by users. Those APIs offered by Twitter are referred to as Twitter Streaming APIs. They come in three main types: public, user, and site streams:

- ✔ **Public streams** allow a user to collect public tweets about a specific topic or user, or support an analytics purpose.

- ✔ **User streams** allow a user to collect tweets that are accessible by the user's account.

- ✔ **Site streams** are for large-scale servers that connect to Twitter on behalf of many users.

Now, suppose you use such a program to download users' data and organize it into a tabular format such as the matrix shown in the next figure. Table 6-10 shows a simple matrix that records the online interactions of Zach's online friends over two different weeks. This dataset consists of seven elements and seven features. The features as shown in the table column are the number of interactions between each member and the other members.

For instance, the number of online interactions between Mike and John over Week 1 is 10. These interactions include — but are not limited to — chat conversations, appearances in the same photos, tweets, and e-mail exchanges. After building this dataset, the flocking behavior will be applied to detect communities (clusters) and visualize this data as a flock of data items.

Let us walk you through how a computer applies bird-flocking behavior to detect communities of common interests.

Take an empty piece of paper and imagine you have information about 20 users in a social network that you want to analyze. On that piece of paper, draw 20 dots randomly distributed all around. Each dot represents a user in the social network. If you move dots as if they were birds, they will move according to two central principles:

- The similarity between those social users in real life
- The rules that produce flocking behavior as you see it in nature

Let's say you have information about online interactions of those 20 members over a period of 10 days. You can gather information about those daily users on a daily basis, including data about their interactions with one another.

For instance, Mike and John appeared in the same photo album, they attended the same event, or they "liked" the same page in an online social network. This information will be processed, analyzed, and converted into a matrix of numbers, with these results:

- The dots (birds) in representing Mike and John move toward each other (flocking attraction rule).
- The dots move with the same speed (flocking alignment and cohesion rules) on that piece of paper (flocking virtual space).
- In one day, several real-world interactions will drive the movements of those dots (birds) in your paper.
- Applying flocking behavior over 20 days will naturally lead to forming swarms of dots (birds) that are similar in some way.

There are many ways to apply the bird-flocking behavior to discover clusters in large datasets. One of the most recent variations is the Flock by Leader machine-learning clustering algorithm, inspired by the discovery of bird leaders in the pigeon species. The algorithm predicts data elements that could potentially lead another group of data objects. A leader is assigned, and then the leader initiates and leads the flocking behavior. Over the course of the algorithm, leaders can become followers or outliers. In essence, this algorithm works in a way that follows the rules of "survival of the fittest."

The Flock by Leader algorithm was first introduced by Abdelghani Bellaachia and Anasse Bari in "Flock by Leader: A Novel Machine Learning Biologically Inspired Clustering Algorithm," published as a chapter in the proceedings of the 2012 Advances in Swarm Intelligence conference.

Tables 6-10 and 6-11 show one possible way to represent data generated by online social exchanges over two weeks. Table 6-10 shows that Zach interacted 41 times with Kellie and four times with Arthur.

Table 6-10 **Week 1 of a Dataset of a Social Network User's Weekly Interactions**

Social Member Network	Interactions with John	Interactions with Mike	Interactions with Zach	Interactions with Emma	Interactions with Kellie	Interactions with Nicole	Interactions with Arthur
John	-	10	10	12	4	4	10
Mike	10	-	5	5	56	57	5
Zach			-	6	41	4	4
Emma				-	28	8	8
Kellie					-	5	5
Nicole						-	4
Arthur							-

Table 6-11 **Week 2 of a Dataset of a Social Network User's Weekly Interactions**

Social Member Network	Interactions with John	Interactions with Mike	Interactions with Zach	Interactions with Emma	Interactions with Kellie	Interactions with Nicole	Interactions with Arthur
John	-	10	12	10	0	10	8
Mike	10	-	50	2	0	0	5
Zach			-	9	0	1	3
Emma				-	2	2	1
Kellie					-	4	9
Nicole						-	1
Arthur							-

Figure 6-2 outlines how to apply the bird-flocking algorithm to analyze social network data. As depicted in the figure, each member is represented by a bird in virtual space. Notice that

✔ The birds are initially dispersed randomly in the virtual space.

✔ Each bird has a velocity and a position associated with it.

✔ Velocity and position are calculated for each bird, using three vectors: separation, attraction, and alignment.

✔ Each bird moves according to the three vectors, and this movement produces the flocking behavior seen in nature.

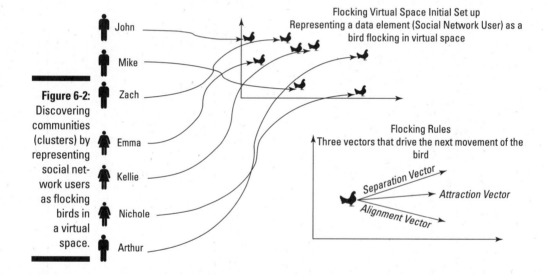

Figure 6-2: Discovering communities (clusters) by representing social network users as flocking birds in a virtual space.

Figure 6-3 illustrates the dynamics of applying flocking behavior to the initial birds shown in Figure 6-2.

Here interaction data is analyzed weekly to find similar social networks' users. Each week the birds can be visualized in a simple grid. The positions of these birds reflect the interactions of actual individuals in the real world.

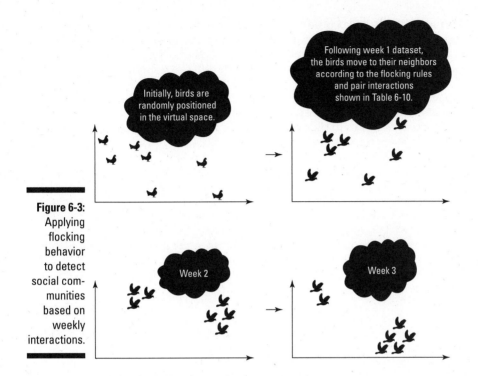

Figure 6-3:
Applying
flocking
behavior
to detect
social com-
munities
based on
weekly
interactions.

Ant colonies

Another natural example of self-organizing group behavior is a colony of
ants hunting for food. The ants collectively optimize their track so that it
always takes the shortest route possible to a food target. Even if you try to
disturb a marching colony of ants and prevent them from getting to the food
target — say, by blocking their track with a finger — they get back on track
quickly and (again) find the shortest way possible to the food target, all of
them avoiding the same obstacles while looking for food. This uniformity of
behavior is possible because every ant deposits a trail of pheromones on the
ground. Okay, how is that related to predictive analytics? Surprisingly closely.
Read on.

Consider an army of ants idle in their nest. When they start looking for food,
they have absolutely no information about where to find it. They march randomly until an individual ant finds food; now the lucky ant (call it Ant X) has
to communicate its find to the rest of the ants — and to do that, it must find
its way back to the nest.

Fortunately, Ant X was producing its own pheromones the whole time it was looking for food; it can follow its own trail of pheromones back to the nest. On its way back to the nest, following its own pheromone trail, Ant X puts more pheromones on the same trail. As a result, the scent on Ant X's trail will be the strongest among all the other ants' trails. The strongest trail of pheromones will attract all the other ants that are still searching for food. They'll stop and follow the strongest scent. As more ants join Ant X's trail, they add more pheromones to it; the scent becomes stronger. Pretty soon, all the other ants have a strong scent to follow.

So far, so good: The first ant that discovers food leads the rest of the ants to it by reinforcing scent. But how do the ants discover the shortest path? Well, the trail with the strongest pheromone will attract the most ants — but when large numbers of ants are involved, the shortest trails that reach the food will allow more trips than the longer trails. If several ants have discovered the same source of food, the ants that took the shortest path will do more trips in comparison to ants that follow longer paths — hence more pheromones will be produced on the shortest path. The relationship between individual and collective behavior is an enlightening natural example.

In Figure 6-4, every dot represents a document. Assume that the black dots are documents about predictive analytics and the white dots are documents about anthropology. Dots representing the different types of documents are randomly distributed in the grid of five cells. "Ants" are deployed randomly in the grid to search for similar documents. Every cell with a value in it represents an instance of a "pheromone." Using the document matrix, each cell's "pheromone" value is calculated from the corresponding document.

Figure 6-4: Setting up the initial phase of clustering documents, using a model based on ant-colony behavior.

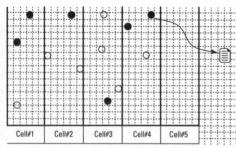 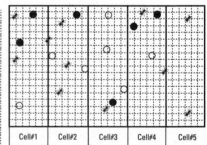

Okay, how does an ant colony's collective intelligence produce a model for effectively clustering data? The answer lies in a simple analogy: Ants are searching for food in their environment, much as we're searching for clusters in a dataset — looking for similar documents within a large set of documents.

Consider a dataset of documents that you want to organize by topic. Similar documents will be grouped in the same cluster. Here's where the ant colony can provide hints on how to group similar documents.

Imagine a two-dimensional (2D) grid where we can represent documents as dots (often referred to as *vectors* with coordinates). The 2D grid is divided into cells. Each cell has a "pheromone" (value) associated with it. (Later in this section, we show how to calculate this value.) Briefly, the "pheromone" value distinguishes each document in a given cell.

The dots are initially distributed randomly — and every dot in the grid represents a unique document. The next step is to deploy other dots randomly on the 2D grid, simulating the ant colony's search for food in its environment. Those dots are initially scattered in the same 2D grid with the documents. Each new dot added to the grid represents an ant. Those "ants," often referred to in the ant-colony algorithm as *agents*, are moving in the 2D grid. Each "ant" will either pick up or drop off the other dots (documents), depending on where the documents best belong. In this analogy, the "food" takes the form of documents sufficiently similar that they can be clustered.

In Figure 6-5, an "ant" walks randomly in the grid; if it encounters a document, it can perform one of two actions: pick or drop. Each cell has a "pheromone intensity" (a relative size of numerical value) that indicates how similar the document is to the other documents (dots) residing near the document in question — the one an "ant" is about to either pick up or drop. Note that the "ant" in Cell 3 will pick up the black-dotted document because the white "pheromone" value is dominating; and move to a cell where the value is close (similar) to what's in Cell 4 (several black dots). The search keeps iterating until the clusters form.

Figure 6-5: Deploying "ants" into the documents' virtual space to discover similar documents.

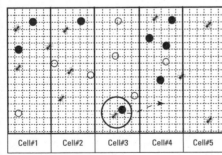 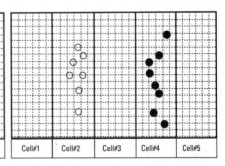

In effect, the "ant" moves documents from one cell to another to form clusters by performing either one of only two actions: picking up a document or dropping a document. When the "ants" started moving randomly on the grid, encountering a dot (document) results in the "ant" picking up a document from its current cell, moving with it, and dropping it into a cell in which it had sufficient similarity to fit.

How would an "ant" determine the best cell in which to drop a document? The answer is that the values in the cells act like "pheromones" — and every cell in the 2D grid contains a numerical value that can be calculated in a way that represents a document in the cell. Remember that each document is represented as a set of numbers or a vector of numerical values. The "intensity of the pheromone" (the numerical value) increases when more documents are dropped into the cell — and that value decreases if the numbers that represent documents are moved out of the cell.

Chapter 7

Predicting the Future Using Data Classification

*T*his chapter introduces an easy and widely used concept that can help you predict the future: *data classification,* a data-mining technique used to make sense of overwhelmingly large and humanly unmanageable datasets to uncover hidden patterns in the data. That could be one possible first step in the direction of building a predictive model.

Predictive models that use this technique are called *classification models,* often referred to as *classifiers.* Behind the scenes of these classifiers is a set of sophisticated machine-learning algorithms that learn from experience — as represented by the historical data — to discover hidden patterns and trends in the data. When these unseen relationships come to light, the model can predict the outcome (a class, category, or numerical value) based on newly input data.

For instance, most financial institutions that issue loans to individuals or corporate entities use *risk modeling* to predict whether the loan will be paid back (or, in the case of mortgage loans, paid back early). Often these models use a classification algorithm. In essence, a classification algorithm predicts the class or category of an unknown event, phenomenon, or future numerical value. The categories or classes are extracted from the data. One way to organize data into categories of similar data objects is by using data clustering (covered in detail in Chapter 6).

FICO Score and credit risk

The FICO Score was initially introduced in 1989 by Fair, Isaac and Company (FICO). Your FICO Score is calculated using several criteria such as length of credit history, bill-payments history, types and balances of credit cards, and also recent applications for credit.

A FICO Score ranges between 300 and 850. The higher the score, the lower the predicted credit risk, and the higher the chances that the applicant will pay back the loan on time. What a high FICO Score means for the applicant is higher chances to be granted a loan.

Financial analysts, mortgage bankers, and underwriters depend heavily on such predictive models when they decide whether to grant loans. Most people have heard of the *FICO Score* — as noted in the accompanying sidebar, it's a number that represents your credit history and creditworthiness. It's also a classic example of the output you get from a classification model.

Besides providing just a number (or score) as output, a classifier may place a credit applicant in one of several categories of risk — such as risky, not risky, or moderately risky. It's up to the modeler or analyst to determine whether the output will be a discrete number or a category. Thus a classification model may play a major role in whether someone buys that new house or car. The predictive model utilizes historical credit data of the user, labels the user as belonging to a specific category, and speculates on the user's future behavior if his or her loan application is approved.

Classification can be also used in fraud detection, spam e-mail identification, medical diagnosis, image recognition, targeted marketing, text analytics, and many other practical applications.

This chapter explains the underlying concepts behind data classification and illustrates techniques used to build classification-based predictors. You also get a look at a general approach to incorporating data classification into your business.

Explaining Data Classification

In data mining, *data classification* is the process of labeling a data item as belonging to a class or category. A data item is also referred to (in the data-mining vocabulary) as *data object, observation,* or *instance.*

Data clustering (see Chapter 6) is different from data classification.

  ✔ **Data clustering** is used to describe data by extracting meaningful groupings or categories from a body of data that contains similar elements.

  ✔ **Data classification** is used to predict the category or the grouping that a new and incoming data object belongs to.

You can use data classification to predict new data element on the basis of the groupings discovered by a data clustering process. The following section walks you through the use of data classification to solve a practical problem.

Lending

A loan can serve as an everyday example of data classification. The loan officer needs to analyze loan applications to decide whether the applicant will be granted or denied a loan.

One way to make such a critical decision is to use a classifier to assist with the decision-making process. In essence, the *classifier* is simply an algorithm that contains instructions (lines of code) that tell a computer how to analyze the information mentioned in the loan application, and how to reference other (outside) sources of information on the applicant. Then the classifier can label the loan application as fitting one of these sample categories, such as "safe," "too risky," or "safe with conditions."

By removing most of the decision process from the hands of the loan officer or underwriter, the model reduces the human work effort and the company's portfolio risk. This increases return on investment (ROI) by allowing employees to originate more loans and/or get better pricing if the company decides to resell the higher-quality loan.

If the classifier comes back with a result that labels an applicant as "safe with conditions," then the loan processor or officer can request that the applicant fulfill the conditions in order to get the loan. If the conditions are met, then the new data can be run through the classifier again for approval. Using machine learning, the loan application classifier will learn from past applications, leverage current information mentioned in the application, and predict the future behavior of the loan applicant.

As ever, predicting the future is about learning from the past and evaluating the present. Data classification relies on both past and current information — and speeds up decision-making by using both faster.

Marketing

To illustrate the use of classifiers in marketing, consider a marketer who has been assigned to design a smart marketing strategy for a specific product. Understanding the customers' demographics drives the design of an effective marketing strategy. Ultimately it helps the company select suitable products to advertise to the customers most likely to buy them.

For instance, one of the criteria you can use to select targeted customers is specific geographical location. You may have an unknown store (or a store that isn't known for selling a particular product — say, a housewares store that could start selling a new food processor) and you want to start a marketing campaign for the new product line.

Using data you collected or bought from a marketing agency, you can build your classifier. You can design a classifier that anticipates whether customers will buy the new product. For each customer profile, the classifier predicts a category that fits each product line you run through it, labeling the customer as (say) "interested," "not interested," or "unknown."

Using the analysis produced by the classifier, you can easily identify the geographical locations that have the most customers who fit the "interested" category. Your model discovers for example that the population of San Francisco includes a large number of customers who have purchased a product similar to what you have for sale.

You jump at this chance to take action on the insight your model just presented to you. You may send an advertisement for that cool new gadget to those customers — and only to them.

To limit operating and marketing costs, you must avoid contacting uninterested customers; the wasted effort would affect your ROI. For that matter, having too much unnecessary contact with customers can dilute the value of your marketing campaigns and increase customer fatigue till your solicitations seem more like a nuisance. You don't want your glossy flyers to land immediately in the garbage can or your e-mails to end up in the spam folder.

As a marketer, you might want to use data about potential customers' profiles that has been collected from different sources or provided by a third party. Such sources include social media and databases of historical online transactions by customers.

Healthcare

In the medical field, a classifier can help a physician settle on the most suitable treatment for a given patient. It can be designed to analyze the patient data, learn from it, and classify the patient as belonging to a category of similar patients. The classifier can approve recommending the same treatment that helped similar patients of the same category in the past.

As in the examples previously described, the classifier predicts a label or class category for the input, using both past and current data. In the case of healthcare, the predictive model can use more data, more quickly, to help the physician arrive at an effective treatment.

To help physicians prescribe individualized medicine, the classifier would assist them in determining the specific stage of a patient's disease. Hypothetically, the data (say, genetic analysis from a blood sample) could be fed to a trained classifier that could label the stage of a new patient's illness. In the case of cancer (for example), the classifier could have such labels — describing the following classes or groupings — as "healthy," "benign," "early stage," "metastatic," or "terminal."

What's next?

Future uses of classifiers promise to be even more ambitious. Suppose you want to predict how much a customer will spend on a specific date. In such a case, you design a classifier that predicts numerical values rather than specified category names. Of course, numeric predictors can be developed using not only statistical methods such as regression but also other data-mining techniques such as neural networks (covered later in this chapter). Given sufficiently sophisticated designs, we can expect classifiers to become commonly used tools in such fields as presidential elections, national security, and climate change. Chapter 5 also presents some current examples of predictive analytics using classification-based modeling.

Introducing Data Classification to Your Business

Getting back down to earth, if your business has yet to use data classification, maybe it's time to introduce it as a way to make better management or operating decisions. This process starts with an investigative step: Identifying a problem area in the business where ample data is available but currently isn't being used to drive business decisions.

One way to identify such a problem area is to hold a meeting with your analysts, managers, and other decision-makers to ask them what risky or difficult decisions they repeatedly make — and what kind of data they need to support their decisions. If you have data that reflects the results of past decisions, be prepared to draw on it. This process of identifying the problem is called the *discovery phase.*

After the discovery phase, you'll want to follow up with individual question-naires addressed to the business stakeholders. Consider asking the following types of questions:

✔ What do you want to know from the data?

✔ What action will you take when you get your answer?

✔ How will you measure the results from the actions taken?

If the predictive analytical model's results produce meaningful insights, then someone must do something with it — take action. Obviously, you'll want to see whether the results of that action add business value to the organization. So you'll have to find a method of measuring that value — whether in terms of savings from operational costs, increased sales, or better customer retention.

As you conduct these interviews, seek to understand why certain tasks are done and how they're being used in the business process. Asking why things are the way they are may help you uncover unexpected realizations. No point in gathering and analyzing data just for the sake of creating more data. You want to use that data to answer specific business needs.

For the data scientist or modeler, this exercise defines what kinds of data must be classified and analyzed — a step essential to developing a data classification model. A basic distinction to begin with is whether the data you'll use to train the model is internal or external:

✔ **Internal data** is specific to your company, usually draws from your company's data sources, and can include many data types — such as structured, semi-structured, or unstructured.

✔ **External data** comes from outside the company, often as data bought from other companies.

Regardless of whether the data you use for your model is internal or external, you'll want to evaluate it first. Several questions are likely to crop up in that evaluation:

✔ How critical and accurate is the data in question? If it's too sensitive, it may not serve your purposes.

✔ How accurate is the data in question and if its accuracy is questionable, then its utility is limited.

✔ How do company policy and applicable laws allow the data to be used and processed? You may want to clear the use of the data with your legal department for any legal issues that could arise. (See the accompanying sidebar for a famous recent example.)

When you've identified data that is appropriate to use in the building of your model, the next step is to classify it — to create and apply useful labels to your data elements. For instance, if you're working on data about customers' buying behavior, the labels could define data categories according to how some groups of customers buy, along these lines:

✔ **Seasonal customers** could be those who shop regularly or semi-regularly.

✔ **Discount-oriented customers** could be those who tend to shop only when major discounts are offered.

✔ **Faithful customers** are those who have bought many of your products over time.

Predicting the category that a new customer will fit can be of great value to the marketing team. The idea is to spend time and money efficiently on identifying which customers to advertise to, determining which products to recommend to them, and choosing the best time to do so. A lot of time and money can be wasted if you target the wrong customers, probably making them less likely to buy than if you hadn't marketed to them in the first place. Using predictive analytics for targeted marketing should aim not only at more successful campaigns, but also at the avoidance of pitfalls and unintended consequences.

Predictions, privacy, and profit

Legal issues resulting from the use of predictive models are especially relevant if your choice of implementation (or target audience) may raise eyebrows with privacy groups or provoke a negative response from social groups.

Recently, Target Corporation got into just such a mess with the press when their predictive model targeted pregnant women. According to a *New York Times* article, the model accurately predicted a pregnant teen before her parents knew about it.

Her parents eventually discovered their daughter's pregnancy when the marketing materials sent to their home were filled with items that an expectant mom would receive. In this case, the targeted marketing campaign resulted in an unintended invasion of privacy.

On the other hand, companies like LinkedIn and Netflix use data and predictive analytics very effectively to drive their business decisions. They have turned the data that their customers generate into a money-making machine.

Exploring the Data-Classification Process

At a brass-tacks level, data classification consists of two stages:

- ✔ **The learning stage** entails training the classification model by running a designated set of past data through the classifier. The goal is to teach your model to extract and discover hidden relationships and rules — the *classification rules* from historical (training) data. The model does so by employing a classification algorithm.

- ✔ **The prediction stage** that follows the learning stage consists of having the model predict new class labels or numerical values that classify data it has not seen before (that is, test data).

To illustrate these stages, suppose you're the owner of an online store that sells watches. You've owned the online store for quite a while, and have gathered a lot of transactional data and personal data about customers who purchased watches from your store. Suppose you've been capturing that data through your site by providing web forms, in addition to the transactional data you've gathered through operations.

You could also purchase data from a third party that provides you with information about your customers outside their interest in watches. That's not as hard as it sounds; there are companies whose business model is to track customers online and collect and sell valuable information about them. Most of those third-party companies gather data from social media sites and apply data-mining methods to discover the relationship of individual users with products. In this case, as the owner of a watch shop, you'd be interested in the relationship between customers and their interest in buying watches.

You can infer this type of information from analyzing, for example, a social network profile of a customer, or a microblog comment of the sort you find on Twitter. To measure an individual's level of interest in watches, you could apply any of several text-analytics tools that can discover such correlations in an individual's written text (social network statuses, tweets, blog postings, and such) or online activity (such as online social interactions, photo uploads, and searches).

After you collect all that data about your customers' past transactions and current interests — the *training data* that shows your model what to look for — you'll need to organize it into a structure that makes it easy to access and use (such as a database).

At this point, you've reached the second phase of data classification: the *prediction stage,* which is all about testing your model and the accuracy of the classification rules it has generated. For that purpose, you'll need additional historical customer data, referred to as *test data* (which is different from the training data). You feed this test data into your model and measure the accuracy of the resulting predictions. You count the times that the model predicted correctly the future behavior of the customers represented in your test data. You also count the times that the model made wrong predictions.

At this point, you have only two possible outcomes: Either you're satisfied with the accuracy of the model or you aren't:

✔ If you're satisfied, then you can start getting your model ready to make predictions as part of a production system.

✔ If you're not happy with the prediction, then you'll need to retrain your model with a new training dataset.

If your original training data was not representative enough of the pool of your customers — or contained noisy data that threw off the model's results by introducing false signals — then there's more work to do to get your model up and running. Either outcome is useful in its way.

Using Data Classification to Predict the Future

When your data is divided into clusters of similar objects, your model is in a better position to make reliable predictions. This section examines a handful of common algorithms used to classify data in predictive analytics.

Decision trees

A *decision tree* is an approach to analysis that can help you make decisions. Suppose, for example, that you need to decide whether to invest a certain amount of money in one of three business projects: a food-truck business, a restaurant, or a bookstore. A business analyst has worked out the rate of failure or success for each of these business ideas as percentages (shown in Table 7-1) and the profit you'd make in each case (shown in Table 7-2).

Table 7-1	Business Success Percentage	
Business	*Success Rate*	*Failure Rate*
Food Truck	60 percent	40 percent
Restaurant	52 percent	48 percent
Bookstore	50 percent	50 percent

Table 7-2	Business Value Changes	
Business	*Gain (USD)*	*Loss (USD)*
Food Truck	20,000	-7,000
Restaurant	40,000	-21,000
Bookstore	6,000	-1,000

From past statistical data shown in Table 7-1, you can construct a decision tree as shown in Figure 7-1.

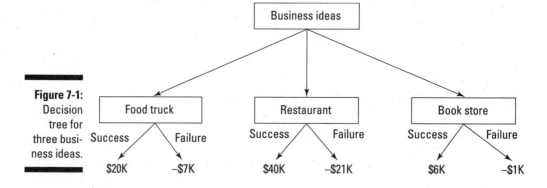

Figure 7-1:
Decision tree for three business ideas.

Using such a decision tree to decide on a business venture begins with calculating the *expected value* for each alternative — a numbered rank that helps you select the best one.

The expected value is calculated in such a way that includes all possible outcomes for a decision. Calculating the expected value for the food-truck business idea looks like this:

> Expected value of food-truck business = (60 percent x 20,000 (USD)) + (40 percent * -7,000 (USD)) = 9,200 (USD)

Here the expected value reflects the average gain from investing in a food-truck business. In this scenario — working with hypothetical numbers, of course — if you attempt to invest in food-truck businesses several times (under the same circumstances each time), your average profit will be 9,200 (USD) per business.

Accordingly, you can calculate the expected values of a restaurant business and bookstore the same way, as follows:

> Expected value of restaurant business = (52 percent x 40,000 (USD)) + (48 percent * -21,000 (USD)) = 10,720 (USD)

Expected value of bookstore business = (50 percent x 6,000 (USD))
+ (50 percent * -1,000 (USD)) = 2,500 (USD)

The expected value of a restaurant business represents a prediction of how much profit you'd make (on average) if you invested in a restaurant business several times. Therefore the expected value becomes one of the criteria you figure into your business decision-making. In this example, the expected values of the three alternatives might incline you to favor investing in the restaurant business.

Decision trees can also be used to visualize classification rules (such as those mentioned in the earlier example of the online watch store).

A decision algorithm generates a decision tree that represents classification rules. In the watch-store example mentioned in the previous section, you want to predict whether a given customer will buy a watch from your store; the decision tree will be, essentially, a flow chart (refer to Figure 7-1): Each *node* of the decision tree represents an attribute identified in the data matrix. The leaves of the tree are the predicted decisions, as shown in Figure 7-2.

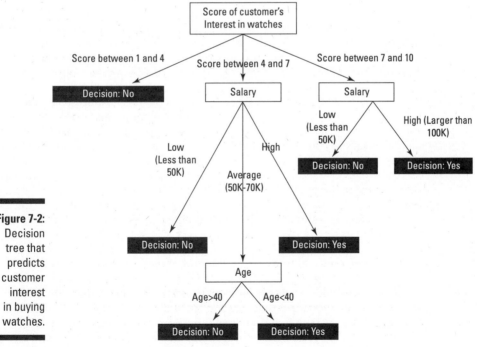

Figure 7-2:
Decision
tree that
predicts
customer
interest
in buying
watches.

This decision tree predicts whether a customer might buy a given watch at the online store. The nodes in this decision tree represent some of the attributes you're analyzing; each is a score — of customer interest in watches, customer age, and customer salary.

Applying the model to a new Customer X, you can trace a path from the root of the tree down to a decision tree's leaf (yes or no) that indicates and maps how that customer would behave toward the watch being advertised.

Support vector machine

The *support vector machine* (SVM) is a data-classification algorithm that assigns new data elements to one of labeled categories

SVM is, in most cases, a *binary* classifier; it assumes that the data in question contains two possible target values. Another version of the SVM algorithm, *multiclass SVM,* augments SVM to be used as classifier on a dataset that contains more than two classes (grouping or category). SVM has been successfully used in many applications such as image recognition, medical diagnosis, and text analytics.

Suppose you're designing a predictive analytics model that will automatically recognize and predict the name of an object in a picture. This is essentially the problem of *image recognition* — or, more specifically, face recognition: You want the classifier to recognize the name of a person in a photo.

Well, before tackling that level of complexity, consider a simpler version of the same problem: Suppose you have pictures of individual pieces of fruit and you'd like your classifier to predict what kind of fruit appears in the picture. Assume you have only two types of fruit: apples and pears, one per picture.

Given a new picture, you'd like to predict whether the fruit is an apple or a pear — without looking at the picture. You want the SVM to classify each picture as apple or pear. As with all other algorithms, the first step is to train the classifier.

Suppose you have 200 pictures of different apples, and 200 pictures of pears. The learning step consists of feeding those pictures to the classifier so it learns what an apple looks like and what a pear looks like. Before getting into this first step, you need to transform each image into a data matrix, using (say) the R statistical package (which is covered in detail in Chapter 14). A simple way to represent an image as numbers in a matrix is to look for geometric forms within the image (such as circles, lines, squares, or rectangles) and also the positions of each instance of each geometric form. Those numbers can also represent coordinates of those objects within the image, as plotted in a coordinate system.

As you might imagine, representing an image as a matrix of numbers is not exactly a straightforward task. A whole distinct area of research is devoted to image representation.

Figure 7-3 shows how a support vector machine can predict the class of a fruit (labeling it mathematically as *apple* or *pear*), based on what the algorithm has learned in the past.

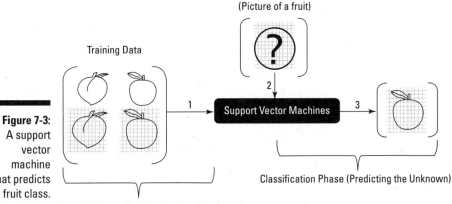

Figure 7-3: A support vector machine that predicts a fruit class.

Suppose you've converted all the images into data matrices. Then the support vector machine takes two main inputs:

- ✔ Previous (training) data: This set of matrices corresponds to previously seen images of apples and pears.

- ✔ The new (unseen) data consists of an image converted to a matrix. The purpose is to predict automatically what is in the picture — an apple or a pear.

The support vector uses a mathematical function, often called a *kernel function* which is a math function that matches the new data to the best image from the training data in order to predict the unknown picture's label (apple or pear).

In comparison to other classifiers, support vector machines produce robust, accurate predictions, are least affected by noisy data, and are less prone to overfitting (see Chapter 15 for more about overfitting). Keep in mind, however, that support vector machines are most suitable for binary classification — when you have only two categories (such as apple or pear).

Naïve Bayes classification algorithm

Naïve Bayes is a data-classification algorithm that is based on probabilistic analysis. The term *probability* is often associated with the term *event*. So you often hear statements along these lines: "The probability of Event X is so and so."

Well, the probability of Event X is a numerical value. You can calculate this numerical value by dividing the number of times Event X can occur by the number of events that are possible in the same circumstances.

Probability as a grab bag

Consider a bag that contains seven fruits: three apples and four oranges. Imagine that you'll be pulling one fruit at a time out of the bag, without looking at the bag. What is the likelihood (the probability) that you'll pull out an orange? In this case, following the definition just mentioned, Event X is *picking an orange out of a bag that contains seven fruits.*

✔ The number of times that the Event X in question *could* happen is four because there are four oranges in the bag.

✔ The total number of *possible* events that can occur is seven because there are seven fruits in the bag.

✔ Each time you pull a fruit out of the bag, it's considered an event. Thus the probability of picking an orange is four divided by seven.

✔ If you follow the same reasoning, you can deduce that the probability of pulling an apple out of the fruit bag is the result of dividing three by seven.

✔ The probability of pulling out a banana from the same bag is zero because the number of times such an event can happen is zero, the total number of possible events is seven, and zero divided by seven equals zero.

Naïve Bayes algorithm and Bayes' Theorem

The Naïve Bayes classification algorithm is based on basic probabilities and on *Bayes' Theorem*, powerful formula that can be used to calculate the probability of an event based on previous knowledge. Such previous knowledge is often referred to as *evidence*.

Let X be the event you want to calculate the probability for; let Y be the prior event that just happened (evidence). Bayes' Theorem states that

Probability of (Event X given Y)
= Probability of (Events X and Y occurring) / Probability of (Event Y)

The same equation can be also written as follows:

$$\text{Prob}(X|Y) = \left[P(X)P(Y|X)\right] \mid \left[P(X)P(Y|X) + P(\text{not-X})P(Y|\text{not-X})\right]$$

where

P (X) is the probability that Event X will happen.

P (not-X) is the probability that Event X will not happen.

P (X|Y) is the probability that Event X will happen, given that Event Y has happened.

P (Y|X) is the probability that Event Y will happen, given that Event X has happened.

P (Y|not-X) is the probability that Event Y will happen, given that X has not happened.

In practice, this last equation in the list is the one most often used when applying Bayes' Theorem.

Fundamentals of the Naïve Bayes classifier

Consider the scenario where you want to advertise Product X to a customer. You've gathered information about your customers, as shown in Figure 7-4. You want to predict whether the customer in question will buy Product X.

customer ID	Income (I)	Credit Rating (CR)	Sentiment Analysis on Social Media about the Product (SA)	Purchased Similar Products (SP)	Purchased Product X
3345	High	Fair	Neutral	Yes	Yes
3346	Medium	Excellent	Positive	Yes	Yes
3347	Poor	Fair	Positive	Yes	No
3348	Medium	Poor	Positive	No	No
3349	Medium	Excellent	Positive	Yes	Yes
3350	High	Poor	Negative	Yes	No
3351	Poor	Fair	Positive	No	Yes
3352	High	Fair	Negaive	No	Yes
3353	High	Excellent	Positive	No	No
3354	High	Fair	Positive	Yes	Yes

Figure 7-4: Customer data.

Figure 7-4 shows customer data you could possibly gather. Each customer has an ID, income, a credit rating, and a purchase history of similar products. Each customer record also has also the sentiment analysis of his or her social media text about Product X.

Consider the following probabilities definitions and notations:

P(X) is the probability of X being purchased.

P(not_X) is the probability of X not being purchased.

P(CR_fair | X) is the probability that a customer's credit rating is fair given the customer purchases Product X.

P(CR_excellent | X) is the probability that a customer's credit rating is excellent given the customer purchases Product X.

P(CR_poor | X) is the probability that a customer's credit rating is poor given the customer purchases Product X.

P(CR_fair | not_X) is the probability that a customer's credit rating is poor given the customer did not purchase Product X.

P(CR_excellent | not_X) is the probability that a customer's credit rating is excellent given the customer did not purchase Product X.

P(CR_poor | not_X) is the probability that a customer's credit rating is poor given the customer did not purchase Product X.

P(I_medium | X) is the probability that a customer's income is medium given the customer did purchase Product X.

P(I_high | X) is the probability that a customer's income is high given the customer did purchase Product X.

P(I_poor | X) is the probability that a customer's income is poor given the customer did purchase Product X.

P(I_medium | not_X) is the probability that a customer's income is medium given the customer did not purchase Product X.

P(I_high | not_X) is the probability that a customer's income is high given the customer did not purchase Product X.

P(I_poor | not_X) is the probability that a customer's income is poor given the customer did not purchase Product X.

P(SA_neutral | X) is the probability that a customer's sentiment on social media is neutral about Product X given the customer did purchase Product X.

P(SA_positive | X) is the probability that a customer's sentiment on social media is positive about Product X given the customer did purchase Product X.

P(SA_negative|X) is the probability that a customer's sentiment on social media is negative about Product X given the customer did purchase Product X.

P(SA_neutral|not_X) is the probability that a customer's sentiment on social media is neutral about Product X given the customer did not purchase Product X.

P(SA_positive|not_X) is the probability that a customer's sentiment on social media is positive about Product X given the customer did not purchase Product X.

P(SA_negative|not_X) is the probability that a customer's sentiment on social media is negative about Product X given the customer did not purchase Product X.

P(SP_yes|X): the probability that a customer has purchased a product similar to X given the customer did purchase Product X.

P(SP_no|X) is the probability that a customer has not purchased a product similar to X given the customer did purchase Product X.

P(SP_yes|not_X) is the probability that a customer has purchased a product similar to X given the customer did not purchase Product X.

P(SP_no|not_X) is the probability that a customer has not purchased a product similar to X given the customer did not purchase Product X.

Those probabilities can be calculated as follows, using the basic explanation of probabilities mentioned at the beginning of this section:

$$P(X) = 6/10 = 0.6$$

$$P(not\_X) = 4/10 = 0.4$$

$$P(CR\_fair | X) = 4/6 = 0.67$$

$$P(CR\_excellent | X) = 2/6 = 0.33$$

$$P(CR\_poor | X) = 0/6 = 0$$

$$P(CR\_fair | not\_X) = 1/4 = 0.25$$

$$P(CR\_excellent | not\_X) = 1/4 = 0.25$$

$$P(CR\_poor | not\_X) = 2/4 = 0.5$$

$$P(I\_medium | X) = 2/6 = 0.33$$

$$P(I\_high | X) = 3/6 = 0.5$$

P(I_poor|X)= 1/6 = 0.17

P(I_medium|not_X) = 1/4 = 0.25

P(I_high|not_X) = 2/4 = 0.5

P(I_poor|not_X) = 1/4 = 0.25

P(SA_neutral|X) =1/6 = 0.17

P(SA_positive|X)=4/6 = 0.67

P(SA_negative|X)=1/6 = 0.17

P(SA_neutral|not_X)=0/4 = 0

P(SA_positive|not_X)=3/4 = 0.75

P(SA_negative|not_X)=1/4 = 0.25

P(SP_yes|X)=4/6 = 0.67

P(SP_no|X)=2/6 = 0.33

P(SP_yes|not_X)=2/4 = 0.5

P(SP_no|not_X)=2/4 = 0.5

Here comes a new customer, whose ID is 3356 and who has the features (evidence) shown in Figure 7-5.

Figure 7-5:
New cus-
tomer data.

customer ID	Income (I)	Credit Rating (CR)	Sentiment Analysis on Social Media about the product (SA)	Pushased Similar Products (SP)
3356	Medium	Fair	positive	Yes

Figure 7-5 shows the data belonging to the new customer (#3356). You want to know whether the company should spend money on advertising Product X to this new customer. In other words, you want to know the probability that the customer will purchase Product X, given what you know already: that the customer is of medium income, has a poor credit rating, has a positive sentiment analysis on social media about Product X, and has a history of purchasing similar products.

The classifier uses historical data (as shown in Figure 7-4) and Bayes' Theorem (mentioned earlier in this section) to label the new customer as a potential buyer of Product X . . . or not.

Let P(X|Customer#3356) be the probability that Product X will be purchased by Customer#3356, given the customer's features.

Let P(not_X|Customer#3356) be the probability that Product X will not be purchased by Customer#3356, given the customer's features.

Following Bayes' Theorem, the following probabilities can be calculated:

P (X | Customer#3356) =

[P(X) * P(Customer#3356 | X)] / [P(X) * P(Customer#3356 | X) + P (not-X) * P (Customer#3356 | not_X)]

P(not_X | Customer#3356) = [P(not_X) * P(Customer#3356 | not_X)] /

[P (not_X) * P (Customer#3356 | not-X) + P(X) * P(Customer#3356 | X)]

Notice that those probabilities have the same denominator. Thus we focus on comparing the numerators, as follows:

P(Customer#3356 | X) is the probability of having customers like Customer#3356, knowing that Customer#3356 purchased Product X.

P(Customer#3356 | X) = P(CR_fair | X) * P(I_medium | X) * P(SA_positive | X) * P(SP_yes | X)

= 0.67 * 0.33 * 0.67 * 0.67 = 0.0993

P(Customer#3356 | not_X) = P(CR_fair | not_X) * P(I_medium | not_X) * P(SA_positive | not_X) * P(SP_yes | not_X)

= 0.25 * 0.25 * 0.75 * 0.5 = 0.0234

P(X | Customer#3356) = [P(X) * P(Customer#3356 | X)] /

[P(X) * P(Customer#3356 | X) + P (not-X) * P (Customer#3356 | not_X)]

= 0.0993 / [P(X) * P(Customer#3356 | X) + P (not-X) * P (Customer#3356 | not_X)]

P(not_X | Customer#3356) = [P(not_X) * P(Customer#3356 | not_X)] / [P(X) * P(Customer#3356 | X) + P (not-X) * P (Customer#3356 | not_X)]

= 0.0234 / [P(X) * P(Customer#3356 | X) + P (not-X) * P (Customer#3356 | not_X)]

Notice that both probabilities P(not_X/Customer#3356) and P(X/Customer#3356) have the same numerator. Through comparing the numerators, the following inequality can be deduced:

P(X | Customer#3356) > P(not_X | Customer#3356)

Thus we can conclude that Customer#3356 is more likely to buy Product X.

Neural networks

A more complex algorithm, the *neural network*, is biologically inspired by the structure of the human brain. A neural network provides a very simple model in comparison to the human brain, but it works well enough for our purposes.

Widely used for data classification, neural networks process past and current data to estimate future values — discovering any complex correlations hidden in the data — in a way analogous to that employed by the human brain.

Neural networks can be used to make predictions on time series data such as weather data. A neural network can be designed to detect pattern in input data and produce an output free of noise.

Figure 7-6 illustrates the structure of a neural-network algorithm and its three layers:

- ✔ **The input layer** feeds past data values into the next (hidden) layer. The black circles represent *nodes* of the neural network.

- ✔ **The hidden layer** encapsulates several complex functions that create predictors; often those functions are hidden from the user. A set of nodes (black circles) at the hidden layer represents mathematical functions that modify the input data; these functions are called *neurons*.

- ✔ **The output layer** collects the predictions made in the hidden layer and produces the final result: the model's prediction.

Figure 7-6:
Neural networks create predictors in the second (hidden) layer of a three-layer structure.

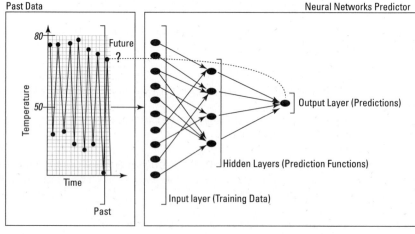

Here's a closer look at how a neural network can produce a predicted output from input data. The hidden layer is the key component of a neural network because of the neurons it contains; they work together to do the major calculations and produce the output.

Each neuron takes a set of input values; each is associated with a *weight* (more about that in a moment) and a numerical value known as *bias*. The output of each neuron is a function of the output of the weighted sum of each input plus the bias.

Most neural networks use mathematical functions to activate the neurons. A *function* in math is a relation between a set of inputs and a set of outputs, with the rule that each input corresponds to an output. (For instance, consider the negative function where a whole number can be an input and the output is its negative equivalent.) In essence, a function in math works like a black box that takes an input and produces an output.

Neurons in a neural network can use *sigmoid* functions to match inputs to outputs. When used that way, a sigmoid function is called a *logistic function* and its formula looks like this:

$$f(input) = \frac{1}{1 + e^{output}}$$

Here *f* is the *activation function* that activates the neuron, and *e* is a widely used mathematical constant that has the approximate value of 2.718.

You might wonder why such a function is used in neurons. Well, most sigmoid functions have derivatives that are positive and easy to calculate. They're continuous, can serve as types of smoothing functions, and are also bounded functions. This combination of characteristics, unique to sigmoid functions, is vital to the workings of a neural network algorithm — especially when a derivative calculation — such as the weight associated with each input to a neuron — is needed.

The weight for each neuron is a numerical value that can be derived using either supervised training or unsupervised training such as data clustering (see Chapter 6).

- ✔ In the case of supervised training, weights are derived by feeding sample inputs and outputs to the algorithm until the weights are *tuned* (that is, there's a near-perfect match between inputs and outputs).

- ✔ In the case of unsupervised training, the neural network is only presented with inputs; the algorithm generates their corresponding outputs. When we present the algorithm with new-but-similar inputs and the algorithm produces new outputs that are similar to previous outputs, then the neurons' weights have been tuned.

Neural networks tend to have high accuracy even if the data has a significant amount of noise. That's a major advantage; when the hidden layer can still discover relationships in the data despite noise, you may be able to use otherwise-unusable data.

One disadvantage of the neural-network algorithms is that the accuracy of the prediction may be valid only within the time period during which the training data was gathered.

The Markov Model

The *Markov Model* is a statistical model that relies heavily on probability theory. (It's named after a Russian mathematician whose primary research was in probability theory.)

Here's a practical scenario that illustrates how it works: Imagine you want to predict whether Team X (let's say a soccer team) will win tomorrow's game. The first thing to do is collect previous statistics about Team X. The question that might arise is how far back you should go in history? Let's assume you were able to get to the last 10 past game outcomes in sequence. You want to know the probability of Team X winning the next game, given the outcomes of the past 10 games (for example, Team X won 3 times and then lost 7 times). The problem is that the further back in history you want to go, the harder and more complex the data collection and probability calculation become.

Believe it or not, the Markov Model simplifies your life by providing you with the *Markov Assumption,* which looks like this when you write it out in words:

> The probability that an event will happen, given *n* past events, is approximately equal to the probability that such an event will happen given just the last past event.

Written as a formula, the Markov Assumption looks like this:

$$P\left(event_t | event_{t-1}, event_2, \ldots, event_n\right) \approx P\left(event_t | event_{t-1}\right)$$

Either way, the Markov Assumption means that you don't need to go too far back in history to predict tomorrow's outcome. You can just use the most recent past event. This is called the *first-order Markov prediction* because you're considering only the last event to predict the future event. A *second order Markov prediction* includes just the last two events that happen in sequence. From the equation just given, the following widely used equation can also be derived:

$$\left(event_1, event_2, \ldots, event_n\right) = \prod_n^2 P\left(event_t | event_{t-1}\right)$$

This equation aims to calculate the probability that some events will happen in sequence: *event₁* after *event₂*, and so on. This probability can be calculated by multiplying the probability of each *eventₜ* (given the event previous to it) by the next event in the sequence. For instance, suppose you want to predict the probability that Team X wins, then loses, and then ties.

A typical Markov Model prediction

Here's how a typical predictive model based on a Markov Model would work. Consider the same example: Suppose you want to predict the results of a soccer game to be played by Team X. The three possible outcomes — called *states* — are win, loss, or tie.

Assume that you've collected past statistical data on the results of Team X's soccer games, and that Team X lost its most recent game. You want to predict the outcome of the next soccer game. It's all about guessing whether Team X will win, lose, or tie — relying only on data from past games. So here's how you use a Markov Model to make that prediction.

1. Calculate some probabilities based on past data.

   For instance, how many times has Team X lost games? How many times has Team X won games? For example, imagine if Team X won 6 games out of ten games in total. Then, Team X has won 60 percent of the time. In other words, the probability of wining for Team X is 60 percent. You arrive at this figure by taking the number of victories and dividing by 10 (the total number of games), which results in a probability of 60 percent.

2. Calculate the probability of a loss, and then the probability of a tie, in the same way.

3. Use the probability equation mentioned in the previous Naïve Bayes section to calculate probabilities such as the following:

   • The probability that Team X will win, given that Team X lost the last game.

   • The probability that Team X will lose, given that Team X won the last game.

Let's arbitrarily assign those probabilities. Note that you can easily calculate $P(X|Y)$ — the probability of X given Y — as shown earlier in the Naïve Bayes section of this chapter.

4. Calculate the probabilities for each state (win, loss, or tie).

Assuming that the team plays only one game per day, the probabilities are as follows:

- P (Win|Loss) is the probability that Team X will win today, given that it lost yesterday.

- P (Win|Tie) is the probability that Team X will win today, given that it tied yesterday.

- P(Win|Win) is the probability that Team X will win today, given that it won yesterday.

5. Using the calculated probabilities, create a chart like the one shown in Figure 7-7.

A circle in this chart represents a possible state that Team X could attain at any given time (win, loss, tie); the numbers on the arrows represent the probabilities that Team X could move from one state to another.

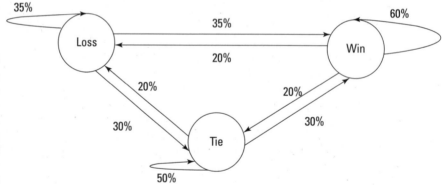

Figure 7-7:
Team X's possible states (win, loss, tie) and past probabilities.

For instance, if Team X has just won today's game (its current state = win), the probability that the team will win again is 60 percent; the probability that they'll lose the next game is 20 percent (in which case they'd move from current state = win to future state = loss).

Suppose you want to know the chances that Team X will win two more games in a row and lose the third one. As you might imagine, that's not a straightforward prediction to make.

However, using the chart just created and the Markov assumption, you can easily predict the chances of such an event occurring. You start with the win state, walk through the win state twice, and record 60 percent twice; then you move to the loss state and record 20 percent. The chances that Team X will win twice and lose the third game become simple to calculate: 60 percent times 60 percent times 20 percent which is 60 percent * 60 percent * 20 percent, which equals 7.2 percent.

So what are the chances that Team X after a win, will tie, and then lose thrice after that? The answer is 20 percent (moving from win state to tie state) times 20 percent (moving from tie to loss), times 35 percent (moving from loss to loss) times 35 percent (moving from loss to loss). The result is 0.49 percent.

Using hidden Markov Models

A *hidden Markov Model* is a Markov Model in which a previous state from which the current state originated can be hidden or unknown. The main inputs to the model are the states transition probabilities and a number of observations. A hidden Markov Model takes observation states into consideration. Let us walk you through an example that predicts a future state on the basis of a previous state and some observations.

Suppose you're currently watching a game that Team X is playing and you make the following observation:

> Team X is winning, so far, by 1 goal to zero (the current score over the first 30 minutes of the game).

Based on only one present observation, you want to predict a hidden future state: Will Team X win, lose, or tie?

Assume you know the past statistical probabilities for Team X, as mentioned earlier in the previous section (refer to Figure 7-7). Here are the steps to predict the next hidden (unknown) state — whether Team X will win, lose, or tie — on the sole basis of your current observation.

The first phase (as mentioned earlier) is the learning phase: You learn about Team X from past data and the outcomes of Team X's games. The following facts turn up:

- ✔ Team X won 55 percent of its past games, lost 40 percent of those games, and tied 5 percent of the time.
- ✔ In all past games, Team X won 60 percent of the time when they scored a goal within the first 30 minutes.

✔ In all past games, Team X lost 35 percent of the time when they scored a goal within the first 30 minutes.

✔ In all past games, Team X tied 5 percent of the time when they scored a goal within the first 30 minutes.

The statistics that reflect the learning outcomes from past games can be summarized like this:

	Win	Loss	Tie
P(X)	55 percent	40 percent	5 percent

The following table shows the probabilities of an outcome X, given observation Y.

	Y = scored a goal within the first 30 minutes
P(X=win/Y)	60 percent
P(X=loss/Y)	35 percent
P(X=tie/Y)	5 percent

Using a probability rule known as Bayes' Theorem (mentioned in the Naïve Bayes section) and the Markov Assumption just mentioned in the previous section, you can easily calculate the probability that Team X will win if you're currently observing that the team has scored a goal within the first 30 minutes of the game. Similarly, you can calculate the probability that Team X will lose if you observe that the team has scored a goal within the first 30 minutes of the game. Also, assume that Team X ties in the previous game, and that the prior probability of Team X scoring in the first 30 minutes in any game is 40 percent. Given these facts and observations, what is the probability Team X will win the game?

Here's how to calculate the probability that Team X will win, given that Team X tied in the last game and you observe that the team scored within the first 30 minutes of the current game. This probability can be written as follows:

$$P\left(\begin{array}{l}event_{t=future}=win|event_{t-1}=tie,\\ observation=scored\ a\ goal\ in\ the\ first\ 30\ minutes\end{array}\right)$$

For simplicity in the equations, consider the following notations:

$X{:}event_{t=future}=win$

$Y{:}event_{t-1}=tie$

$Z{:}observation=scored\ a\ goal\ in\ the\ first\ 30\ minutes$

Now you can write that same probability — that Team X will win, given that Team X tied in the last game and you observe that the team scored within the first 30 minutes of the current game — like this:

P(X|Y, Z) = P(X, Y|Z) / P(Y|Z)

= P(X, Y|Z) / P(Y)

Applying the Naïve Bayes rules explained earlier, we get this:

= P(Z|Y, X) * P(X, Y) / [P(Y) * P (Z)]

Applying Markov's Assumption equation (mentioned in the previous section) gives you this result:

= P(Z|X) * P(X, Y) / [P(Y) * P (Z)]

= P(Z|X) * P(X|Y) * P(Y) / [P(Y) * P (Z)]

= P(Z|X) * P(X|Y) / P (Z)

= 60 percent * 30 percent / 40 percent = 45 percent

Written out, it looks like this:

$$\left(\begin{array}{l} event_{t=future} = win | event_{t-1} = tie, \\ observation = scored\ a\ goal\ in\ the\ first\ 30\ minutes \end{array} \right) = 45\ percent$$

Hidden Markov Models have been successfully used in time series predictions and in practical applications such as speech recognition and biological sequence analysis.

Linear regression

Linear regression is a statistical method that analyzes and finds relationships between two variables. It can be used to predict a future numerical value of a variable.

Consider an example of data that contains two variables: past data consisting of the arrival times of a train and its corresponding delay time. Suppose you want to predict what the delay would be for the next train. If you apply linear regression to these two variables — the arrival and delay times — you can generate a linear equation such as

Delay = a + (b * Arrival time) + d

This equation expresses the relationship between delay time and arrival time. The constants *a* and *b* are the model's parameters. The variable *d* is the *error term* (also known as the *remainder*) — a numerical value that represents the mismatch between the two variables *delay* and *arrival time*. If the error is not equal to zero, then that might indicate that there are criteria affecting the variable *delay*.

If you're sitting at the train station, you can simply plug the arrival time into the preceding equation and you can compute the expected delay, using the linear regression model's given parameters *a, b,* and *d*.

Linear regression is (as you might imagine) most suitable for linear data. But it's very sensitive toward outliers in the data points. The outliers in your data can have a significant impact on the model (for more about outliers, see Chapter 15). We recommend that you remove those outliers from the training set if you're planning to use linear regression for your predictive model.

Ensemble Methods to Boost Prediction Accuracy

As in the real world, so with the multiplicity of predictive models: Where there is unity, there is strength. Several models can be combined in different ways to make predictions. You can then apply the combined model — called an *ensemble model* — at the learning stage, at the classification stage, or at both stages.

Here's one way to use an ensemble model:

1. Split the training data into several sets.
2. Have each of the individual models that make up the ensemble model process parts of the data and learn from it.
3. Have each model produce its learning outcome from that data.

So far, so good. But in order to get the ensemble model to predict a future class or category label for new data and make a decision, you have to run the new data through all of the trained models; each model predicts a class label. Then, on the basis of the collective classification or prediction, you can generate an overall prediction.

You can generate that overall prediction by simply implementing a voting mechanism that decides the final result. One voting technique could use the label that the majority of the models predict as the label that the ensemble model produces as its result.

Suppose you want to build a model that will predict whether an incoming e-mail is spam. Assume that the training data consists of a set of e-mails in which some are spam and others are not. Then you can distribute that dataset to a number of models for training purposes.

Then the trained models process an incoming e-mail. If the majority of the models classify it as spam, then the ensemble model gives the e-mail the final label of spam.

Another way to implement an ensemble model is to weigh the accuracy of each model you're building into the ensemble model against the accuracy of all the other models in the *set*:

1. You assign a specific weight (accuracy) to each model.

   This weight will vary from one dataset to the next and from one business problem to the next.

2. After the models are trained, you can use test data where you know the classification of each data point in the test data.

3. Evaluate the prediction made by each model for each test case.

4. Increase the weight for the models that predicted correctly and decrease the weight for the models that classified the data incorrectly.

Part III
Developing a Roadmap

In this part . . .

- ✔ Evaluating results
- ✔ Creating proposals
- ✔ Processing data
- ✔ Building and maintaining models
- ✔ Visualizing predictions and results
- ✔ Visit `www.dummies.com/extras/predictiveanalytics` for great Dummies content online.

Chapter 8

Convincing Your Management to Adopt Predictive Analytics

In This Chapter

▶ Measuring the benefits of adopting predictive analytics

▶ Optimizing operational decisions

▶ Developing unambiguous success metrics

▶ Creating a proposal to management

*P*redictive analytics should be on every company's radar. If it is not in your company's toolkit, take a good look at the surrounding competitive landscape: Margins are thinner; customers are more demanding and selective; customers have more and more choices. Companies that thrive in this environment are those that adapt to these changes and innovate to get ahead of the competition. They're lean; they're agile; they have embraced predictive analytics.

For examples of the effective use of predictive analytics, consider the success of Amazon, Netflix, LinkedIn, and Facebook. Amazon and Netflix have been around for about two decades, publicly traded for roughly half that time; LinkedIn and Facebook have been around for about a decade, publicly traded for only a few years. Although these companies are relatively new in comparison to blue-chip giants like Walmart or IBM, they are some of the biggest companies in the world. One major reason: These companies have pioneered the use of predictive analytics in managing customer relationships and targeted marketing.

Within the last couple of years, the stock market has seen a huge shift towards investing, especially in the initial public offering (IPO) market, in companies that deal with data in all forms. Companies like Facebook, LinkedIn, and Tableau (a vendor of big-data visualization software) have had successful recent IPOs. (Facebook had a bit of a bumpy ride immediately following the IPO, but as of this writing, Facebook's stock price has surpassed its IPO price and currently sits at an all-time high. Given these precedents, the Twitter IPO is a sure draw for investor interest.)

The market has rewarded this new generation of companies with very high stock valuations — and equally high expectations. To justify those high valuations, these companies are expected to grow their earnings at a very rapid pace for the next several years. The velocity of growth in these young companies reflects the explosive growth in data generation — and the use of that data to grow.

During this shift toward using big data for analytics and decision-making, an astonishing 90 percent of the data in use has been created in just two years (2011-2013). As more people start using social media, businesses collect more data on various things — including users and their online behavior — which further contributes to rapid data growth. As data is being used, even more data is being generated as a result. Unless the market and its analysts are terribly wrong, we can expect to see further exponential data growth and usage.

The companies just mentioned are no longer just retail or service companies; they have transformed themselves into data companies. They used data wisely to grow their businesses. They collect, analyze, and monetize their data by using it to understand their customers' needs and offer them compelling and customized products. Without using data in innovative and ingenious ways, these companies probably would not have grown as fast and as large as they have.

So, if your company wants to follow suit, the questions to ask are

- ✔ How did the analytics team or middle management (for companies that lacked data-science teams at the time) convince upper management to adopt predictive analytics?
- ✔ How did the executive management team have (or acquire) the insight to create data science teams?

Nothing like that had been done before in the open, which makes it all the more remarkable. At least we don't have to worry about that now. You can use the success of the pioneering companies as a real-world example to convince your management about the importance of applying predictive analytics to your organization.

Making the Business Case

Many CMOs and CIOs may already be including predictive analytics in the company roadmap, but may not yet know how to incorporate it into their business. Others may not have even heard of predictive analytics, or may confuse it with traditional descriptive analytics. After reading this chapter, you'll have an understanding of that distinction. If you're a company executive, you'll have a handle on the benefits of predictive analytics as part of your overall business strategy.

If you're in a middle management role, you're probably looking for ways to make effective recommendations to upper management. You want to take advantage of the buzz surrounding big data and predictive analytics — and find out how you can use it to benefit your company. After reading this chapter, you'll be armed with what you need to propose a predictive analytics solution for decision management to the executive team.

Benefits to the business

The benefits of adopting predictive analytics can be achieved in any company. However, larger companies see greater benefits than smaller ones due to the multitude of inefficiencies that can be found in large corporations.

In general, more established companies see greater benefits and have greater opportunity to

- ✔ Optimize their operations
- ✔ Look for new opportunities
- ✔ Acquire new customers
- ✔ Retain current customers
- ✔ Find new revenue streams from their current customer base

Startup companies may see a smaller benefit and defer adopting predictive analytics because opportunities are initially obvious and their strategies are already focused. Smaller companies may also consider a predictive solution too costly and complex to implement. They may think differently later on: After all the core business strategies have been executed and the company has begun to search for ways to grow customer lifetime value and improve customer loyalty, the time is right to add predictive analytics to standard operations.

An exception to the previous paragraph would be a startup company that has already centered its business around data and analytics. If such a company has already be doing predictive analytics or already has the staff and tools to create a predictive analytics solution, cost and barrier may not be a barrier.

Companies are having a much more difficult time gaining an advantage over their competitors. Many competitive advantages that leading companies enjoyed were eventually eliminated as competitors adjusted or copied the leaders' practices. This is especially true for companies offering the same types of products.

Adopting predictive analytics is one of the last process enhancements that many companies pursue to gain a competitive edge. Most companies start with traditional business intelligence to answer:

- ✔ What has happened in their business?
- ✔ Why did it happen?

They use dashboards and ad hoc queries against their databases to create reports for the management team.

- ✔ A *dashboard* is a graphical display where users, at a glance, can view summaries of predefined key information about the business.
- ✔ *Ad hoc queries* are non-predefined and non-routine queries on the database, used when specific information is needed.

Using these tools just gives those businesses an understanding of what has happened in the past. It does not give them any insight as to what will happen in the future. You can, of course, use standard math and statistics to try to forecast the future by extrapolating from historical data. But sometimes that approach leads to incorrect or non-optimized results.

There is very little chance that a data analyst, using standard math or statistics, can find relationships among the hundreds or thousands of variables that can affect the outcome that he or she is trying to forecast. For example, using just a few predictor variables may lead the analyst to forecast an uptick in sales for the next few months for a product. But predictive analytics may present an entirely different picture.

By taking more variables into account, and faster, predictive analytics can provide a more reliable answer to the question that every business wants answered: What will happen in the future? In this case, suppose the predictive model has predicted a sales decline instead of an uptick for the next few months. The machine-learning algorithm discovered dozens of highly useful predictor variables that affect the outcome, sometimes too subtly to be easily understood as a contributing reason or cause. Not until a particular predictor has presented itself can the team think analytically about why the outcome would depend on it; here the subtler predictors were brought to light. The power you gain from predictive analytics is the insight to make better-informed decisions.

Even so, predictive analytics is still currently under-adopted (and incompletely understood) by many companies. The companies that have invested the time and money to understand and implement a predictive solution for their operational processes have enjoyed a return on investment (ROI) nearly double that provided by non-predictive solutions.

In this tough competitive landscape, predictive analytics offer a way to differentiate from the competition.

Improving operational processes

The primary benefit of adopting predictive analytics is its ability to discover actionable insights that are not easily found by the naked eye. With these insights, the company can optimize business processes.

Predictive analytics are typically applied to operational business decisions such as

- **Predicting trends in sales:**
  - Forecasting sales of a particular product
  - Forecasting the revenue contribution of a company division
  - Lead scoring (predicting the value of a sales lead)
- **Predicting trends in marketing:**
  - Target marketing: Predicting which customers will respond to advertisement
  - Cross-selling: Predicting which products a customer will also be interested in.
- **Predicting which customers will *churn* (leave the business relationship):**
  - Predicting which customers will leave to a competitor
  - Predicting which customers will cancel a subscription
- **Prediction of fraud:**
  - Predicting which retail transactions are likely to be fraudulent
  - Predicting unauthorized access to accounts

Historically, the specific applications of predictive analytics are usually associated with the particular industry a company does business in. However, predictive analytics can be applied to many more domains and problems. The applications are only limited to the imagination of your staff and available resources. Start small with a prototype and then scale up from there.

Using predictive analytics to make data-driven decisions provides a couple of major advantages:

- It alleviates the stresses and inefficiencies of traditional processes.

  This relief not only optimizes decision-making throughout the organization, but also establishes a consistent decision, free of potentially harmful influences from other outside factors.
- It frees up human resources to handle other operational issues that can't be (or haven't been) automated.

The result is an improvement in the overall quality of operational processes, allowing the company to scale up its operations without having to add an equal amount of human resources.

Knowing the score

The predictive "score" is the best example of using predictive analytics to make data-driven decisions for operational processes. The best way to describe the score is in terms of a familiar example — the credit score created by the FICO company to help creditors make decisions on consumer loans. Several other credit companies create and sell their own credit scores, but the FICO Score is by far the most popular. Here are some examples of scoring decisions and their benefits:

- ✔ Only contacting those sales leads in the CRM (customer relations management) database who have high lead scores.

  Sales managers save valuable time and money by not calling contacts who won't buy.

- ✔ Only targeting a segment of the customer database that has high response scores for a particular marketing campaign.

  Saves marketing costs, decreases opt-out from e-mail campaigns, and improves overall customer satisfaction rates by not contacting customers who aren't interested.

- ✔ Contact customers who have high churn scores.

  Send a retention offer, such as a discount, to prevent customers from defecting.

- ✔ Fraud system will deny transaction and/or send inquiry to customer regarding the suspicious transaction with a high fraud score.

  Saves fraudulent payments made to criminals and enhances customer loyalty.

Table 8-1 shows some typical uses of predictive scoring.

Table 8-1	Typical Uses of Predictive Analytics		
Use Cases	**Predictive Model**	**Output**	**Take Action**
Mobile phone contracts, cable subscriptions	Churn model	Customer churn score	Send retention offer when score is high.
Insurance claims, eCommerce transactions	Fraud detection model	Transaction fraud score	Send claims to investigator or risk management when score is high

Use Cases	Predictive Model	Output	Take Action
Stock trading account	Risk model	Portfolio risk score	Send notification or route transaction to risk management when score is high.
eCommerce, marketing	Response model	Customer response score	Send advertisement to customers with high scores.

Operational decisions are generally scored along a range of numbers. If the range is from 0 to 100, you can treat each score value as a percentage and allow the user to make a decision based on that information. Or you can create a rule that tells the system always to take action when a score is higher than a particular number (provided your business rules allow it).

Sales and marketing teams are among the largest users of predictive analytics. A 2013 survey by Gartner reported that analytics and business intelligence form the top priority for CIOs. That result is almost certainly in response to the rapidly growing trend among sales and marketing teams to use big data to deliver business insights. One popular and widely respected CEO even goes so far as to cite a Gartner prediction that a company's chief marketing officer will spend more on technology than the chief information officer by 2017.

Building relationships with your customers

Company representatives spend many hours trying to get to know their customers and build a relationship. As the relationship grows, so does the *customer lifetime value* (CLV): Loyal customers will continue to add to future profits. Loyal customers also refer new customers to your business. Your cost of customer acquisition eases off and your revenues improve — the result is closer to an ideal business environment.

Obviously, it takes time to know each customer — and it's practically impossible to get to know each and every one of your customers in equal detail. Most businesses find the acquisition cost for each customer way too high using the one-at-a-time method.

Predictive analytics offers a way to get a virtual understanding of the customer by combining and analyzing data from

- Registration forms filled out by customers
- Customer surveys
- Social networks
- Customer purchase histories

The machine-learning algorithm learns and predicts the customers' behavior. The data can be thought of as the aggregate of the customers' experiences; thus the algorithm is learning from experiences of all the customers. By scoring each customer for churn or responses, you can optimize operational processes across all customer *touchpoints* (instances of company contact with the customer, whether in person or through a message conveyed by salespeople, store cashiers, call centers, websites, direct mail, television, radio, billboards, and the like). This is the competitive edge you gain by applying predictive analytics on the customer.

Don't freak out your customer by obtaining or using data analytics in socially unacceptable ways. The result of doing so may be the complete opposite of what you're trying to accomplish. Customers are very sensitive to data privacy issues. For example, there was a big backlash when consumers found out that Target Corporation was using predictive analytics to predict pregnancy in customers.

Improve customer retention

As the company grows, the cost of getting new customers (*customer acquisition cost*) generally increases. The supply of easy customers declines, so companies must work hard to keep the customers they spent so much to acquire.

Churn modeling is the application of predictive analytics for predicting a customer's propensity to leave the relationship with the company. If you know which customers are ready to leave, you can implement some type of retention program before they leave. It can be as simple as a discount offer for a product or service. The key is that you only offer these incentives to high-risk customers — keeping retention costs low and margins high.

Typical adopters of churn modeling are providers of service subscriptions such as those for mobile phone service. One implementation of such modeling is to integrate the churn score into the customer service application. Then the customer service representative can get a real-time notification to offer a discount for a new phone or service when the churn score is high, even during contact with the customer. The system can also generate a discount offer via e-mail or standard mail, if a customer's churn score is high when approaching renewal time.

Improve response rates

Wouldn't it be nice to launch marketing campaigns that have higher response rates than you're used to? By applying predictive analytics, you can target customers with advertisements that make better sense in terms of expected return. The model can segment out a portion of your entire contact list with customers that have a high response score (those most likely to respond) for a particular product or marketing campaign. To increase response rates, companies must shift from mass marketing to such *segmented marketing*.

Segmented marketing also reduces the expensive side effects incurred by mass marketing. When enough ads miss the target, customers start to see your marketing messages as spam. Customers eventually become irritated and opt out of future contact. This in turn will reduce your contact list, customer satisfaction, and company image.

Many customers are only willing to spend a limited amount of money. By marketing products to them that are customized and have ranked high in the recommendation list, not only do you increase your response rate, you also increase customer satisfaction and loyalty.

 Check your data regularly. Customers often change their e-mails or create multiple user profiles with different e-mails (that get forwarded to their main e-mail). Find the e-mail that is valid and try not to pollute their inboxes with repetitions of the same advertisement. You don't want them to get irritated and opt out.

Gathering Support from Stakeholders

Most people don't like change; convincing management or other stakeholders to adopt change is hard. To make matters worse, the adoption of predictive analytics is low compared to other forms of analytics. Company executives either don't know what it is or they've heard of it but don't believe in its value, so convincing them to see the value in it will require some work.

The good news is that, as hard as it sounds to make the pitch, it can be accomplished. Many new CMOs, VPs, marketing directors and marketing managers are technically savvy and value the benefits of technology. Some companies have product management executives that are also engineering executives. Some software engineering managers are changing roles into engineering product managers. These executives are looking hard for technological ways to find an advantage over their competitors and using predictive analytics is an innovative and unique way to distinguish them from the competition.

In any case, starting a predictive analytics initiative begins with the leadership team, as shown in Figure 8-1.

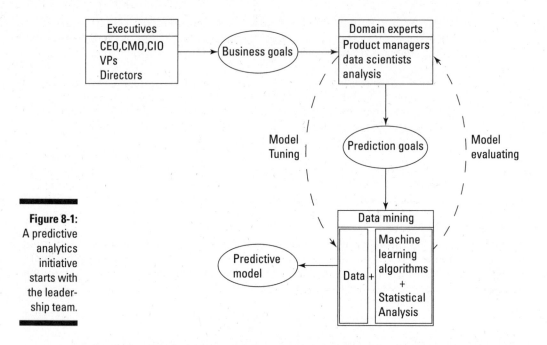

Figure 8-1:
A predictive
analytics
initiative
starts with
the leader-
ship team.

Working with your sponsors

In order to develop a successful and optimal predictive analytics initiative, the sponsors must think collectively about the problem(s) that they're trying to solve and how they will solve it. Developing a predictive analytics solution includes some indispensable activities:

- Thinking strategically
- Asking questions
- Defining success as a group at the beginning of the process
- Investing in human resources and tools

The upcoming subsections examine these developmental aspects.

Strategic thinking

As with most company initiatives, getting the executive team together in a room and having them agree on the strategy is critical to the success of this initiative. Doing so requires a lot of thinking about current objectives, business practices, investments, resources, and competition. Having a clearly defined plan from the executive team allows middle managers to prioritize and deploy the necessary resources to execute the plan.

Asking the right questions

You need to know what insights you're looking for — and what operational decisions they help solve. If those are not known right off the bat, then asking some concrete questions will help flesh out the answers. The executive team must answer these apparently simple questions in great detail:

- ✔ What do you want to know?
- ✔ What actions will you take when you get the answers?
- ✔ What is the expected outcome?
- ✔ What are the success metrics?

These questions should lead to a series of follow-up questions. When the team is satisfied with the degree of detail in the answers, you should have a picture of the business problem they want most to solve. The time that the team invests in the beginning of this process — to define and clearly understand all aspects of the task — will contribute to the success of the project.

Try to think from the customers' point of view. Creating customer personas will help you understand who your customers are, their needs and *pain points* (problems that the business wants to solve). Ask questions that you think your customers would ask. Doing so helps identify the most important operational goals.

Defining success

To measure the expected ROI of the predictive analytics solution, you must be very specific when defining the prediction goals. Having an ambiguous definition of success can lead to misleading results and conflicting interpretations among stakeholders. Start with small projects that have clear outcomes. A clear win gives the executive team more confidence in predictive analytics generally, and can lead to additional projects of larger scope and value. A track record of success also boosts the confidence of the teams that work on the project, and can improve cross-functional and cross-organizational collaboration.

Time to market

Your first predictive analytics project will take some time, and that time will vary greatly depending on many factors such as the size of the company and what prediction goal is being attempted. Ask your analytics, IT, or data-science team to determine a timeframe for a small project. An alternative is to get an expert consultant who can discuss the project plan and review your infrastructure. Such a consultant can provide a cost estimate and a realistic timeframe.

Typically, most of the time spent is in data preparation. All the vendors mentioned in the bonus chapter online at www.dummies.com/go/predictive analytics can provide capabilities to help you prepare your data for analysis. For example: After you load the data, you can explore the data and decide whether (and how) to handle columns that have missing data.

You may have the option to use your data in its current state — rather than having to spend precious time cleaning it — as you build a predictive model with. If you do so, your results may be less accurate than they'd be with thoroughly prepared data; it really depends on your specific situation. Your company may feel the time pressure to get the solution deployed quickly; dirty data may be less important than speed in such a case.

Budgeting

Realistically, implementing a predictive analytics project will cost more than doing a non-predictive project. Such costs can include the addition of human resources in marketing, analytics, IT, and engineering. You need both people and tools to store the data, prepare the data, model the data, and deploy the model — which can make the whole undertaking appear too costly to many smaller companies. Larger companies can absorb the initial cost more easily, and may already have staff who can be reassigned to handle the task.

To determine whether to do a predictive analytics project, you have to evaluate whether the projected benefits exceed the costs. Predictive projects have returned up to two times the ROI realized by their non-predictive counterparts. If building a custom solution is not feasible, products available from predictive analytics vendors can be of help. Check out the bonus chapter online at www.dummies.com/go/predictiveanalytics for a descriptive list of 10 such vendors.

Getting business and operations buy-in

After the strategy has been defined and the solution deployed, the key players in the success of the project will be the business and operations personnel.

You need people managers (such as program managers and project managers) to shepherd the team and coordinate with the other stakeholders. This group of people will keep the project on track, resolve road blocks, schedule cross-functional training, and help resolve any difficult cross-organizational issues that may arise.

Your product managers and analysts will have to create requirements, find meaning in the model's output (throughout the various stages of the project), and report the performance metrics to upper levels of management. Your customer operations team will make sure that the data is flowing smoothly between the company and the customer.

To get the full support of these people, you must be able to explain to them why these initiatives are being implemented — and why their routine operational processes are being altered. The project is about optimizing operational decisions, which targets the core of what many employees have been doing over time. The changes in their work requirements will take getting used to. They will also be the first people to feel the effects if the project is working — or if it's not.

Cross-organizational training

Cross-organizational training will be required for members who have customer contact, whether in person, by phone, or online. Salespeople will need to understand what the lead scores mean. And they may want to know how those scores were derived so they can use that information to strengthen their knowledge of the customer.

You must also train your customer support team not only to understand data scoring but also to apply it when the customer contact happens. Your customer service representatives must know how to respond to a high fraud score (ask for further verification or decline high-risk transactions) or a high churn score (offer a specific discount or freebie).

Standard operating procedures must be created to guide the interaction when such situations occur. To make things simpler, you can display the score as a color that shows the level of attention. You can also embed the correct decisions directly into the application.

A simple scenario between Customer Service and a mobile phone customer would look like this:

1. The customer calls Customer Service to inquire about her abnormally high bill this month.

2. In Customer Service, a red indicator on the screen shows that the churn score is high; the customer is predicted to cancel her service.

   The model scored this high because:

   - Her service contract has about one month left.

   - She has called numerous times in the past complaining about the high cost of service.

   - She has only been a customer for a year.

3. Action taken: The Customer Service representative offers a discount for a new phone if she renews for another year.

A more advanced version of this same scenario would change the churn score dynamically as the customer service representative inputs notes from the conversation. The model uses text and sentiment analysis to predict the likelihood that the customer will terminate her service contract.

Fostering a data-sharing environment

Being a data-driven company doesn't stop with using predictive analytics to create data in silos. The data should be shared across all business functions. As each team produces more data from the existing data they have, they should store it *and* make it readily available for other teams to use.

Another team may find just the piece of data they're looking for — which would otherwise be a waste of resources to redo the effort. Just as data should be shared, so should the techniques used to produce the data. To make efficient use of the knowledge across the entire business ensures that the business reaps the maximum return on investment.

Getting IT buy-in

Predictive analytics is a science. To ensure that you get the best possible results, you need the talents and skill-sets of your engineering team. IT plays a critical role in the success of your predictive analytics projects.

In addition to data scientists (especially if your company lacks data scientists), you need computer scientists and software engineers who are experienced in machine learning, natural language processing, and data mining. They can help you choose the appropriate algorithm (say, a clustering or classification algorithm or decision tree) to build your predictive model. IT may also own the databases to which you would need access. They're the ones who set up access rights so the data doesn't get accidentally modified or deleted during the creation of the model. After building your predictive model, coordinating with IT again becomes necessary to deploy the model you've built.

From its inception, to data access, data preparation, data mining and applying statistical analysis, and finally to model deployment and maintenance, getting IT buy-in will be critical to the success of your project.

Building a data-science team

Building a data-science team is an essential part of your predictive project. This is the team that helps you create the predictive model to solve the business problem.

You can hire new talent if your organization doesn't have qualified employees who can perform the task. Or you can recruit from within the organization. Recruiting personnel from within to be part of your data-science team may actually increase your chance of success; these people already have the much-needed business domain knowledge. Nevertheless, the team must have a strong lead member who has experience with the whole predictive analytics lifecycle.

The team's background should be diverse; the team should encompass business domain experts, data scientists, and IT personnel. All business departments should have representation in the makeup of your data-science team. Your data scientists should have deep mathematical knowledge and preferably proficiency in your line of business, and broader experience building different kinds of models. IT staff should include computer scientists who know machine-learning algorithms, software architects who can help in the design and implementation of the whole project, database and data warehouse experts, and personnel experienced in running IT operations.

If your organization lacks the skill-sets you need to produce a predictive analytics solution, you can look into the trade-off between hiring a consulting company versus building a team in-house. Many enterprise-level software solutions are available that managers and business analysts can use to build predictive models without having to know much about machine learning or algorithms. You can hire consultants to build the initial models with the software and also train your team to use the models. Your team can maintain and enhance the models.

Depending on your specific needs, it may be easier and more cost effective for you to buy a simple-but-powerful tool designed to enable business users to build predictive models. Such software products have built-in templates for predictive modeling. The tools make assumptions based on the data you're loading into the program, which can get you started right away. This option may be faster than hiring specialized and diverse professionals to build your data-science team.

Choosing your tools

If you buy a software tool for your predictive analytics project, which tool should you use? As with all important business decisions, you have several factors to evaluate. Choosing the right tool(s) depends on

- The budget
- The scope of your project
- The data you'll be analyzing
- Who will be the main users of the tool

You may need to hire consultants to do a feasibility study for you to see what tools are available and which ones would work best for you, given the business questions you'd like to answer. Experienced consultants who have working knowledge of at least a few predictive analytics tools — who know the pros and cons of those tools, as well as the business problems they're built to solve — will be best able to help you choose a tool. Or you can have them build a pilot model if that's within your company's budget.

As with all information technologies, predictive analytics tools are getting more powerful and less expensive all the time. This is an impressive trend, given that data is only getting bigger and more complex. Look for predictive analytics to become more widely adopted as data availability increases and the technology to analyze it becomes more accessible.

The tools are being built with user-friendly interfaces. They're easy to use and come already powered with all necessary features for managers and analysts to start using them to derive value right away. Analysts can select the data, process it, run multiple algorithms on it, and view results as visualizations or reports; all in a few clicks.

There are also *open-source* tools available online: They're mostly free of charge and have active communities where you can discuss and post questions. Keep in mind, however, that open-source tools

- ✔ Target more advanced users (some, for example, require programming knowledge)
- ✔ Are often less user-friendly (some lack advanced graphical user interfaces)
- ✔ Have limited capacity for handling big-data problems
- ✔ May run out of memory when handling big datasets
- ✔ May not be able to handle real-time analytics or streaming data
- ✔ Require that you invest time in learning them.

The learning curve and lack of commercial support may make an open-source tool unsuitable for wide adoption in a large corporation. Using a commercial tool designed as an enterprise solution can lead to a much smoother deployment.

The bonus chapter online at www.dummies.com/go/predictiveanalytics highlights ten vendors who provide predictive analytics as enterprise solutions. Most such products aim at hiding complex algorithms and mathematical equations and focusing on results. They enable users of all disciplines to run statistical analyses and/or data-mining algorithms, make sense of the data, and build predictive models.

Having too little or too much data

Data is abundant and getting more so; *big data* has become a familiar buzzword. Everyone is collecting it and talking about the large amount of data that is available. Organizations are amassing more data than ever before.

In this environment, it's hard to imagine a scenario where a company has a shortage of data. If such a scenario exists, the quickest way to get more data is to ask your customers to fill out surveys, or ask your customers to rate the products they've already purchased. Here the goal is to generate valuable feedback that you can put to use for data analysis.

You should have already stored all past transactions that your business has conducted. Building a database that contains detailed profiles of your customers can be of great value to your predictive analytics model. You can even buy third-party data.

On the other hand, having too much data also poses challenges. How do you determine which items are important? Where do you begin? How do you handle the constant influx? Increasingly, software tools and industry literature are addressing such big-data issues. These challenges will continue to grow as data complexities, in terms of data velocity and data volume, deepen.

Leading software products in predictive analytics are making it much easier to use big data, rendering its analysis more manageable. By the same token, those same software leaders are providing tools that smaller companies can use and apply effectively, even on smaller datasets.

Employing data you're already storing

As a result of normal operations, your organization must have already collected a fair amount of data it can use for predictive analytics. That data may not be analysis-ready, but with some effort you can make that data work for you.

One of the important steps in data preparation is to remove your duplicate entries. Make sure you don't have (for example) multiple IDs for the same customer profile. When you merged your data, you may have brought over the same customer with a different e-mail address. The same customer may have registered multiple times by accident or through different channels. For openers, make sure that the e-mail address you have for each customer is the most recent.

You can also buy third-party data, such as that derived from (and by) social media for the purpose of selling it to interested parties such as (perhaps) your company. Adding such data can help you build a better picture and richer profile of your customers — and it's readily available. Increasingly, data and its storage are affordable commodities.

To cut down on data preparation, you can enforce input checking at the time your customer information is collected, or (better yet) provide customers with multiple-choice surveys, and limited ranges of responses to choose from, to minimize data-input errors.

Buying data from third-party vendors

By itself, the data your company has may not be enough to provide you with a good basis for predictive analytics. For example, to produce actionable insights at today's ever-increasing pace, simply using demographics and basic inferences from your data is not enough. The demographics of loyal customers may look exactly the same as demographics of churning customers.

To generate those actionable insights, you'd need more complete data. To get it, you'd probably need to pull that data from various sources; one way of doing that is to buy it from third-party suppliers. If you can get hold of third-party data that's relevant to your predictive model, the next step is to integrate it into your existing datasets.

With the rise of social media, an abundance of data is being generated, some of which is collected by companies whose business model involves collecting this data, packaging it, and selling it. Such companies view that data as their product. Your company may have a use for that product.

Rapid prototyping

Predictive analytics is a complex science in every aspect. It requires a lot of strategic thinking by executives and domain experts. It requires technology and specialized skills. It requires time and money. When companies finally decide to take the plunge, they have to know where to start.

After the executive team has come to a consensus on what operational problem they want to solve, the spotlight is on you. You want to prove to them that predictive analytics will work. You want them to see some results in a month or two, not in six months to a year. Without their confidence in the science of predictive modeling, any attempt to launch a company-wide predictive initiative won't get off the ground.

When an executive wants something, time is your enemy. We know that most of the time creating a predictive model is in the data preparation. Don't spend that much time doing it. Creating a rapid prototype of the predictive model is the way to go. Such a prototype doesn't necessarily have to be pin-point-accurate to be valuable; the idea is to prove the concept. You just want to build something for the executive team to see in action.

Take a clean subset of the data and use that for starters; that should be plenty for most prototypes. Once the execs see the model at work, they may just get that "aha" moment that demonstrates the value of predictive analytics and makes a full adoption a lot more likely. Even if they don't get it right away, you may be buying some time with the demonstration. If they see that you're capable of building a predictive model, they'll probably wait a little longer to see clearer results.

You can build on the prototype and show incremental progress to the executive team. That way they can evaluate your progress and make recommendations along the way — which also firms up their relationship with the project. The investment is also allocated in small chunks instead of one big lump sum, which can make the decision to do the project much easier. Upper management loves small investments and quick returns.

Presenting Your Proposal

When you're ready to sit down with your executive management to propose a predictive analytics initiative, you must be able to explain predictive analytics clearly, and in simple terms. Granted, many executives already know about it (or have at least heard of it), but be prepared for those who have not. We've spoken to some executives who don't understand what it is or how it's different from business intelligence, so be prepared to frame that explanation in many different ways.

Here are several definitions of predictive analytics that you can use for your specific needs:

- ✔ A tool that uses data to assist a business to make smarter operational and strategic decisions.

- ✔ A tool that uses advanced machine-learning and data-mining algorithms to extract hidden patterns that produce actionable business insights.

- ✔ A tool that uses computer science to compute the best action from data.

- ✔ Software that models future events based on historical data.

- ✔ Software that allows you to simulate business decisions and see their predicted outcomes.

- ✔ A technology that predicts customer behavior by using data from purchase histories, demographics, social media, and web logs.

Okay, here's another business truism: Executives are (by definition) busy, so they're generally pressed for time and skeptical of being sold to. You need to be concise. They got to where they are because they have been making decisions that got these results. They know what initiatives not to do, what initiatives to do, and probably have strong opinions about both. You had better have a thoroughly well-thought-out proposal.

With the right message, you may get their attention. To seal the deal, you'll have to wow them with a vision and a demo. When you have them interested, ask them to sponsor a rapid prototype.

Here are some tips on presenting the proposal.

- ✔ This is a complex topic, so expect — and be prepared — to answer a lot of questions.

- ✔ No presentation is complete without providing a summary and answering questions at the end. You can find answers to many of these questions in this chapter. Other questions will be specific to your situation. Generally you'll need to answer

    - • How will predictive analytics add value to the business?

    - • How long will it take?

    - • How much will it cost?

    - • Who's going to do it?

- ✔ Tell them at least one interesting story about who is using it and how they're reaping the benefits, before trotting out the details of how to implement predictive analytics.

✔ Be armed with success stories of predictive analytics as implemented by other companies — especially your competitors. If you can't find something specific to your domain, talk about these more famous success stories:

  • Amazon's product recommendation engine

  • Netflix's movie recommendation engine

  • Facebook's recommendations based on users' "likes"

  • LinkedIn's "people you may know" feature

✔ Show them a list of specific benefits that your company will get from applying predictive analytics.

For a refresher, see the "Benefits to the Business" section of this chapter.

✔ You can frame the benefits in terms of an overarching goal: to gain a competitive advantage over your competitors by

  • Optimizing company operations

  • Looking for new business opportunities

  • Acquiring new customers

  • Retaining current customers

  • Finding new revenue streams from your current customer base

✔ Show that the costs of missing these benefits are greater than the small cost of approving the pilot program.

✔ Have a list of employees (and the reasons why) you think are ideal prospective members of your data-science team.

The pilot program should be short-term and small in scope. The employees on your team can still work on their current projects if they cannot be dedicated full-time to the predictive analytics pilot.

Employees may find it fun and rewarding to work on something new to the company. Finding meaning in data is very challenging and gratifying. Big data and predictive analytics form one of the hottest topics in technology right now — and employees are sure to dive right in to learn these new skills if given the opportunity.

✔ Ask them to sponsor you to build a pilot model in a short period of time.

Use open-source tools to create the predictive model to solve a simple problem. For example, build a simple recommendation engine that would address a small percentage of your overall web traffic or a small targeted mailing.

Chapter 9

Preparing Data

· ·

· ·

*T*he roadmap to building a successful predictive model involves defining business objectives, preparing the data, and then building and deploying the model. This chapter delves into data preparation, which involves:

- ✔ Acquiring the data

- ✔ Exploring the data

- ✔ Cleaning the data

- ✔ Selecting variables of interest

- ✔ Generating derived variables

- ✔ Extracting, loading, and transforming the data

- ✔ Sampling the data into training and test datasets

Data is a four-letter word. It's amazing that such a small word can describe trillions of gigabytes of information: customer names, addresses, products, discounted versus original prices, store codes, times of purchase, supplier locations, run rates for print advertising, the color of your delivery vans. And that's just for openers. Data is, or can be, literally everything.

Not every source or type of data will be relevant to the business question you're trying to answer. Predictive analytics models are built from multiple data sources, and one of the first critical steps is to determine which sources to include in your model. If you're trying to determine (for example) whether customers who subscribe to e-magazines in the spring are more likely to purchase hardcover print books in the fall, you may decide to omit the January paperback sales records. Then you have to vet the specific records and attributes of each possible source for format, quantity, and quality. Data may be a small word, but it brings on a lot of big tasks.

Listing the Business Objectives

At this stage, presumably, you've already sat down with the business mangers and collected the objectives they're after. Now you have to go into detail, evaluate what information sources will help achieve the objectives, and choose the variables you'll analyze for operational use.

Understanding what the stakeholders really want from the project is challenging; you may encounter multiple competing needs as well as limitations on what can be realistically done.

For this stage, you and the intended recipient of the results have to roll up your sleeves and brainstorm potential information sources. The goal is to determine what information, from which sources, will be relevant to reaching the type of concrete outcome that will provide true value for both the business and the customer. Without this in-the-trenches activity, your results may be no more than academic — of little practical value to your client. You may uncover fascinating inferences from (say) the accessory division's second-quarter sales records — and discover just how likely cross-dressers who wear flat shoes are to purchase faux leather purses — but this will fall on deaf ears if the accessories division is discontinuing its faux leather product line next quarter.

A business objective can be quantifiable and objective — for example, "identify two currently unknown major customer groups with a greater-than-50-percent likelihood of churning in the next six months" or "identify three supplier groups in Asia with decreasing delivery timeframes over the next five years." You might also list more subjective goals such as "provide valuable insights into the effectiveness of customer rewards incentives programs."

In the subjective cases, be sure to define what you mean by "valuable."

Identifying related objectives

Typically, there will be many subsets of business questions that the customer would like to address — any and all of which can provide insights into the main question. For example, the primary business goal might be to identify unhappy customers before they *churn* (move to a competing product). Related business questions could be: "How many times does a customer abandon a shopping cart online before purchasing from another online retailer?" "Does decreasing the threshold for free shipping from $100 to $75 prevent churn?" Table 9-1 shows some handy examples of primary and secondary business questions.

Table 9-1	Primary and Secondary Business Questions
Primary	**Secondary**
How do we increase print book sales?	What percentage of people who bought or downloaded a fiction e-book in FY12 then bought a print fiction paperback in FY13?
How do we predict the effect of health-based decisions on fitness-related products more accurately?	If customers are buying fewer French fries this year, will they buy more or fewer yoga mats next year?
How will a new tablet affect sales of existing digital products?	Are iPad users less likely to purchase laptops?

Collecting user requirements

Okay, suppose the high-level objectives have been documented and now you're moving into the details. What are the project requirements and timeframes you'll need to fulfill and follow? What are the requirements for your business, project, system, models, and data?

In order to avoid mismatched expectations, project managers should meet with all relevant groups in the client department. For marketing, this could include social media marketing managers, marketing analytics specialists, or database marketing managers. Information sources to specify can include (for example) customer lists, budgets, schedules and other logistics.

Thorough documentation — and key management sign-off — are critical to ensure that everyone is embarking on the coming intensive effort with the same understanding, commitment, and expectations.

Processing Your Data

Don't be surprised if preparing your data to be fed into the predictive model is as tedious a task as it is crucial. Understanding data quality, availability, sources, and any existing constraints will have a direct effect on the successful implementation of your predictive analytics project.

The raw data usually has to be cleaned — and possibly integrated, combined with other datasets, and used to derive new data variables. Hence data quality and quantity should be carefully and thoroughly examined across all data sources used to build the model.

In this exploration phase, you'll gain intimate knowledge of your data —
which in turn will help you choose the relevant variables to analyze. This
understanding will also help you evaluate the results of your model.

Identifying the data

For your analytics project, you'll need to identify appropriate sources of
data, pool data from those sources, and put it in a structured, well-organized
format. These tasks can be very challenging and will likely require careful
coordination among different data stewards across your organization.

You'll also need to select the variables you're going to analyze. This process
must take data constraints, project constraints, and business objectives into
consideration.

The variables you select must have predictive power. Also, you need to
consider variables that are both valuable and feasible for your project within
the budget and timeframes. For example, if you're analyzing bank transactions
in a criminal investigation, phone records for all parties involved may be
relevant to the analysis but not accessible to the analysts.

Expect to spend considerable time on this phase of the project. Data collection, data analysis, and the process of addressing data content, quality, and
structure can add up to a time-consuming to-do list.

During the process of data identification, it helps to understand your data
and its properties; this knowledge will help you choose which algorithm
to use to build your model. For example, time series data can be analyzed
by regression algorithms; classification algorithms can be used to analyze
discrete data.

Variable selection is affected by how well you understand the data. Don't be
surprised if you have to look at and evaluate hundreds of variables, at least
at first. Fortunately, as you work with those variables and start gaining key
insights, you start narrowing them down to a few dozen. Also, expect variable
selection to change as your understanding of the data changes throughout
the project.

You may find it beneficial to build a data inventory that you can use to track
what you know, what you don't know, and what might be missing. The data
inventory should include a listing of the various data elements and any attributes that are relevant in the subsequent steps of the process. For example,
you may want to document whether any segments are missing zip codes or
missing records for a specific period of time.

Your go-to people for business knowledge (also known as *domain knowledge experts*) will help you select the key variables that can positively influence the results of your project. They can help explain to you the importance of these variables, as well as where and how to get them, among other valuable input.

Cleaning the data

You'll need to make sure that the data is clean of extraneous stuff before you can use it in your model. This includes finding and correcting any records that contain erroneous values, and attempting to fill in any missing values. You'll also need to decide whether to include duplicate records (two customer accounts, for example). The overall goal is to ensure the integrity of the information you're using to build your predictive model. Pay particular attention to the completeness, correctness, and timeliness of the data.

It's useful to create *descriptive statistics* (quantitative characteristics) for various fields, such as calculating min and max, checking *frequency distribution* (how often something occurs) and verifying the expected ranges. Running a regular check can help you flag any data that is outside the expected range for further investigation. Any records showing retirees with birth dates in the 1990s can be flagged by this method. Also, cross-checking the information is important so that you make sure the data is accurate. For deeper analysis of the data characteristics and the identification of the relationship between data records, you can make use of *data profiling* (analyzing data availability and gathering statistics on the data quality), and visualization tools.

Missing data could be due to the fact that particular information was not recorded. In such a case, you can attempt to fill in as much as you can; suitable defaults can easily be added to fill the blanks of certain fields. For example, for patients in a hospital maternity ward where the gender field is missing a value, the application can simply fill it in as female. For that matter, for any male who was admitted to a hospital with a missing record for the pregnancy status, that record can similarly be filled in as not applicable. A missing zip code for an address can be inferred from the street name and the city provided in that address.

In the cases where the information is unknown or cannot be inferred, then you would need to use values *other* than a blank space to indicate that the data is missing without affecting the correctness of the analysis. A blank in the data can mean multiple things, most of them not good or useful. Whenever you can, you should specify the nature of that blank by meaningful place filler.

Just as it's possible to define a rose in a cornfield as a weed, outliers can mean different things to different analyses. It's common for some models to be built solely to track those outliers and flag them. Fraud-detection models and criminal activities monitoring are interested in those outliers, which in such cases indicate something unwanted taking place. So keeping the outliers in the dataset in cases like these is recommended. However, when outliers are considered anomalies within the data — and will only skew the analyses and lead to erroneous results — remove them from your data.

Duplication in the data can also be useful or a nuisance; some of it can be necessary, can indicate value, and can reflect an accurate state of the data. For example, a record of a customer with multiple accounts can be represented with multiple entries that are (technically, anyway) duplicate and repetitive of the same records. By the same token, when the duplicate records don't contribute value to the analysis and aren't necessary, then removing them can be of tremendous value. This is especially true for large datasets where removing duplicate records can simplify the complexity of the data and reduce the time needed for analysis.

You can pre-emptively prevent incorrect data from entering your systems by adopting some specific procedures:

- ✔ Institute quality checks and data validation for all data being collected.
- ✔ Allow your customers to validate and self-correct their personal data.
- ✔ Provide your clients with possible and expected values to choose from.
- ✔ Routinely run checks on the integrity, consistency, and accuracy of the data.

Generating any derived data

Derived attributes are entirely new records constructed from one or more existing attributes. An example would be the creation of records identifying books that are bestsellers at book fairs. Raw data may not capture such records — but for modeling purposes, those derived records can be important. Price-per-earnings ratio and 200-day moving average are two examples of derived data that are heavily used in financial applications.

Derived attributes can be obtained from simple calculation such as deducing age from birth date. Derived attributes can also be computed by summarizing information from multiple records. For example, converting a table of customers and their purchased books into a table can enable you to track the number of books sold via a recommender system, through targeted marketing, and at a book fair — and identify the demographic of customers who bought those books.

Generating such additional attributes bring additional predictive power to the analysis. In fact, many such attributes are created so as to probe their potential predictive power. Some predictive models may use more derived attributes than the attributes in their raw state. If some derived attributes prove especially predictive and their power is proven to be relevant, then it makes sense to automate the process that generates them.

Derived records are new records that bring in new information and provide new ways of presenting raw data; they can be of tremendous value to predictive modeling.

Reducing the dimensionality of your data

The data used in predictive models is usually pooled from multiple sources. Your analysis can draw from data scattered across multiple data formats, files, and databases, or multiple tables within the same database. Pooling the data together and combining it into an integrated format for the data modelers to use is essential.

If your data contains any hierarchical content, it may need to be *flattened*. Some data has some hierarchical characteristics such as parent-child relationships, or a record that is made up of other records. For example, a product such as a car may have multiple makers; flattening data, in this case, means including each maker as an additional feature of the record you're analyzing.

Flattening data is essential when it merged from multiple related records to form a better picture. For example, analyzing adverse events for several drugs made by several companies may require that the data be flattened at the substance level. By doing so, you end up removing the *one-to-many relationships* (in this case, many makers and many substances for one product) that can cause too much duplication of data by repeating multiple substance entries that repeat product and maker information at each entry.

Flattening reduces the *dimensionality* of the data, which is represented by the number of features a record or an observation has. For example, a customer can have the following features: name, age, address, items purchased. When you start your analysis, you may find yourself evaluating records with many features, only some of which are important to the analysis. So you should eliminate all but the very few features that have the most predictive power for your specific project.

Reducing the dimensionality of the data can be achieved by putting all the data in a single table that uses multiple columns to represent attributes of interest. At the beginning of the analysis, of course, the analysis has to evaluate a large number of columns — but that number can be narrowed down as the analysis progresses. This process can be aided by reconstituting the fields — for example, by grouping the data in categories that have similar characteristics.

The resultant dataset — the cleaned dataset — is usually put in a separate database for the analysts to use. During the modeling process, this data should be easily accessed, managed, and kept up to date.

Structuring Your Data

Raw data is a potential resource, but it can't be usefully analyzed until it's been given a consistent structure. Data residing in multiple systems has to be collected and transformed to get it ready for analysis. The collected data should reside in a separate system so it won't interfere with the live production system. While building your model, split your dataset into a training dataset to train the model, and a test dataset to validate the model.

Extracting, transforming and loading your data

After it's initially collected, data is usually in a dispersed state; it resides in multiple systems or databases. Before you can use it for a predictive analytics model, you have to consolidate it into one place. Also, you don't want to work on data that resides in operational systems — that's asking for trouble. Instead, place a portion of it somewhere where you can work on it freely without affecting operations. *ETL (extract, transform and load)* is the process that achieves that desirable state.

Many organizations have multiple databases; your predictive model will likely utilize data from all of them. ETL is the process that collects all the information needed and places it in a separate environment where you can run your analysis. ETL is not, however, a once-and-for-all operation; usually it's an ongoing process that refreshes the data and keeps it up to date. Be sure you run your ETL processes at night or at other times when the load on the operational system is low.

- **The extraction step** collects the desired data in its raw form from operational systems.

- **The transformation step** makes the collected data ready to be used in your predictive model — merging it, generating the desired derived attributes, and putting the transformed data in the appropriate format to fit business requirements.

- **The loading step** places the data in its designated location, where you can run your analysis on it — for example, in a data mart, data warehouse, or another database.

You should follow a systematic approach to build your ETL processes to fulfill the business requirements. It's a good practice to keep a copy of the original data in a separate area so you can always go back to it in case an error disrupts the transformation or the loading steps of the processes. The copy of the original data serves as a backup that you can use to rebuild the entire dataset employed by your analysis if necessary. The goal is to head off Murphy's Law and get back on your feet quickly if you have to rerun the entire ETL process from scratch.

Your ETL process should incorporate *modularity* — separating the tasks and accomplishing the work in stages. This approach has advantages in case you want to reprocess or reload the data, or if you want to use some of that data for a different analysis or to build different predictive models. The design of your ETL should be able to accommodate even major business requirement changes — with only minimal changes to your ETL process.

Keeping the data up to date

After the loading step of ETL, after you get your data into that separate database, data mart, or warehouse, you'll need to keep the data fresh so the modelers can rerun previously built models on new data.

Implementing a data mart for the data you want to analyze and keeping it up to date will enable you to refresh the models. You should, for that matter, refresh the operational models regularly after they're deployed; new data can increase the predictive power of your models. New data can allow the model to depict new insights, trends, and relationships.

Having a separate environment for the data also allows you to achieve better performance for the systems used to run the models. That's because you're not overloading operational systems with the intensive queries or analysis required for the models to run.

Data keeps on coming — more of it, faster, and in greater variety all the time. Implementing automation and the separation of tasks and environments can help you manage that flood of data and support the real-time response of your predictive models.

To ensure that you're capturing the data streams and that you're refreshing your models while supporting automated ETL processes, analytical architecture should be highly modular and adaptive. If you keep this design goal in mind for every part you build for your overall predictive analytic project, the continuous improvement and tweaking that go along with predictive analytics will be smoother to maintain and will achieve better success.

Outlining testing and test data

When your data is ready and you're about to start building your predictive model, it's useful to outline your testing methodology and draft a test plan. Testing should be driven by the business goals you've gathered, documented, and collected all necessary data to help you achieve.

Right off the bat, you should devise a method to test whether a business goal has been attained successfully. Since predictive analytics measure the likelihood of a future outcome — and the only way to be ready to run such a test is by training your model on past data, you still have to see what it can do when it's up against future data. Of course, you can't risk running an untried model on real future data, so you'll need to use existing data to simulate future data realistically. To do so, you have to split the data you're working on into training and test datasets.

Be sure that you select these two datasets at random, and that both datasets contain and cover all the data parameters you're measuring.

When you split your data into test and training datasets, you're effectively avoiding any overfitting issues that could arise from overtraining the model on the entire dataset and picking up all the noise patterns or specific features that only belong to the sample dataset and are not applicable to other datasets. (See Chapter 15 for more on the pitfalls of overfitting.)

Separating your data into training and test datasets, about 70 percent and 30 percent respectively, ensures an accurate measurement of the performance of the predictive analytics model you're building. You want to evaluate your model against the test data because it's a straightforward way to measure whether the model's predictions are accurate. Succeeding here is an indication that the model will succeed when it's deployed. A test dataset will serve as an independent set of data that the model has not yet seen; running your model against the test dataset provides a preview of how the model will perform when it goes live.

Chapter 10

Building a Predictive Model

In This Chapter

▶ Defining your business objective

▶ Preparing your data

▶ Developing, testing, and evaluating the model

▶ Deploying and maintaining the model

S ome claims are fraudulent. Some customers will churn. Some transactions are fraudulent. Some investments will be a loss. Some employees will leave. But the burning question in everyone's mind is: Which ones?

Building a predictive analytics model can help your business answer such questions. The model will look at the data you have about your customers, for example, and tell you the probability of customer churning. But such questions merely touch upon the surface of what predictive analytics can do; the potential applications of this fascinating discipline are endless.

As mentioned earlier in the book, a *model* is a mathematical representation of a real-world phenomenon we're interested in making sense of. For example, you can use the data you have to build a model that mimics the stock market in which your firm is actively engaged in all sort of trades — and then your job is to sort out the winning trades from the losing ones. In such a case, your model helps you select a strategy to make money by trading on the stock market.

Building a predictive analytics model becomes vital when the consequences of not acting — or of making the wrong decision — would be costly. Fraudulent transactions, for example, can drain resources such as time, money, and personnel; they can break the financial health of a company. Using predictive analytics to detect and counteract fraud then becomes part of your risk management strategy — and again, this function only scratches the surface of the potential value that a predictive model can bring to your company.

Getting Started

Predictive analytics aims at finding answers to business questions by examining data and presenting a range of possible outcomes, ranked with a score for each outcome. It helps organizations predict future outcomes and trends with confidence. It improves an organization's ability to plan, adopt, and execute strategies that improve its competitive edge. After your organization has put a predictive model in place, it then has the responsibility to act upon those findings.

Creating a successful predictive model involves these general steps:

1. Define the business objectives. (See Chapter 8.)

2. Prepare the data for use in the model. (See Chapter 9.)

3. Apply statistical and/or data-mining algorithms to the data. (See Chapters 6 and 7.)

4. Build, test, deploy, and maintain the model. (This chapter delves into this stage.)

Building a predictive model is the essence of predictive analytics. The specific model-building stage of the whole process is when you're ready to run some mathematical algorithms to see what interesting patterns and relationships you can find in the data. As you do so, keep these questions in mind:

✔ How can you answer business questions?

✔ What can you contribute to business decision-making?

✔ How can you increase return on investment?

For you to be at this stage, you must already have convinced your management about the worthiness of predictive analytics. You've sealed the business case; sat down with management and stakeholders to ask all the relevant questions; and chosen to address one or a few related business questions. Then you've gathered a talented group of people of data scientists, IT personnel, and business experts to form your data analytical group.

Of course, the analytics team (or if you're a "group" consisting of one person running from cubicle to office, verifying and asking questions at each step), the team or you've already done mighty deeds of preparation:

✔ You've identified the data sources that you'll use to run the model. (See Chapters 3 and 9.)

✔ You've performed any required data preprocessing (such as cleansing and integration), and created any derived data that you expect to have predictive power. (See Chapter 9 and 15.)

✔ You've selected and identified all these variables. (See Chapter 9.)

Now, at last, it's time to run the mathematical algorithm and see what you can learn from it.

The essential steps of the preparatory process leading up to this point are making the business case and preparing your data. Now for the fun part: running those specialized algorithms and see what you can learn.

We address a few practical questions here:

✔ What is the process of running the algorithm?

✔ How do I go about it?

✔ Which algorithm do I choose?

✔ How do I test my model?

✔ What's next?

Building a predictive analytics model starts with clearly defining the business objectives you want it to attain, and then identifying and preparing the data that will be used to train and test the model.

Defining your business objectives

A predictive analytics model aims at solving a business problem or accomplishing a desired business outcome. Those business objectives become the model's goals. Knowing those ensures the business value of the model you build — which is not to be confused with the accuracy of the model. After all, hypothetically you can build an accurate model to solve an imaginary business problem — but it's a whole other task to build a model that contributes to attaining business goals in the real world.

Defining the problem or the business question you want your model to solve is a vital first step in this process. A relevant and realistic definition of the problem will ensure that if you're successful in your endeavor of building this model and once it is used, it will add value to your business.

In addition to defining the business objectives and the overall vision for your predictive analytics model, you need to define the scope of the overall project. Here are some general questions that must be answered at this stage:

✔ What business problems would your stakeholders like to solve? Here are some immediately useful examples:

  • Classify transactions into legitimate versus fraudulent.

  • Identify the customers who are most likely to respond to a marketing campaign.

  • Identify what products to recommend to your customers.

- Solve operational issues such as the optimal scheduling of employees' work — days or hours.

- Cluster the patients according to their different stages of the disease.

- Identify individualized treatments for patients.

- Pick the next best-performing stock for today, the quarter, or the year.

✔ If you develop your predictive model as a solution, you have another range of questions to address:

- What would stakeholders do with that solution?

- How would they use the model?

- What is the current status with no model in place?

- How is this business problem handled today?

- What are the consequences of predicting the wrong solution?

- What is the cost of a false positive?

- How will the model be deployed?

- Who is going to use the model?

- How will the output of the model be represented?

Preparing your data

When you've defined the objectives of the model, the next step is to identify and prepare the data you'll use to build your model. (Chapter 9 addresses this step in detail.) This section touches upon the most important activities. The general sequence of steps looks like this:

1. Identify your data sources.

   Data could be in different formats or reside in various locations.

2. Identify how you will access that data.

   Sometimes, you would need to acquire third-party data, or data owned by a different division in your organization, etc.

3. Consider which variables to include in your analysis.

   One standard approach is to start off with a wide range of variables and eliminate the ones that offer no predictive values for the model.

4. Determine whether to use derived variables (See Chapter 9).

   In many cases, a derived variable (such as the price-per-earning ratio used to analyze stock prices) would have a greater direct impact on the model than would the raw variable.

5. Explore the quality of your data, seeking to understand both its state and limitations.

   The accuracy of the model's predictions is directly related to the variables you select and the quality of your data. You would want to answer some data-specific questions at this point:

   • Is the data complete?

   • Does it have any outliers?

   • Does the data need cleansing?

   • Do you need to fill in missing values, keep them as they are, or eliminate them altogether?

Understanding your data and its properties can help you choose the algorithm that will be most useful in building your model. For example:

✔ Regression algorithms can be used to analyze time-series data.

✔ Classification algorithms can be used to analyze discrete data.

✔ Association algorithms can be used for data with correlated attributes.

The dataset used to train and test the model must contain relevant business information to answer the problem you're trying to solve. If your goal is (for example) to determine which customer is likely to churn, then the dataset you choose must contain information about customers who have churned in the past in addition to customers who have not.

Some models created to mine data and make sense of its underlying relationships — for example, those built with clustering algorithms — need not have a particular end result in mind.

Two problems arise when dealing with data as you're building your model: underfitting and overfitting.

Underfitting

Underfitting is when your model can't detect any relationships in your data. This is usually an indication that essential variables — those with predictive power — weren't included in your analysis. For example, a stock analysis that includes only data from a bull market (where overall stock prices are going up) doesn't account for crises or bubbles that can bring major corrections to the overall performance of stocks. Failing to include data that spans both bull *and* bear markets (when overall stock prices are falling) keeps the model from producing the best possible portfolio selection.

Overfitting

Overfitting is when your model includes data that has no predictive power but it is only specific to the dataset you're analyzing. *Noise* — random variations in the dataset — can find its way into the model, such that running the model on a different dataset produces a major drop in the model's predictive performance and accuracy. The accompanying sidebar provides an example.

If your model performs just fine on a particular dataset and only underperforms when you test it on a different dataset, suspect overfitting. (For more about overfitting, see Chapter 15.)

Choosing an algorithm

Various statistical, data-mining, and machine-learning algorithms are available for use in your model. You're in a better position to select an algorithm after you've defined the objectives of your model and selected the data you'll work on. Some of these algorithms were developed to solve specific business problems, enhance existing algorithms, or provide new capabilities — which may make some of them more appropriate for your purposes than others. You can choose from a range of algorithms to address business concerns such as the following:

- ✔ For customer segmentation and/or community detection in the social sphere, for example, you'd need clustering algorithms.
- ✔ For customer retention or to develop a recommender system, you'd use classification algorithms.
- ✔ For credit scoring or predicting the next outcome of time-driven events, you'd use a regression algorithm.

These genes fit wrong

A classic example of overfitting might cause trouble in a gene classification analysis that measures the proteins in particular genes. Imagine what happens when a lab technician calibrates the machine while it's taking measurements that turn out to be erroneous — or a particular machine used for the experiment suffers an electrical disruption, or a specific technique goes awry during the experiments: The erroneous measurements end up in the data, and the model's predictive potential goes out the window.

As time and resources permit, you should run as many algorithms of the appropriate type as you can. Comparing different runs of different algorithms can bring surprising findings about the data or the business intelligence embedded in the data. Doing so gives you more detailed insight into the business problem, and helps you identify which variables within your data have predictive power.

Some predictive analytics projects succeed best by building an *ensemble model,* a group of models that operate on the same data. An ensemble model uses a predefined mechanism to gather outcomes from all its component models and provide a final outcome for the user.

Models can take various forms — a query, a collection of scenarios, a decision tree, or an advanced mathematical analysis. In addition, certain models work best for certain data and analyses. You can (for example) use classification algorithms that employ decision rules to decide the outcome of a given scenario or transaction, addressing questions like these:

- ✔ Is this customer likely to respond to our marketing campaign?
- ✔ Is this money-transfer likely to be part of a money-laundering scheme?
- ✔ Is this loan applicant likely to default on the loan?

You can use unsupervised clustering algorithms to find what relationships exist within your dataset. (For more about the use of unsupervised clustering, see Chapter 6.) You can use these algorithms to find different groupings among your customers, determine what services can be grouped together, or decide for example which products can be upsold.

Regression algorithms can be used to forecast continuous data, such as predicting the trend for a stock movement given its past prices.

Data and business objectives aren't the only factors to consider when you're selecting an algorithm. The expertise of your data scientists is of tremendous value at this point; picking an algorithm that will get the job done is often a tricky combination of science and art. The art part comes from experience and proficiency in the business domain, which also plays a critical role in identifying a model that can serve business objectives accurately.

Developing and Testing the Model

Let the magic begin! Model development starts at this stage, followed by testing the results of the runs. You use training and test datasets to align the model more closely to its business objectives, and refine the model's output through careful selection of variables, further training, and evaluating the output.

Developing the model

Developing a predictive model almost can never be a one-time deal; it requires an iterative process. You have to narrow the list of variables you're working with — starting with more variables than you think you'll need, and using multiple runs on the training dataset to narrow down the variables to those that truly count.

Run each algorithm several times while tweaking and changing the input variables fed to that model. With each run, you're examining a new hypothesis, changing input variables, and digging deeper for better solutions and more accurate predictions.

Okay, an iterative process can be overwhelming; you can easily lose track of what you've changed, or of what combinations of hypotheses and variables you've already run. Be sure to document each experiment thoroughly. Include inputs, the algorithm, and the outputs of each experiment. In addition, document any relevant observations you may have such as the specific assumptions made, your initial assessment, and the next step planned. This way you can avoid duplicate efforts.

Consulting with business domain experts at this stage can help you keep your model relevant while you're building it. Your domain experts can

- ✔ Identify the variables that have greater predictive power.
- ✔ Provide you with business language necessary for you to report your findings.
- ✔ Help you explain the business significance of your preliminary results.

Testing the model

To be able to test the model you need to split your dataset into two sets: training and test datasets. These datasets should be selected at random and should be a good representation of the actual population.

- ✔ Similar data should be used for both the training and test datasets.
- ✔ Normally the training dataset is significantly larger than the test dataset.
- ✔ Using the test dataset helps you avoid errors such as overfitting.
- ✔ The trained model is run against test data to see how well the model will perform.

Some data scientists prefer to have a third dataset that has characteristics similar to those of the first two: a *validation dataset*. The idea is that if you're actively using your test data to refine your model, you should use a separate (third) set to check the accuracy of the model. Having a validation dataset, that wasn't used as part of the development process of your model, helps ensure a neutral estimation of the model's accuracy and efficacy.

If you've built multiple models using various algorithms, the validation sample can also help you evaluate which model performs best.

Make sure you double-check your work developing and testing the model. In particular, be skeptical if the performance or the accuracy of the model seems too good to be true. Errors can happen where you least expect them. Incorrectly calculating dates for time series data, for example, can lead to erroneous results.

Employing cross-validation

Cross-validation is a popular technique you can use to evaluate and validate your model. The same principle of using separate datasets for testing and training applies here: The training data is used to build the model; the model is run against the testing set to predict data it hasn't seen before, which is one way to evaluate its accuracy.

In cross-validation, the historical data is split into X numbers of subsets. Each time a subset is chosen to be used as test data, the rest of the subsets are used as training data. Then, on the next run, the former test set becomes one of the training sets and one of the former training sets becomes the test set. The process continues until every subset of that X number of sets has been used as a test set.

For example, imagine we have a dataset that we have divided into 5 sets numbered 1 to 5. In the first run, we use set 1 as the test set and use sets 2, 3, 4 and 5 as the training set. Then, on the second run, we use set 2 as the test set and sets 1, 3, 4, and 5 as training set. We continue this process until every subset of the 5 sets has been used as a test set.

Cross-validation allows you to use every data point in your historical data for both training and testing. This technique is more effective than just splitting your historical data into two sets, using the set with the most data for training, using the other set for testing, and leaving it at that. When you cross-validate your data, you're protecting yourself against randomly picking test data that's too easy to predict — which would give you the false impression that your model is accurate. Or, if you happen to pick test data that's too hard to predict, you might falsely conclude that your model isn't performing as you had hoped.

Cross-validation is widely used not only to validate the accuracy of models but also to compare the performance of multiple models.

Balancing bias and variance

Bias and variance are two sources of errors that can take place as you're building your analytical model.

Bias is the result of building a model that significantly simplifies the presentation of the relationships among data points in the historical data used to build the model.

Variance is the result of building a model that is explicitly specific to the data used to build the model.

Achieving a balance between bias and variance — by reducing the variance and tolerating some bias — can lead to a better predictive model. This trade-off usually leads to building less complex predictive models.

Many data-mining algorithms have been created to take into account this trade-off between bias and variance.

Troubleshooting ideas

When you're testing your model and you find yourself going nowhere, here are a few ideas to consider that may help you get back on track:

- Always double-check your work. You may have overlooked something you assumed was correct but isn't. Such flaws could show up (for example) among the values of a predictive variable in your dataset, or in the preprocessing you applied to the data.

- If the algorithm you chose isn't yielding any results, try another algorithm. For example, you try several classification algorithms available and depending on your data and the business objectives of your model, one of those may perform better than the others.

- Try selecting different variables or creating new derived variables. Be always on the lookout for variables that have predictive powers.

- Frequently consult with the business domain experts who can help you make sense of the data, select variables, and interpret the model's results.

Evaluating the model

At this stage, you're trying to make sure that your model is accurate, can meet its business objective, and can be deployed.

Before presenting your findings, make sure that the steps you took to build the model are all correct. Verification of those steps, from data processing to data analysis, is essential.

After partitioning your data into training and test sets and performing a cross-validation, you still need to evaluate whether the model meets its business objectives and interpret its results in familiar business terms; domain experts can help with that.

Here's where you address the model's performance in terms of its speed and accuracy when deployed. You want to know how well your model will run against larger datasets — especially in the production environment.

To determine what measures you can take so as to judge the quality of your model, start by comparing the outputs of multiple models (or multiple versions of the same model). You want to have confidence that the model you built is sound, and that you can defend its findings. Be sure you can explain and interpret the results in business terms that the stakeholders can readily understand and apply.

You should be able to pinpoint why your model gives a particular recommendation or prediction. Doing so makes the model's outputs transparent, which allows business stakeholders to transform the predictions more easily into actionable decisions. If you're lucky, you may stumble over some new insights that only make sense after the model brings them to light. Those are rare, but when you get such results, the rewards can be substantial.

Going Live with the Model

After developing the model and successfully testing it, you're ready to deploy it into the production environment.

Deploying the model

The ultimate goal of a predictive analytics project is to put the model you build into the production process so it becomes an integral part of business decision-making.

The model can be deployed as a standalone tool or as part of an application. Either way, deploying the model can bring its own challenges.

✔ Because the goal is to make use of the model's predictive results and act upon them, you have to come up with an efficient way to feed data to the model and retrieve results from the model after it analyzes that data.

✔ Not all predictive decisions are automated; sometimes human intervention is needed. If a model flags a claim as fraudulent or high-risk, a claim processor may examine the claim more thoroughly and find it to be sound, saving the company from the loss of opportunity.

The higher the stakes of a predictive decision, the more necessary it is to incorporate human oversight and approval into those decisions.

The model accrues real value only when it's incorporated into business processes — and when its predictions are turned into actionable decisions that drive business growth higher. This becomes especially useful when the deployed model provides recommendations, some of them in real time, during customers' interactions — or assesses risk during transactions, or evaluates business applications. This business contribution is especially powerful when repeated across several transactions, seamlessly.

Monitoring and maintaining the model

The longer the model is deployed, the more likely it will lose its predictive relevance as the market changes. Business conditions are constantly changing, new data keeps coming in, and new trends are evolving. To keep your model relevant, monitor its performance and refresh it as necessary:

✔ Run the deployed model on the newly acquired data.

✔ Use new algorithms to refine the model's output.

A model tends to degrade over time. A successful model must be revisited, revaluated in light of new data and changing conditions, and probably retrained to account for the changes. Refreshing the model should be an ongoing part of the overall planning process.

Chapter 11

Visualization of Analytical Results

• •

In This Chapter

▶ Applying visualization to the predictive analytics lifecycle

▶ Evaluating data visualization

▶ Using visualization on different predictive analytics models

• •

*V*isualization is an art. In predictive analytics, it's the art of being able to analyze and tell a story from your data and analytical results. The story may not only be about the present or the past, but also about the future.

Quick, easy-to-generate visualizations would enhance the decision-making process, making it faster and more effective. Data visualization would also provide executives with a basis for asking better and smarter questions about the organization.

This chapter zooms in on the importance, benefits, and complexities of data visualization. You become familiar with four criteria you can use to evaluate a visualization of analytical results. You're also introduced to the different types of visualizations that you can deploy for different types of prediction models.

This chapter focuses on the specific use of data visualization: making sense of the analytical results and using the visualization as part of your reporting back to the business stakeholders. See Chapter 4 for other data visualization techniques that can help you get a closer look at your data and understand it better.

Visualization As a Predictive Tool

Napoleon Bonaparte said, "A good sketch is better than a long speech." The reason for this truism is that the human brain finds pictures easier to digest than text or numbers. Since the early days, mankind has been relying on pictorial representations to communicate and share information. Maps were one of the very first widespread visualizations, becoming indispensable enough to originate the field of cartography. Maps have played a far-reaching role in sharing ideas and distributing them widely to many generations, reinforcing the human tendency to communicate information visually.

In predictive analytics, data visualization presents analytical results as a picture that can be easily used to build realistic, actionable narratives of possible futures; such narratives can be archived and transmitted throughout your organization, helping to form the basis of its approach to its business.

So, how does visualization figure into the lifecycle of predictive analytics? Read on.

Why visualization matters

Reading rows of spreadsheets, scanning pages and pages of reports, and going through stacks of analytical results generated by predictive models can be painstaking, time-consuming, and — let's face it — boring. Looking at a few graphs representing that same data is faster and easier, while imparting the same meaning. The graphs can bring more understanding more quickly, and drive the point home efficiently. Such advantages are behind the increased demand for data visualization. Companies are starving for visualization tools that can help them understand the key drivers of their businesses.

Arming your data analysts with visualization tools changes the way they analyze data: They can derive more insights and respond to risks more quickly. And they will be empowered to utilize imagination and creativity in their digging and mining for deeper insights. Additionally, through visualization tools, your analysts can present their findings to executives in a way that provides easy, user-friendly access to analytical results.

For instance, if you're dealing with content analytics and have to analyze text, e-mails, and presentations (for openers), you can use visualization tools to convert the content and ideas mentioned in raw content (usually as text) into a clear pictorial representation.

One such visualization is the graphs shown in Figure 11-5; they represent the correlation between concepts mentioned in text sources. Think of it as a labor-saving device: Now someone doesn't have to read thousands of pages, analyze them, extract the most relevant concepts, and derive a relationship among the items of data.

Analytics tools provide such visualizations as output, which goes beyond traditional visualizations by helping you with a sequence of tasks:

1. Do the reading efficiently.

2. Understand lengthy texts.

3. Extract the most important concepts.

4. Derive a clear visualization of the relationship between those concepts.

5. Present the concepts in ways that your stakeholders find meaningful.

This process is known as *interactive data visualization*. It's different from a simple visualization because

✔ You can analyze and drill down into the data represented by the graphs and charts for more details and insights.

✔ You can dynamically change the data used in those charts and graphs.

✔ You can select the different predictive models or preprocessing techniques to apply to the data that generated the graph.

These visualization tools save the data analyst a tremendous amount of time when generating reports, graphs, and (most importantly) effective communication about the results of predictive analysis.

That effective communication includes getting people together in a room, presenting the visualizations, and leading discussions that emerge from questions such as these:

"What does that point in the graph mean?"

"Does everyone see what I see?"

"What would happen if we added or removed certain data elements or variables?"

"What would happen if we changed this or that variable?"

Such discussions could unveil aspects of the data that weren't evident before, remove ambiguity, and answer some new questions about data patterns.

Getting the benefits of visualization

Using visualizations to present the results of your predictive analytics model can save you a lot of time when you're conveying your ideas to management. Visualization can make the business case for you, providing an instant under-standing of complex analytical results.

Another benefit of using charts and graphs is to ease the process of decision-making. For example, you can use visualizations to identify areas in your business that need attention, as when you show maps that present compara-tive sales of your product by location and can more easily identify areas that might need more advertising. Doing several such analyses and presentations over time can create a narrative of predicting sales volume by location.

Similarly, in political campaigns maps are powerful communication tools that can be used to convey visually the up-to-date status of votes and eventually help predict the chances of winning. They can also aid with rethinking the campaign strategy.

Walking into a meeting with eye-catching graphics rather than spreadsheets of numbers can make your meeting more effective because visualizations are easy to explain to a diverse audience. Meetings can then become opportunities for discussion, focused imagination, and ingenuity, leading to the discovery of new insights.

Visualization can be used to confirm or disprove assumptions made about a specific topic or phenomenon in your data. It can also validate your predictive model by helping you determine whether the output of the model is in line with the business requirements, and the data supports the claims made for the model.

In summary, visualization:

- ✔ Is easy to understand
- ✔ Is visually appealing
- ✔ Simplifies the complexities of the analysis
- ✔ Is an efficient medium for communicating results
- ✔ Makes the business case
- ✔ Validates the output of your model
- ✔ Enables the decision-making process

Dealing with complexities

Let's face it: Visualization may help simplify communication, but making effective use of visualization isn't exactly simple. Using data visualization to draft the storylines of scenarios that portray the future of your organization can be both powerful and complex.

The complexities of using visualization in predictive analytics can crop up in various areas:

- ✔ Visualization requires a wide range of multi-disciplinary skills in (for example) statistics, analysis, graphic design, computer programming, and narrative.

- ✔ A large body of data that comes from a variety of sources can be unruly to handle. Finding innovative ways to plot all that data — and represent it to the decision-makers in ways they find meaningful — can be challenging.

- ✔ Visualizing analytical results can accidentally convey misleading patterns or predictions. Different interpretations and various possible insights might come from the same visualization.

To head off this difficulty, you might want to have different analysts discuss these possibilities and their meanings beforehand, in depth; get them to agree on a single, consistent story derived from the visualization before you present it to management.

Evaluating Your Visualization

There are several ways to visualize data; but what defines a good visualization? The short answer: Whatever gets the meaning across is your best choice. To help you find that best choice, this section lists four criteria you can use to judge your visualization. This is not a comprehensive list, but it should point you toward the best visualization to drive your idea home.

How relevant is this picture?

Your data visualization must have a clear, well-defined purpose — have a goal in mind and convey a clear idea of how to get there. That purpose could be the answering of the business need that brought you to apply predictive analytics in the first place. A subsidiary, immediately practical purpose could be your need to convey complex ideas through visualization. To answer both needs, first keep in mind that the data presented in the visualization has to be relevant to the overall theme of your analytics project. (That relevance won't be far to seek; your analytical project started with selecting the relevant data to feed into your predictive model.)

With the theme in mind, the next step is to create a narrative that presents the relevant data, highlights the results that point toward the goal, and uses a relevant visualization medium. (If your company has a room that's ideal for, say, PowerPoint presentations, consider that a big hint.)

How interpretable is the picture?

If you apply analytics to your data, build a predictive model, and then display your analytical results visually, you should be able to derive well-defined interpretations from your visualizations. Deriving those meaningful interpretations leads, in turn, to deriving insights, and that's the linchpin for the whole predictive analytics process.

The story you tell via your visualization medium must be clear and unambiguous. A roomful of conflicting interpretations is usually a sign that something is amiss. To keep the interpretation of the visualization on track, be sure you keep it firmly in line with the model's output — which in turn aligns the whole effort with the business questions that prompted the predictive analytics quest.

In cases where a visualization might allow several interpretations, those interpretations should converge to tell the same story in the end. As with many undertakings, multiple interpretations are often possible. Try to anticipate, discuss, and tweak them beforehand until they all convey the same underlying idea or support the same overarching concept.

Is the picture simple enough?

A visualization that's too complex can be misleading or confusing. To achieve simplicity, your visualization needs clarity and elegance.

You should always aim for clarity by adding as many *legends* (guides to what the parts of the image mean) as needed, and making them as clear as possible. You can use legends to define all the symbols, figures, axes, colors, data ranges, and other graphical components you have in your visualization.

Choosing the right combination of colors and objects to represent your data can enhance elegance. The medium you choose to present your data is also critical. The medium refers to the images, graphs, and charts in your presentations, in addition to the conference room, and to the visual aids you use to present your analytical results, such as TV screen, white board, or projector.

As a rule, the simpler the visualization and the more straightforward its meaning is, the better it is. You know you've succeeded when the visualization does the talking for you.

Does the picture lead to new insights?

Your visualization should add something new to your predictive analytics project. Ideally, it should help you find new insights that were not known before. During the building of your predictive analytics model, you can use visualization to fine-tune the output of your model, examine the data, and plot the result of the analysis. Visualization can be your guide to discovering new insights, or discerning and learning new relationships among items of data in the sea of data you're analyzing.

Visualization should help you seal the deal and erase any doubts about the analysis; it should support the findings and the output of the model. If it does so effectively, then presenting these findings to management will help them embrace and act upon the results.

Visualizing Your Model's Analytical Results

This section presents some ways to use visualization techniques to report the results of your models to the stakeholders.

Visualizing hidden groupings in your data

As discussed in Chapter 6, data clustering is the process of discovering hidden groups of related items within your data. In most cases, a *cluster* (grouping) consists of data objects of the same type such as social network users, text documents, or e-mails. One way to visualize the results of a data-clustering model is shown in Figure 11-1, where the graph represents social communities (clusters) that were discovered in data collected from social network users. In Figure 11-1, the data about customers was collected in a tabular format; then a clustering algorithm was applied to the data, and the three clusters (groups) were discovered: loyal customers, wandering customers, and discount customers.

Here the visual relationship among the three groups already suggests where enhanced marketing efforts might do the most good.

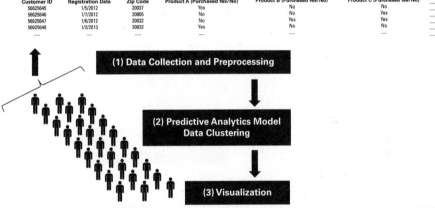

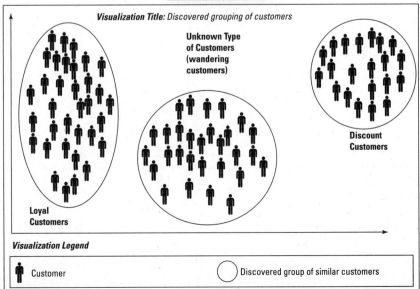

Figure 11-1: Clustering customers in three groups: loyal, wandering, and discount.

Visualizing data classification results

A classification model assigns a specific class to each new data point it examines. The specific classes, in this case, could be the groups that result from your clustering work (see the previous section). The output highlighted in the graph (refer to Figure 11-1) can define your target sets. For any given new customer, a predictive classification model attempts to predict which group the new customer will belong to.

After you've applied a clustering algorithm and discovered groupings in the customer data, you come to a moment of truth: Here comes a new customer — you want the model to predict which type of customer he or she will be.

Figure 11-2 shows how a new customer's information is fed to your predictive analytics model, which in turn predicts which group of customers this new customer belongs to. In Figure 11-2, new Customers A, B, and C are about to be assigned to clusters according the classification model. Applying the

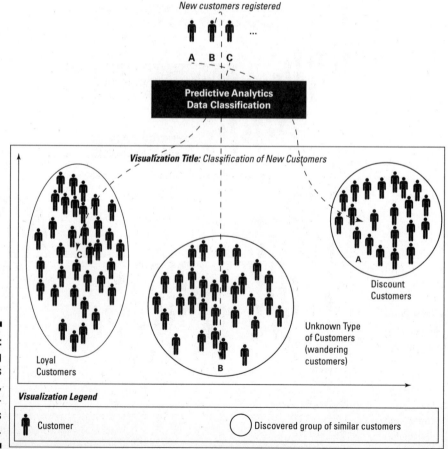

Figure 11-2:
Assigning Customers A, B, and C, to their classifications (clusters).

classification model resulted in a prediction that Customer A would belong with the loyal customers, Customer B would be a wanderer, and Customer C was only showing up for the discount.

Visualizing outliers in your data

In the course of clustering or classifying new customers, every now and then you run into *outliers* — special cases that don't fit the existing divisions.

Figure 11-3 shows a few outliers that don't fit well into the predefined clusters. In Figure 11-3, six outlier customers have been detected and visualized. They behave differently enough that the model can't tell whether they belong to any of defined categories of customers. (Is there such a thing as, say, a loyal wandering customer who's only interested in the discount? And if there is, should your business care?)

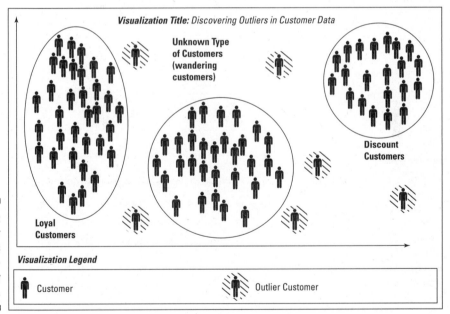

Figure 11-3:
Six outlier customers defy categorization just by showing up.

Visualization of Decision Trees

Many models use *decision trees* as their outputs: These diagrams show the possible results from alternative courses of action, laid out like the branches of a tree. Figure 11-4 shows an example of a decision tree used as a classifier: It classifies baseball fans based on a few criteria, mainly the amount spent on tickets and the purchase dates. From this visualization, you can predict the type of fan that a new ticket-buyer will be: casual, loyal, bandwagon, diehard, or some other type. Attributes of each fan are mentioned at each level in the tree (total number of attended games, total amount spent, season); you can follow a path from a particular "root" to a specific "leaf" on the tree, where you hit one of the fan classes (c1, c2, c3, c4, c5).

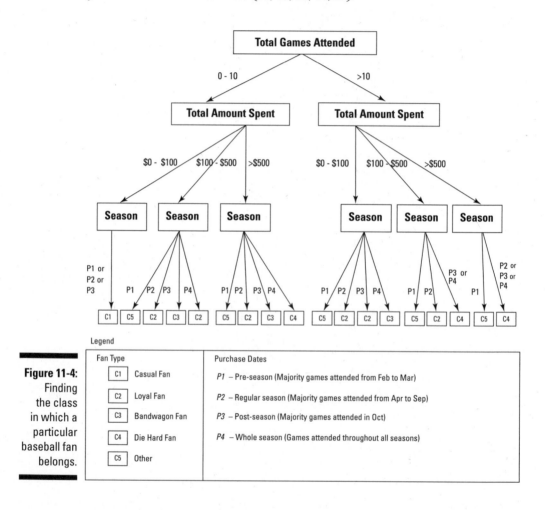

Figure 11-4: Finding the class in which a particular baseball fan belongs.

Suppose we want to determine the type of baseball fan a customer is so that we can determine what type of marketing ads to send to the customer. We want to know whether the customer is a baseball fanatic or someone who just rides the bandwagon. Suppose we hypothesize that baseball fanatics and bandwagon fans can be persuaded to buy a new car (or other discretionary goods) when their team is doing well and headed for the playoffs. We may want to send them marketing ads and discounts to persuade them to make the purchase. Further,

suppose we hypothesize that bandwagon fans can be persuaded to vote in support of certain political issues. We can send them marketing ads asking them for
that support. If you know what type of fan base you have, using decision trees
can help you decide how to approach it as a range of customer types.

Visualizing predictions

Assume you've run an array of predictive analytics models, including decision trees, random forests, and flocking algorithms. You can combine all those
results and present a consistent narrative that they all support, as shown in
Figure 11-5. Here confidence is a numerical percentage that can be calculated
using a mathematical function. The result of the calculation encapsulates a
score of how probable a possible occurrence is. On the x axis, the supporting
evidence represents the content source that was analyzed with content-analytics
models that identified the possible outcomes. In most cases, your predictive
model would have processed a large dataset, using data from various sources,
to derive those possible outcomes. Thus you need show only the most important supporting evidence in your visualization, as depicted in Figure 11-5.

In Figure 11-5, a summary of the results obtained from applying predictive
analytics is presented as a visualization that illustrates possible outcomes,
along with a confidence score and supporting evidence for each one. Three
possible scenarios are shown:

- ✔ The inventory of Item A will not keep up with demand if you don't ship
  at least 100 units weekly to Store S. (Confidence score: 98 percent.)

- ✔ The number of sales will increase by 40 percent if you increase the production of Item A by at least 56 percent. (Confidence score: 83 percent.)

- ✔ A marketing campaign in California will increase sales of Items A and D
  but not Item K. (Confidence score: 72 percent.)

The confidence score represents the likelihood that each scenario will
happen, according to your predictive analytics model. Note that they are
listed here in descending order of likelihood.

Here the most important supporting evidence consists of how excerpts from
several content sources are presented over the x axis. You can refer to them
if you need to explain how you got to a particular possible scenario — and
trot out the evidence that supports it.

The power behind this visualization is its simplicity. Imagine, after months of
applying predictive analytics to your data, working your way through several
iterations, that you walk into a meeting with decision-maker. You're armed
with one slide visualization of three possible scenarios that might have a
huge impact on the business. Such a visualization creates effective discussions and can lead management to "aha" moments.

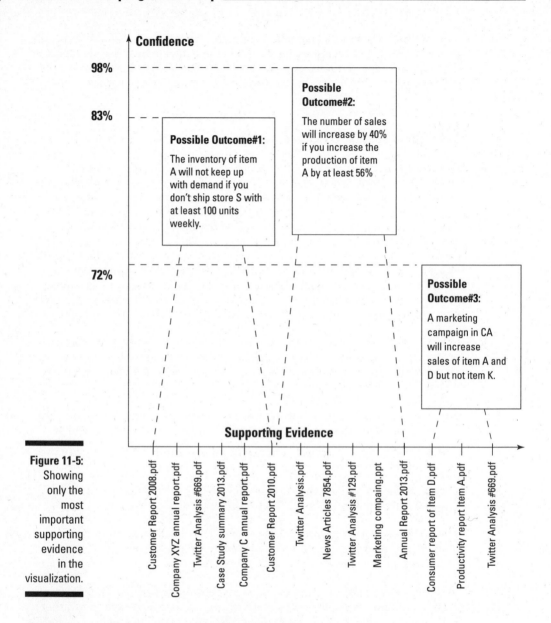

Figure 11-5:
Showing
only the
most
important
supporting
evidence
in the
visualization.

Other Types of Visualizations in Predictive Analytics

A visualization can also represent a *simulation* — a pictorial representation of a what-if scenario. You can follow up a visualization of a prediction with a simulation that overlaps and supports the prediction. For instance, what happens if the company stops manufacturing Product D? What happens if a natural disaster strikes the home office? What happens if your customers lose interest in a particular product? You can use visualization to simulate the future behavior of a company, a market, a weather system — you name it.

A *dashboard* is another type of visualization you can use to display a comprehensive predictive analytics model. The dashboard will allow you, using a control button, to change any step in the predictive analytics pipeline. This can include selecting the data, data preprocessing, selecting a predictive model, and selecting the right evaluation versions. You can easily modify any part of the pipeline at anytime using the control button on the dashboard. A dashboard is an interactive type of visualization where you have control and you can change the diagrams, tables, or maps dynamically based on the inputs you choose to include in the analyses that genearte those charts and graphs.

Bird-flocking behavior data visualization

At least one predictive analytics technique is purely inspired by the natural phenomenon of birds flocking (refer to Chapter 2). The bird-flocking model not only identifies groupings in data, it shows them in dynamic action. The same technique can be used to picture hidden patterns in your data.

The model represents data objects as birds flying in a virtual space, following *flocking rules* that orchestrate how a migrating swarm of birds moves in nature.

Representing several data objects as birds reveals that similar data objects will flock together to form *subflocks* (groupings). The similarity among objects in the real world is what drives the movements of the corresponding birds in the virtual space. For instance, as shown in Figure 11-6, imagine that you want to analyze the online data collected from several Internet users (also known as *netizens*).

Figure 11-6: Using bird flocking to analyze the online behavior of Internet users.

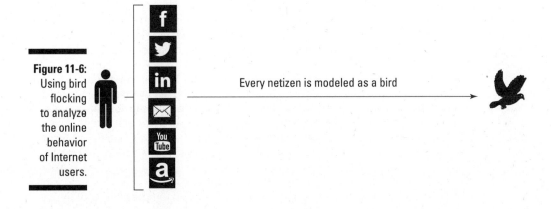

Every netizen is modeled as a bird

Every piece of information (gleaned from such sources as social network user information, customer online transactions, and so on) will be represented as a corresponding bird in the virtual space, as shown in Figure 11-7.

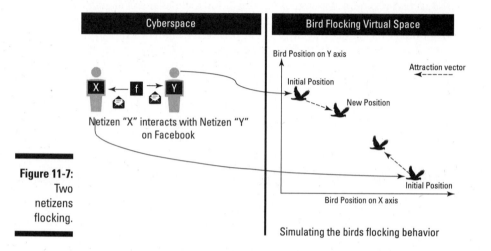

Figure 11-7:
Two
netizens
flocking.

If the model finds that two or more users interact with each other through e-mail or chat, appear in the same online photo, buy the same product, or share the same interests, the model shows those two netizens as birds that flock together, following natural flocking rules.

The interaction (that is, how close the representative birds get to each other) is expressed as a mathematical function that depends on the frequency of social interaction, or the intensity with which the users buy the same products or share the same interests. This latest mathematical function depends purely on the type of analytics you're applying.

Figure 11-7 depicts the interaction on Facebook between Netizens X and Y in cyberspace as bird-flocking virtual space, where both X and Y are represented as birds. Because Netizens X and Y have interacted with each other, the next flocking iteration will show their two birds as closer together.

An algorithm known as "flock by leader," created by Professor Bellaachia's team (see Chapter 6), was inspired by a recent discovery that revealed the leadership dynamics in pigeons. This algorithm can mine user input for data points that enable it to detect leaders, discover their followers, and initiate flocking behavior in virtual space that closely mimics what happens when flocks form naturally — except the flocks, in this case, are data clusters called *data flocks*.

This technique not only detects patterns in data, but also provides a clear pictorial representation of the results obtained by applying predictive analytics models. The rules that orchestrate natural flocking behavior in nature were extended to create new flocking rules that conform to data analytics:

- ✔ **Data flock homogeneity:** Members of the flock show similarity in data.
- ✔ **Data flock leadership:** The model anticipates information leaders.

Representing a large dataset as a flock of birds is one way to easily visualize big data in a dashboard.

This visualization model can be used to detect pieces of data that are outliers, leaders, or followers. One political application could be to visualize community outliers, community leaders, or community followers. In the biomedical field, the model can be used to visualize outliers' genomes and leaders among genetic samples of a particular disease (say, those that show a particular mutation most consistently).

A bird-flocking visualization can also be used to predict future patterns of unknown phenomena in cyberspace — civil unrest, an emerging social movement, a future customer's lineage.

The flocking visualization is especially useful if you're receiving a large volume of streamed data at high velocity: You can see the formation of flocking in the virtual space that contains the birds that represent your data objects. The results of data analytics are reflected (literally) on the fly on the virtual space. Reality given a fictional, yet observable and analytically meaningful, representation purely inspired from nature. Such visualizations can also work well as simulations or what-if scenarios.

In Figure 11-8, a visualization based on flocking behavior starts by indexing each netizen to a virtual bird. Initially, all the birds are idle. As data comes in, each bird starts flocking in the virtual space according to the analytics results and the flocking rules.

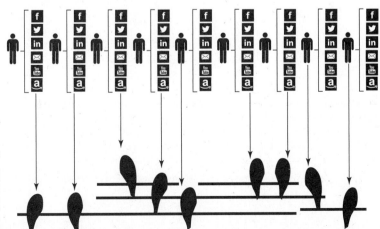

Figure 11-8:
Tracking
the flocking
netizens.

In Figure 11-9, the emerging flock is formed as the analytics are presented.

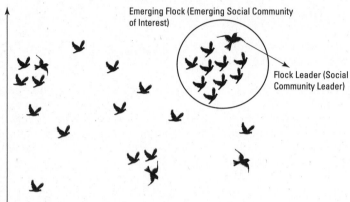

Simulating Flocking Behavior based on Netizen Cyberspace behavior at Time = t

Figure 11-9:
What the
flock is
doing.

After analyzing data over a large period of time ending at t+k, the results of this application of predictive analytics results can be depicted as shown in Figure 11-10: The flock-by-leader algorithm differentiates the members of the flock into three classes: a leader, followers, and outliers.

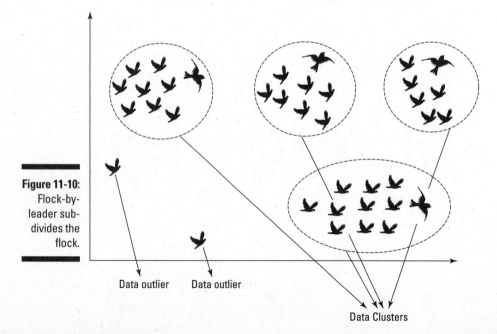

Simulating Flocking Behavior on Netizens Cyberspace behavior at Time = t+k

Figure 11-10:
Flock-by-
leader sub-
divides the
flock.

Part IV
Programming Predictive Analytics

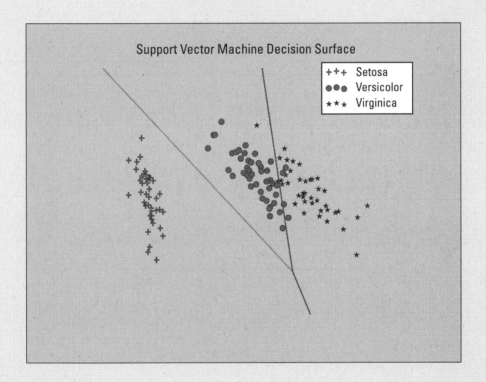

Support Vector Machine Decision Surface

+++ Setosa
●●● Versicolor
★★★ Virginica

Visit www.dummies.com/extras/predictiveanalytics for great Dummies content online.

In this part . . .

- ✔ Installing software
- ✔ Applying algorithms
- ✔ Programming models with R
- ✔ Maximizing accuracy
- ✔ Applying predictive analytics to big data
- ✔ Visit `www.dummies.com/extras/ predictiveanalytics` for great Dummies content online.

Chapter 12

Creating Basic Prediction Examples

In This Chapter

▶ Installing the machine-learning software

▶ Working with a sample dataset

▶ Creating simple predictive models

▶ Visualizing and evaluating your results

*T*his chapter is about installing and setting up the machine-learning software and using the Python programming language to create a couple of simple predictive models. There are a few modules to install and it will take a bit of time, so make sure you have plenty of battery life left if you're working on your laptop. If you already have Python installed prior to reading this book, make sure you're installing the correct versions of the machine-learning modules and dependencies for the Python version you're using. In this book, Python version 2.7.6 is being used on a Windows machine.

If you're following along in this chapter, you'll dive right in and start working with a sample dataset. Don't worry too much about the coding involved; most of the code will be provided and you can run it directly in the Python interactive interpreter, line by line. For most lines of code, you'll see what the output is. If, for some reason, an error crops up, you'll know exactly which line caused the error. Easy stuff.

Installing the Software Packages

The goal here is to build a couple of predictive models using different classification algorithms. To do that, you'll need to install Python, its machine-learning modules, and its dependencies. The setup process can take from 30 minutes to an hour, depending on your available Internet speed and your experience level in installing projects that require multiple other projects.

You can choose from a variety of programming languages and add-on packages to create and run predictive models. Python, together with the `scikit-learn` module, is an easy combination of programming language and machine-learning package to use, learn, and get started with quickly.

Compared to other programming languages, Python is relatively easy to learn. Its syntax is straightforward and the code can be executed directly in an interactive console. You'll know immediately if you wrote a successful statement, and can learn quickly from trial and error in many cases.

Installing Python

Installing Python is an easy process that takes less than thirty minutes and just several clicks of the mouse. All of the default settings can be accepted during the installation process. You can install Python by downloading the installation program for Windows and other operating systems from the Python website at `www.python.org`. This chapter guides you through the installation process for the Windows operating system and Python release version 2.7.6. After you get to the Python website, you can look for the downloads link to get the file. After you've downloaded the file, just double-click it to begin the installation process.

Here is a direct link to the download for your convenience:

```
http://www.python.org/ftp/python/2.7.6/python-2.7.6.msi
```

Installing the machine-learning module

Go to the `scikit-learn` website (`http://scikit-learn.org`) to get the machine learning package.

1. **Click the link to the Installation page and from there, look for the link to the installer in the Windows Installer section.**

   You get a download link that takes you to the SourceForge website where you can get the latest version for your operating system.

   Here is a direct link to the `scikit` project at SourceForge:

   ```
   http://sourceforge.net/projects/scikit-learn/files/.
   ```

   You'll be using the executable file `scikit-learn-0.14.1.win32-py2.7.exe` for your installation.

2. **Click the link with the executable filename.**

   Within a few seconds, you may receive a prompt to download the `scikit-learn` machine-learning module, as shown in Figure 12-1.

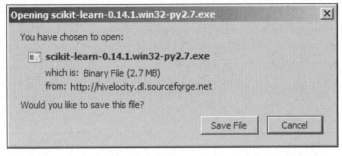

Figure 12-1:
A prompt to download the scikit-learn machine-learning module.

3. **Click the Save File button and wait for the download to finish.**

4. **When the download is finished, go to your downloads folder (or wherever you saved the file) and run the file by double-clicking the filename.**

   This may open a series of prompts or warnings (similar to Figure 12-2 and Figure 12-3) that ask whether you want to proceed with running an executable file.

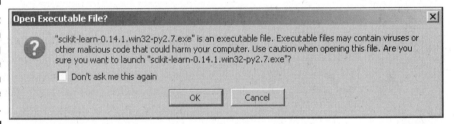

Figure 12-2:
System warning that you're opening an executable file.

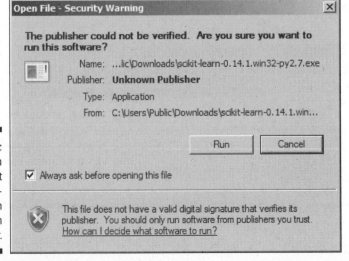

Figure 12-3:
System warning that this software is from an unknown publisher.

5. **Click the OK / Run button and continue.**

   The next screen, shown in Figure 12-4 offers some important and useful information about the `scikit-learn` project.

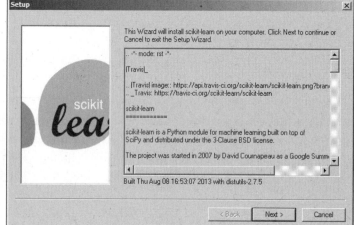

Figure 12-4:
Important
information
about the
scikit-learn
project.

6. **After you finish reading the information, click the Next button.**

   When actual installation begins, the `scikit` installer may ask you to select some custom options during the installation process. In most cases, accepting the default selections will be sufficient for running the examples.

   When a screen that asks where you want the module installed (as shown in Figure 12-5), we recommend accepting the default directory. Doing so simplifies the installation process, as there are other dependent modules you need to install. `C:\Python27\Lib\site-packages\` is the default installation directory for third-party modules.

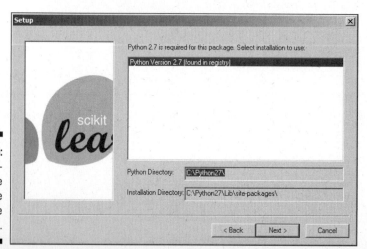

Figure 12-5:
The direc-
tory where
the module
is to be
installed.

7. Click the Next button.

You're now ready to install `scikit-learn`. Figure 12-6 shows one final prompt that appears before installation begins.

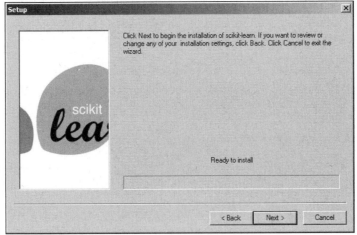

Figure 12-6:
Ready to
install.

8. Click the Next button.

After the status bar is complete, you're notified that your installation is complete (as shown in Figure 12-7).

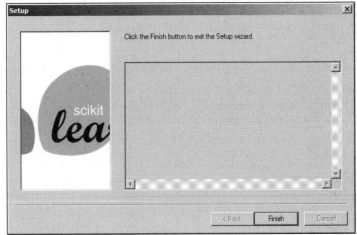

Figure 12-7:
Finished
installation
message.

9. Click the Finish button.

You're done installing the main module for `scikit`. You're now ready to install its dependencies.

Installing the dependencies

The scikit-learn module requires (or is dependent on) a few other modules to be installed before you can start using it. Modules that are dependent on other modules are called *dependencies*. In this case, the dependencies are numpy, scipy, and matplotlib.

You need to install the following dependencies:

- ✔ numpy
- ✔ scipy
- ✔ matplotlib

These packages may be available from several locations:

- ✔ The Python Package Index website at https://pypi.python.org/pypi
- ✔ The SourceForge website at http://sourceforge.net
- ✔ The matplotlib website http://matplotlib.org/downloads.html

Choosing the versions that have Windows installers will make the installation process quicker and as simple as possible.

Installing the dependencies is similar to installing scikit-learn. It's a series of prompts and clicks. To stay consistent across all dependencies, choose the default options.

Installing numpy

The following section details the steps needed to install numpy. You may download numpy from the SourceForge website.

1. **From the SourceForge website, do a search for** *numpy* **in the search form.**

   Many listings show up. The needed module is numpy-1.8.0. If you search for it, it should appear as the top listing onscreen. To be sure that you have the same file, check to make sure it has the following description:

   ```
   Numerical Python: Numerical Python adds a fast and
           sophisticated array facility to the Python
           language.
   ```

2. **Click the Download Now button to download the latest version of** numpy.

   Doing so takes you to the download page; in a few seconds, a prompt appears, asking you to accept the download of the file (as shown in Figure 12-8).

   Here is a direct link to the download page:

   http://sourceforge.net/projects/numpy/files/latest/download

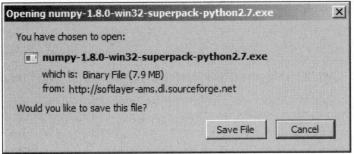

Opening numpy-1.8.0-win32-superpack-python2.7.exe ☒

You have chosen to open:

🔲 **numpy-1.8.0-win32-superpack-python2.7.exe**

which is: Binary File (7.9 MB)

from: http://softlayer-ams.dl.sourceforge.net

Would you like to save this file?

Save File   Cancel

Figure 12-8:
A prompt to download numpy module.

3. **Click the Save File button and wait for the download to finish.**

The file `numpy-1.8.0.win32-superpack-python2.7.exe` will be downloaded.

4. **Go to your downloads folder (or wherever you saved the file) and run the file by double-clicking the filename.**

This may open a series of prompts or warnings that will ask whether you want to proceed with running an executable file. They'll be similar to those that show up when you install `scikit`, as shown earlier in Figure 12-2 and Figure 12-3.

5. **Click the OK/Run/Allow button and continue.**

A screen showing some important and useful information about the `numpy` project (similar to Figure 12-4) appears.

6. **Click the Next button.**

A screen similar to Figure 12-5 appears, asking where you want the `numpy` module installed.

7. **Accept the default location of the setup and click Next.**

A screen appears, displaying one final prompt before installation begins, as shown in Figure 12-6.

8. **Clicking Next begins the installation process.**

When the status bar is finished, you're notified that your installation is complete, as shown in Figure 12-7.

9. **Click the Finish button and then the Close button.**

That's it for this dependency — `numpy` is installed.

Installing scipy

The following section details the steps needed to install `scipy`. You may download `scipy` from the SourceForge website. The installation process is pretty much the same as the installation for `numpy`.

1. **From the SourceForge website, do a search for** *scipy* **in the search form.**

   The top listing from the search should be

   ```
   SciPy: Scientific Library for Python
   ```

2. **Click the Download Now button to download the latest version of scipy.**

   Doing so takes you to the download page. In a few seconds, a prompt appears, asking you to accept the download of the file (as shown in Figure 12-9).

   Here is a direct link to the download page:

   ```
   http://sourceforge.net/projects/scipy/files/latest/
   download
   ```

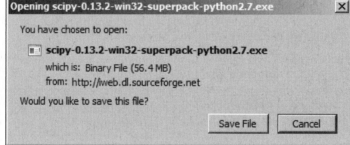

Figure 12-9:
A prompt to download scipy module.

The rest of the installation process is the same as listed for numpy.

Installing matplotlib

The final module to install is matplotlib. To get the executable file, go to http://matplotlib.org/downloads.html and click the link to matplotlib-1.2.1.win32-py2.7.exe. Doing so takes you to the SourceForge website; the download prompt appears in a few seconds, as shown in Figure 12-10. Once again, the rest of the installation process is the same as listed for numpy.

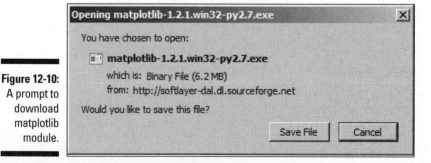

Figure 12-10:
A prompt to download matplotlib module.

Here is a direct link to the download page:

```
sourceforge.net/projects/matplotlib/files/matplotlib/
matplotlib-1.2.1/matplotlib-1.2.1.win32-py2.7.exe/download
```

Checking your installation

When you've installed scikit-learn and all its dependencies, be sure you confirm that the installation went as expected. You want to avoid running into any problem or unexpected errors later on.

1. **Go to the Python interactive shell by choosing Windows Start button➪Python2.7➪Python (command line).**

   The process is similar if you did a custom installation of Python.

2. **In the interactive shell, try running in the following statement to import all the modules that you installed:**

   ```
   >>> import sklearn, numpy, scipy, matplotlib
   ```

   If the Python interpreter returns no errors, then your installation succeeded, as shown in Figure 12-11.

   If you get an error like the one shown in Figure 12-12, then something went wrong in the installation process. You'll have to reinstall the module that is listed in the line that begins with ImportError.

   Assuming everything went as planned, then you're ready to begin using scikit-learn to build a predictive model.

Figure 12-11: Here's what you see if Python successfully imported the modules.

```
C:\Python27\python.exe
Python 2.7.6 (default, Nov 10 2013, 19:24:18) [MSC v.1500 32 bit (Intel)] on win
32
Type "help", "copyright", "credits" or "license" for more information.
>>> import sklearn, numpy, scipy, matplotlib
>>>
```

Figure 12-12: Here an error message states that Python can't import a module.

```
C:\Python27\python.exe
Python 2.7.6 (default, Nov 10 2013, 19:24:18) [MSC v.1500 32 bit (Intel)] on win
32
Type "help", "copyright", "credits" or "license" for more information.
>>> import sklearn, numpy, scipy, matplotlib
Traceback (most recent call last):
  File "<stdin>", line 1, in <module>
ImportError: No module named matplotlib
>>>
```

Preparing the Data

When you're learning a new programming language, it's customary to write the "hello world" program. For machine learning and predictive analytics, creating a model to classify the Iris dataset is its "hello world" equivalent program. This is a rather simple example, but it's very effective in teaching the basics of machine learning and predictive analytics.

Getting the sample dataset

To create our predictive model, you'll need to download the sample Iris dataset. This dataset is freely available from many sources, especially at academic institutions that have machine-learning departments. Fortunately, the folks at scikit-learn were nice enough to include some sample datasets and data-loading functions along with their package. So, for the purposes of these examples, you'll only need to run a couple of simple lines of code to load the data.

Labeling your data

Table 12-1 shows one observation and its features from each class of the Iris Flower dataset.

Table 12-1		The Iris Flower Dataset		
Sepal Length	**Sepal Width**	**Petal Length**	**Petal Width**	**Target Class/ Label**
5.1	3.5	1.4	0.2	Setosa (0)
7.0	3.2	4.7	1.4	Versicolor (1)
6.3	3.3	6.0	2.5	Virginica (2)

The Iris Flower dataset is a real multivariate dataset of three classes of the Iris flower (*Iris setosa, Iris virginica,* and *Iris versicolor*) introduced by Ronald Fisher in his 1936 article, "The Use of Multiple Measurements in Taxonomic Problems." This dataset is best known for its extensive use in academia for machine learning and statistics. The dataset consists of 150 total instances, with 50 instances from each of the 3 classes of the Iris flower. The sample has 4 features (also commonly called *attributes*), which are the length and width measurements of the sepals and petals.

The interesting part of this dataset is that the three classes are somewhat linearly separable. The *Setosa* class can be separated from the other two classes by drawing a straight line on the graph between them. The *Virginica* and *Versicolor* classes can't be perfectly separated using a straight line — although it is close. This makes it a perfect candidate dataset to do classification analysis but not so good for clustering analysis.

The sample data was already labeled. The right column (Label) of Table 12-1 shows the names of each class of the Iris flower. The class name is called a *label* or a *target;* it's usually assigned to a variable named *y*. It is basically the outcome or the result of what is being predicted. In statistics and modeling, it is often referred to as the *dependent variable*. It depends on the inputs that correspond to sepal length and width and to petal length and width.

You may also want to know what's different about the `scikit` preprocessed Iris dataset, as compared to the original dataset. To find out, you need to obtain the original data file. You can do a Google search for *iris dataset* and download it or view it from any one of the academic institutions. The result that usually comes up first is the University of California Irvine's (UCI) machine-learning repository of datasets. Here is a direct link to the Iris dataset in its original state from the UCI machine-learning repository:

```
http://archive.ics.uci.edu/ml/machine-learning-databases/
iris/iris.data
```

If you download it, you should be able to view it with any text editor. Upon viewing the data in the file, you'll notice that there are five columns in each row. The first four columns are the measurements (referred to as the *features*) and the last column is the label. The label differs between the original and `scikit` versions of the Iris dataset. Another difference is the first row of the `sckit` data file. It includes a header row used by the `scikit` data-loading function. It has no effect on the algorithms themselves.

Normalizing features to numbers rather than keeping them as text makes it easier for the algorithms to process — and it's much more memory-efficient. This is especially evident if you run very large datasets with many features — which is often the case in real scenarios.

Table 12-2 shows sample data from both files. All the data columns are the same except for `Col5`. Note that `scikit` has class names with numerical labels; the original file has text labels.

Table 12-2			Sample Data		
Source	*Col1*	*Col2*	*Col3*	*Col4*	*Col5*
scikit	5.1	3.5	1.4	0.2	0
original	5.1	3.5	1.4	0.2	Iris-setosa
scikit	7.0	3.2	4.7	1.4	1
original	7.0	3.2	4.7	1.4	Iris-versicolor
scikit	6.3	3.3	6.0	2.5	2
original	6.3	3.3	6.0	2.5	Iris-virginica

Making Predictions Using Classification Algorithms

You have all the tools and data necessary to start creating a predictive model. Now the fun begins.

In general, creating a learning model for classification tasks will entail the following steps:

1. Load the data.

2. Choose a classifier.

3. Train the model.

4. Visualize the model.

5. Test the model.

6. Evaluate the model.

Creating a supervised learning model with SVM

Supervised learning is a machine-learning task that learns from data that has been labeled. One way to think about supervised learning is that the labeling of data is done under the supervision of the modeler; *unsupervised learning,* by contrast, doesn't require labeled data. Supervised learning is commonly performed using a classification algorithm. In this section, you use the Support Vector Machine classification algorithm to create a supervised learning model.

Loading your data

You need to load the data for your algorithms to use. Loading the Iris dataset in scikit is as simple as issuing a couple of lines of code because scikit has already created a function to load the dataset.

1. **Open a new Python interactive shell session.**

    Use a new Python session so there isn't anything left over in memory and you have a clean slate to work with.

2. **Enter the following code in the prompt and observe the output:**

    ```
    >>> from sklearn.datasets import load_iris
    >>> iris = load_iris()
    ```

    After running those two statements, you should not see any messages from the interpreter. The variable iris should contain all the data from the iris.csv file.

Before you create a predictive model, it's important to understand a little about the new variable iris and what you can do with it. It makes the code easier to follow and the process much simpler to grasp. You can inspect the value of iris by typing it in the interpreter.

```
>>> iris
```

The output will be all the content from the iris.csv file, along with some other information about the dataset that the load_iris function loaded into the iris variable. The iris variable is a dictionary data structure with four main properties. The important properties of iris are listed on Table 12-3.

Table 12-3	Main Properties of Iris Variable
Property Name	**Description**
data	Contains all the measurements of the observations.
feature_name	Contains the name of the feature (attribute name).
target	Contains all the targets (labels) of the observations.
target_names	Contains the names of the iris classes.

You can print out the values in the interpreter by typing the variable name followed by dot followed by property name. An example is using iris.data to access the data property of iris, like this:

```
>>> iris.data
```

This is a standard way of accessing properties of an object in many programming languages.

To create an instance of the SVM classifier, type the following code in the interpreter:

```
>>> from sklearn.svm import LinearSVC
>>> svmClassifier = LinearSVC(random_state=111)
```

The first line of code imports the LinearSVC library into the session. The linear Support Vector Classifier (SVC) is an implementation of SVM for linear classification and has multi-class support. The dataset is somewhat linearly separable and has three classes, so it would be a good idea to experiment with LinearSVC to see how it performs. (You can read more about SVM in Chapter 7.)

The second line creates the instance using the variable svmClassifier. This is an important variable to remember; you'll see it used several more times in the chapter. The random_state parameter allows us to reproduce these examples and get the same results. If you didn't put in the random_state parameter, your results may differ from the ones shown here.

Running the training data

Before you can feed the SVM classifier with the data that was loaded, you must split the full dataset into a training set and test set.

Fortunately, scikit-learn has implemented a function that will help you to easily split the full dataset. The train_test_split function takes as input a single dataset and a percentage value. The percentage value is used to determine the size of the test set. The function returns two datasets: the test dataset (with its size specified) and the training dataset (which uses the remaining data).

Typically, one can take around 70-80 percent of the data to use as a training set and use the remaining data as the test set. But the Iris dataset is very small (only 150 instances), so you can take 90 percent of it to train the model and use the other 10 percent as test data to see how your predictive model will perform.

Type in the following code to split your dataset:

```
>>> from sklearn import cross_validation
>>> X_train, X_test, y_train, y_test =
        cross_validation.train_test_split(iris.data,
        iris.target, test_size=0.10, random_state=111)
```

The first line imports cross-validation library into your session. The second line creates the test set from 10 percent of the sample.

> X_train will contain 135 observations and its features.

> y_train will contain 135 labels in the same order as the 135 observations.

> X_test will contain 15 (or 10 percent) observations and its features.

> y_test will contain 15 labels in the same order as the 15 observations.

The following code verifies that the split is what you expected:

```
>>> X_train.shape
(135, 4)
>>> y_train.shape
(135,)
>>> X_test.shape
(15, 4)
>>> y_test.shape
(15,)
```

You can see from the output that there are 135 observations with 4 features and 135 labels in the training set. The test set has 15 observations with 4 features and 15 labels.

Many beginners in the field of predictive analytics forget to split the datasets — which introduces a serious design flaw into the project. If the full 150 instances were loaded into the machine as training data, that would leave no unseen data for testing the model. Then you'd have to resort to reusing some of the training instances to test the predictive model. You'll see that in such a situation, the model always predicts the correct class — because you're using the same exact data you used to train the model. The model has already seen this pattern before; it will have no problem just repeating what it's seen. A working predictive model needs to make predictions for data that it hasn't seen yet.

When you have an instance of an SVM classifier, a training dataset, and a test dataset, you're ready to train the model with the training data. Typing the following code into the interpreter will do exactly that:

```
>>> svmClassifier.fit(X_train,y_train)
```

This line of code creates a working model to make predictions from. Specifically, a predictive model that will predict what class of Iris a new unlabeled dataset belongs to. The svmClassifier instance will have several methods that you can call to do various things. For example, after calling the fit method, the most useful method to call is the predict method. That's the method to which you'll feed new data; in return, it predicts the outcome.

Visualizing the classifier

The Iris dataset is not easy to graph in its original form because you cannot plot all four coordinates (from the features) of the dataset onto a two-dimensional screen. Therefore you have to reduce the dimensions by applying a *dimensionality reduction* algorithm to the features. In this case, the algorithm you'll be using to do the data transformation (reducing the dimensions of the features) is called Principal Component Analysis (PCA).

The PCA algorithm takes all four features (numbers), does some math on them, and outputs two new numbers that you can use to do the plot. Think of PCA as following two general steps:

1. It takes as input a dataset with many features.

2. It reduces that input to a smaller set of features (user-defined or algorithm-determined) by transforming the components of the feature set into what it considers as the main (principal) components.

This transformation of the feature set is also called *feature extraction*. The following code does the dimension reduction:

```
>>> from sklearn.decomposition import PCA
>>> pca = PCA(n_components=2).fit(X_train)
>>> pca_2d = pca.transform(X_train)
```

If you've already imported any libraries or datasets listed in this code section, it's not necessary to re-import or load them in your current Python session. If you do so, however, it should not affect your program.

After you run the code, you can type the `pca_2d` variable in the interpreter and see that it outputs arrays with two items instead of four. These two new numbers are mathematical representations of the four old numbers. When the reduced feature set, you can plot the results by using the following code:

```
>>> import pylab as pl
>>> for i in range(0, pca_2d.shape[0]):
>>>     if y_train[i] == 0:
>>>         c1 = pl.scatter(pca_2d[i,0],pca_2d[i,1],c='r',
                marker='+')
>>>     elif y_train[i] == 1:
>>>         c2 = pl.scatter(pca_2d[i,0],pca_2d[i,1],c='g',
                marker='o')
>>>     elif y_train[i] == 2:
>>>         c3 = pl.scatter(pca_2d[i,0],pca_2d[i,1],c='b',
                marker='*')
>>> pl.legend([c1, c2, c3], ['Setosa', 'Versicolor',
                'Virginica'])
>>> pl.title('Iris training dataset with 3 classes and
                known outcomes')
>>> pl.show()
```

Figure 12-13 is a *scatter plot* — a visualization of plotted points representing observations on a graph. This particular scatter plot represents the known outcomes of the Iris training dataset. There are 135 plotted points (observations) from our training dataset. (You can see a similar plot, using all 150 observations, in Chapter 13.) The training dataset consists of

- ✔ 45 pluses that represent the Setosa class.
- ✔ 48 circles that represent the Versicolor class.
- ✔ 42 stars that represent the Virginica class.

You can confirm the stated number of classes by entering following code:

```
>>> sum(y_train==0)
45
>>> sum(y_train==1)
48
>>> sum(y_train==2)
42
```

From this plot you can clearly tell that the Setosa class is linearly separable from the other two classes. While the Versicolor and Virginica classes are not completely separable by a straight line, they're not overlapping by very much. From a simple visual perspective, the classifiers should do pretty well.

Figure 12-14 shows a plot of the Support Vector Machine (SVM) model trained with a dataset that has been dimensionally reduced to two features. This is not the same SVM model that you trained earlier in the previous section; that SVM model used all four features. Four features is a small feature set; we want to keep all four so that the data can retain most of its useful information. The plot is shown here as a visual aid.

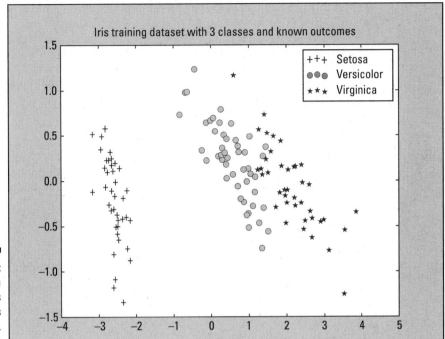

Figure 12-13:
Plotting data
elements
from the Iris
dataset.

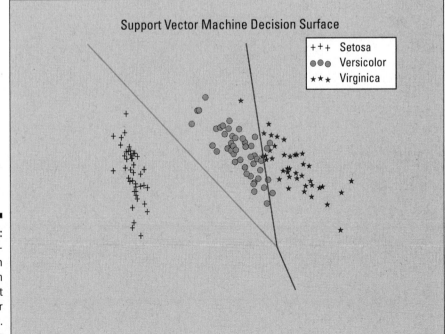

Figure 12-14:
Classi-
fication
based on
Support
Vector
Machine.

This plot includes the *decision surface* for the classifier — the area in the graph that represents the decision function that SVM uses to determine the outcome of new data input. The lines separate the areas where the model will predict the particular class that a data point belongs to. The left section of the plot will predict the Setosa class, the middle section will predict the Versicolor class, and the right section will predict the Virginica class.

The SVM model that you created did not use the dimensionally reduced feature set. We only use dimensionality reduction here to generate a plot of the decision surface of the SVM model — as a visual aid. The full listing of the code that creates the plot is provided as reference. *It should not be run in sequence with our current example if you're following along.* It may overwrite some of the variables that you may already have in the session. The code to produce this plot is based on the sample code provided on the scikit-learn website. You can learn more about creating plots like these at the scikit-learn website.

Here is the full listing of the code that creates the plot:

```
>>> from sklearn.decomposition import PCA
>>> from sklearn.datasets import load_iris
>>> from sklearn import svm
>>> from sklearn import cross_validation
>>> import pylab as pl
>>> import numpy as np
>>> iris = load_iris()
>>> X_train, X_test, y_train, y_test =
        cross_validation.train_test_split(iris.data,
        iris.target, test_size=0.10, random_state=111)
>>> pca = PCA(n_components=2).fit(X_train)
>>> pca_2d = pca.transform(X_train)
>>> svmClassifier_2d =
        svm.LinearSVC(random_state=111).fit(
        pca_2d, y_train)
>>> for i in range(0, pca_2d.shape[0]):
>>>     if y_train[i] == 0:
>>>         c1 = pl.scatter(pca_2d[i,0],pca_2d[i,1],c='r',
                s=50,marker='+')
>>>     elif y_train[i] == 1:
>>>         c2 = pl.scatter(pca_2d[i,0],pca_2d[i,1],c='g',
                s=50,marker='o')
>>>     elif y_train[i] == 2:
>>>         c3 = pl.scatter(pca_2d[i,0],pca_2d[i,1],c='b',
                s=50,marker='*')
>>> pl.legend([c1, c2, c3], ['Setosa', 'Versicolor',
        'Virginica'])
>>> x_min, x_max = pca_2d[:, 0].min() - 1,
        pca_2d[:,0].max() + 1
>>> y_min, y_max = pca_2d[:, 1].min() - 1,
        pca_2d[:, 1].max() + 1
>>> xx, yy = np.meshgrid(np.arange(x_min, x_max, .01),
        np.arange(y_min, y_max, .01))
>>> Z = svmClassifier_2d.predict(np.c_[xx.ravel(),
```

```
              yy.ravel()])
>>> Z = Z.reshape(xx.shape)
>>> pl.contour(xx, yy, Z)
>>> pl.title('Support Vector Machine Decision Surface')
>>> pl.axis('off')
>>> pl.show()
```

Running the test data

Using 10 percent of the 150 instances from the dataset gives you 15 test-data points to run through the model. Let's see how your predictive model will perform. Type the following code listing into the interpreter:

```
>>> predicted = svmClassifier.predict(X_test)
>>> predicted
array([0, 0, 2, 2, 1, 0, 0, 2, 2, 1, 2, 0, 1, 2, 2])
```

The `predict` function in the first line of code is what does the prediction, as you may have guessed. It takes the test data as input and outputs the results into the variable `predicted`. The second line prints the output. The last line in the code section is the output, or prediction: an array of 15 — that is, 10 percent of the sample dataset, which is the size of the test dataset. The numbers in the array represent the Iris Flower classes.

Evaluating the model

To evaluate the accuracy of your model, you can compare the output array with the `y_test` array. For this small sample dataset, you can easily tell how it performed by seeing that the output array from the predict function is almost the same as the `y_test` array. The last line in the code is a simple equality check between the two arrays, sufficient for this simple test case. Here's the code:

```
>>> predicted
array([0, 0, 2, 2, 1, 0, 0, 2, 2, 1, 2, 0, 1, 2, 2])
>>> y_test
array([0, 0, 2, 2, 1, 0, 0, 2, 2, 1, 2, 0, 2, 2, 2])
>>> predicted == y_test
array([ True,   True,   True,   True,   True,   True,   True,
        True,   True,   True,   True,   True,  False,   True,
        True], dtype=bool)
```

Looking at the output array with all the Boolean (`True` and `False`) values, you can see that the model predicted all but one outcome. On the thirteenth data point, it predicted 1 (Versicolor) when it should have been 2 (Virginica). The `False` value(s) indicate that the model predicted the incorrect Iris class for that data point. The percentage of correct predictions will determine the accuracy of the predictive model. In this case you can simply use basic division and get the accuracy:

correct outcomes / test size => 14 / 15 => 0.9333 or 93.33 percent

It's no surprise that the model failed to predict Virginica or Versicolor; they're clearly not separable by a straight line. A failure to predict Setosa, however, would be surprising because Setosa *is* clearly linearly separable. Still, the accuracy was 14 out of 15, or 93.33 percent.

For a test set with more data points, you may want to use the `metrics` module to do your measurements. The following code will get the accuracy of the model:

```
>>> from sklearn import metrics
>>> metrics.accuracy_score(y_test, predicted)
0.93333333333333335
```

Another useful measurement tool is the *confusion matrix*. Yes, it's real. It's a matrix (tabular format) that shows the predictions that the model made on the test data. Here is the code that displays the confusion matrix:

```
>>> metrics.confusion_matrix(y_test, predicted)
array([[5, 0, 0],
       [0, 2, 0],
       [0, 1, 7]])
```

The diagonal line from the top-left corner to the bottom-right corner is the number of correct predictions for each row. Each row corresponds to a class of Iris. For example: The first row corresponds to the Setosa class. The model predicted five correct test data points and had no errors predicting the Setosa class. If it had an error, a number other than zero would be present in any of the columns in that row. The second row corresponds to the Versicolor class. The model predicted two correct test data points and no errors. The third row corresponds to the Virginica class. The model predicted seven correct test data points but also had one error. The model mistakenly predicted one observation of Virginica for a Versicolor. You can tell that by looking at the column where the error is showing up. Column 1 belongs to Versicolor.

The accuracy of a predictive model's results will directly affect the decision to deploy that model; the higher the accuracy, the more easily you can gather support for deploying the model.

When creating a predictive model, start by building a simple working solution quickly — and then continue to build iteratively until you get the desired out-come. Spending months building a predictive model — and not being able to show your stakeholders any results — is a sure way to lose the attention and support of your stakeholders.

Here is the full listing of the code to create and evaluate a SVM classification model:

```
>>> from sklearn.datasets import load_iris
>>> from sklearn.svm import LinearSVC
>>> from sklearn import cross_validation
>>> from sklearn import metrics
>>> iris = load_iris()
>>> X_train, X_test, y_train, y_test =
        cross_validation.train_test_split(iris.data,
        iris.target, test_size=0.10, random_state=111)
>>> svmClassifier = LinearSVC(random_state=111)
>>> svmClassifier.fit(X_train, y_train)
>>> predicted = svmClassifier.predict(X_test)
>>> predicted
array([0, 0, 2, 2, 1, 0, 0, 2, 2, 1, 2, 0, 1, 2, 2])
>>> y_test
array([0, 0, 2, 2, 1, 0, 0, 2, 2, 1, 2, 0, 2, 2, 2])
>>> metrics.accuracy_score(y_test, predicted)
0.93333333333333335
>>> predicted == y_test
array([ True,   True,   True,   True,   True,   True,   True,
        True,   True,   True,   True,   True,  False,   True,
        True], dtype=bool)
```

Creating a supervised learning model with logistic regression

After you build your first classification predictive model, creating more models like it is a really straightforward task in `scikit`. The only real difference from one model to the next is that you may have to tune the parameters from algorithm to algorithm. We felt it was important to include two examples of the classification technique so that you can feel comfortable trying other algorithms from the `scikit` library.

Loading your data

This code listing will load the `iris` dataset into your session:

```
>>> from sklearn.datasets import load_iris
>>> iris = load_iris()
```

Creating an instance of the classifier

The following two lines of code create an instance of the classifier. The first line imports the logistic regression library. The second line creates an instance of the logistic regression algorithm.

```
>>> from sklearn import linear_model
>>> logClassifier = linear_model.LogisticRegression(C=1,
        random_state=111)
```

Notice the C parameter (regularization parameter) in the constructor. The *regularization parameter* is used to prevent overfitting (see Chapter 15 for more about overfitting). The parameter isn't strictly necessary (the constructor will work fine without it because it will default to C=1). In a later section, however, we'll be creating a logistic regression classifier, using C=150 because it creates a better plot of the decision surface, so we're just introducing it here. (You can see both plots in the "Visualizing the classifier" section later in the chapter, in Figures 12-15 and 12-16.)

Running the training data

You'll need to split the dataset into training and test sets before you can create an instance of the logistic regression classifier. The following code will accomplish that task:

```
>>> from sklearn import cross_validation
>>> X_train, X_test, y_train, y_test =
        cross_validation.train_test_split(iris.data,
        iris.target, test_size=0.10, random_state-111)
>>> logClassifier.fit(X_train, y_train)
```

Line 1 imports the library that allows us to split the dataset into two parts.

Line 2 calls the function from the library that splits the dataset into two parts and assigns the now-divided datasets to two pairs of variables.

Line 3 takes the instance of the logistic regression classifier you just created and calls the fit method to train the model with the training dataset.

Visualizing the classifier

Looking at the decision surface area on the plot, as shown in Figure 12-15, it looks like some tuning has to be done. If you look near the middle of the plot, you can see that many of the data points belonging to the middle area (Versicolor) are lying in the area to the right side (Virginica).

Figure 12-16 shows the decision surface with a C value of 150. It visually looks better, so choosing to use this setting for your logistic regression model seems appropriate.

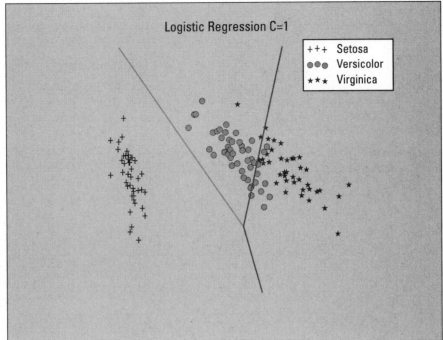

Figure 12-15:
Classi-
fication
based on
logistic
regression
with C=1.

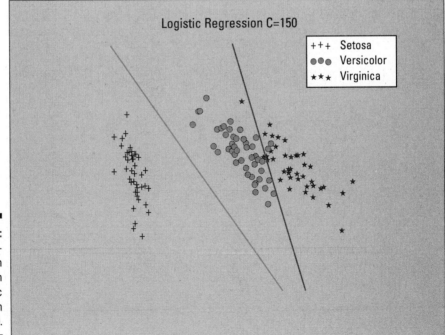

Figure 12-16:
Classi-
fication
based on
logistic
regression
with C=150.

Running the test data

In the following code, the first line feeds the test dataset to the model and the third line displays the output:

```
>>> predicted = logClassifier.predict(X_test)
>>> predicted
array([0, 0, 2, 2, 1, 0, 0, 2, 2, 1, 2, 0, 2, 2, 2])
```

Evaluating the model

You can cross-reference the output from the prediction against the y_test array. As a result, you can see that it predicted all the test data points correctly. Here's the code:

```
>>> from sklearn import metrics
>>> predicted
array([0, 0, 2, 2, 1, 0, 0, 2, 2, 1, 2, 0, 2, 2, 2])
>>> y_test
array([0, 0, 2, 2, 1, 0, 0, 2, 2, 1, 2, 0, 2, 2, 2])
>>> metrics.accuracy_score(y_test, predicted)
1.0                # 1.0 is 100 percent accuracy
>>> predicted == y_test
array([ True,    True,    True,    True,    True,    True,    True,
        True,    True,    True,    True,    True,    True,    True,
        True], dtype=bool)
```

So how does the logistic regression model with parameter C=150 compare to that? We expected that it would do better because the visualization looked better, but you can't beat 100 percent. Here is the code to create and evaluate the logistic classifier with C=150:

```
>>> logClassifier_2 = linear_model.LogisticRegression(
        C=150, random_state=111)
>>> logClassifier_2.fit(X_train, y_train)
>>> predicted = logClassifier_2.predict(X_test)
>>> metrics.accuracy_score(y_test, predicted)
0.93333333333333335
>>> metrics.confusion_matrix(y_test, predicted)
array([[5, 0, 0],
       [0, 2, 0],
       [0, 1, 7]])
```

We expected better, but it was actually worse. There was one error in the predictions. The result is the same as that of the SVM model built earlier in the chapter.

Here is the full listing of the code to create and evaluate a logistic regression classification model with the default parameters:

```
>>> from sklearn.datasets import load_iris
>>> from sklearn import linear_model
>>> from sklearn import cross_validation
>>> from sklearn import metrics
>>> iris = load_iris()
>>> X_train, X_test, y_train, y_test =
        cross_validation.train_test_split(iris.data,
        iris.target, test_size=0.10, random_state=111)
>>> logClassifier = linear_model.LogisticRegression(,
        random_state=111)
>>> logClassifier.fit(X_train, y_train)
>>> predicted = logClassifier.predict(X_test)
>>> predicted
array([0, 0, 2, 2, 1, 0, 0, 2, 2, 1, 2, 0, 2, 2, 2])
>>> y_test
array([0, 0, 2, 2, 1, 0, 0, 2, 2, 1, 2, 0, 2, 2, 2])
>>> metrics.accuracy_score(y_test, predicted)
1.0             # 1.0 is 100 percent accuracy
>>> predicted == y_test
array([ True,   True,   True,   True,   True,   True,   True,
        True,   True,   True,   True,   True,   True,   True,
        True], dtype=bool)
```

Comparing two classification models

Both classification models perform rather well using the Iris dataset. The logistic regression model with parameter C=1 was perfect in its predictions, while the SVM model and the logistic regression model with C=150 missed only one prediction. Indeed, the high accuracy of both models is a result of having a small dataset that has data points that are pretty close to linearly separable.

Interestingly, the logistic regression model with C=150 had a better-looking decision surface plot than the one with C=1, but it didn't perform better. That's not such a big deal, considering that the test set is so small. If another random split between training set and test set had been selected, the results could have easily been different.

This reveals another source of complexity that crops up in model evaluation: the effect of sampling, and how choosing the training and testing sets can affect the model's output. Cross-validation techniques (see Chapter 15) can help minimize the impact of random sampling on the model's performance.

For a larger dataset with non-linearly separable data, you would expect the results to deviate even more. In addition, choosing the appropriate model becomes increasingly difficult due to the complexity and size of the data. Be prepared to spend a great deal of time tuning your parameters to get an ideal fit.

When creating predictive models, try a few algorithms and exhaustively tune their parameters until you find what works best for your data. Then compare their outputs against each other.

Chapter 13

Creating Basic Examples of Unsupervised Predictions

In This Chapter

▶ Working with a sample dataset

▶ Creating simple predictive models using clustering algorithms

▶ Visualizing and evaluating your results

*T*his chapter is about creating a couple of simple predictive models using unsupervised learning with clustering algorithms such as K-means and DBSCAN. These examples use the Python programming language, version 2.7.4, on a Windows machine. Please refer to Chapter 12 if you need instructions on installing Python and `scikit-learn` machine-learning package.

No prior knowledge of supervised learning is required to understand the concepts of unsupervised learning. *Supervised learning* is when the output categories are known; *unsupervised learning* is when the output categories are unknown. Chapter 12 covers examples of supervised learning with classification and regression algorithms.

You can read Chapters 12 and 13 independently. One advantage of reading both chapters in the same session is that you'll be able to reuse the work that you did to load the Iris dataset into the Python *interpreter* (the command line where you enter the code statements or commands). So if you're continuing from Chapter 12, you may skip the next section.

Getting the Sample Dataset

The sample Iris dataset is included in the installation of `scikit-learn` — along with a set of functions that load data into the Python session.

To load the Iris dataset, follow these steps:

1. **Open a new Python interactive shell session.**

   Use a new Python session so there isn't anything left over in memory and you have a clean slate to work with.

2. **Paste the following code at the prompt and press Enter:**

   ```
   >>> from sklearn.datasets import load_iris
   >>> iris = load_iris()
   ```

   After you run those two statements, you should not see any messages from the interpreter. The variable `iris` should contain all the data from the `iris.csv` file.

3. **Enter the following command to confirm that variable `iris` contains the data:**

   ```
   >>> iris
   ```

   The command prints out a verbose description of the Iris dataset, followed by a list of all the data members. Please refer to Table 12-3 for the main properties and descriptions of the iris variable.

You don't use a training dataset for an unsupervised learning task because you normally don't know the outcomes. Hence the dataset is not labeled and the clustering algorithm doesn't accept a target value in its creation.

Using Clustering Algorithms to Make Predictions

In general, the use of clustering algorithms to create an unsupervised learning model entails the following general steps:

1. Prepare and load the data.

2. Fit the model.

3. Visualize the clusters.

4. Tune the parameters.

5. Repeat Steps 2 to 4 until you get the clustering output that you think yields the best output.

6. Evaluate the model.

Comparing two clustering models

Unsupervised learning has many challenges — including not knowing what to expect when you run an algorithm. Each algorithm will produce different results; you'll never be certain whether one result is better than the other — or even whether the result is of any value.

In the case of the Iris dataset, you know what the outcomes should be; as a result, you can tweak the algorithms to produce the desired outcomes. In real-world datasets, you won't have this luxury. You'll have to depend on some prior knowledge of the data — or intuition — to decide which initialization parameters and algorithms to use as you create your model.

In real unsupervised learning tasks, however, this prior knowledge is unavailable and the desired result is difficult to find. Choosing the right number of clusters is the key problem. If you happen to stumble upon the right number of clusters, your data will yield insights with which you can make highly accurate predictions. On the flip side, guessing the wrong number of clusters may yield subpar results.

K-means algorithm is a good choice for datasets that have a small number of clusters with proportional sizes and linearly separable data — and you can scale it up to use the algorithm on very large datasets.

Think of *linearly separable* data as a bunch of points in a graph that can be separated using a straight line. If the data is not linearly separable, then more advanced versions of K-means will have to be employed — which will become more expensive computationally and may not be suitable for very large datasets. In its standard implementation, the complexity to compute the cluster centers and distances is low.

K-means is widely employed to solve big-data problems because it's simple to use, effective, and highly scalable. No wonder most commercial vendors use the K-means algorithm as a key component of their predictive analytics packages.

The DBSCAN (Density-Based Spatial Clustering of Applications with Noise) implementation in `scikit-learn` does not require any user-defined initialization parameters to create an instance. You can override the default parameters during initialization if you want. Unfortunately, if you're using the default parameters, the algorithm can't provide a close match to the desired outcome.

That said, DBSCAN does not perform well with the Iris dataset. Even after exhaustive tweaking of the initialization parameters, it's still very hard to get an output that mimics the known outcomes for Iris. DBSCAN is better suited for datasets that have disproportional cluster sizes, and whose data can be separated in a non-linear fashion. Like K-means, DBSCAN is scalable, but using it on very large datasets requires more memory and computing power. You get a closer look at DBSCAN in action later in this chapter.

Creating an unsupervised learning model with K-means

The K-means algorithm requires one initialization parameter from the user in order to create an instance. It needs to know how many *K* clusters to use to perform its work.

Since you're using the Iris dataset, you already know that it has three clusters. As described in Chapter 12, the Iris dataset has three classes of the Iris flower (Setosa, Versicolor, and Virginica). In general, when you're creating an unsupervised learning task with a clustering algorithm, you wouldn't know how many clusters to specify. Some algorithms are available that try to determine the best number of clusters, but their results can be dubious. One such method iterates from a range of clusters and then selects a number of clusters that best fits its mathematical criteria. This approach requires heavy computation, may take a long time, and still may not produce the best *K* (number of clusters).

The best way to get immediate results is to make an educated guess about the number of clusters to use — basing your estimate on features present in the data (whether one or multiple features), or on some other knowledge of the data you may have from the business domain expert.

This falling back on guesswork (even educated guesswork) is a major limitation of the K-means clustering algorithm. An upcoming section explores another clustering algorithm, DBSCAN, that doesn't need the number of clusters in order to do its work.

Running the full dataset

To create an instance of the K-means clustering algorithm and run the data through it, type the following code in the interpreter.

```
>>> from sklearn.cluster import KMeans
>>> kmeans = KMeans(n_clusters=3, random_state=111)
>>> kmeans.fit(iris.data)
```

The first line of code imports the KMeans library into the session. The second line creates the model and stores it in a variable named kmeans. The model is created with the number of clusters set to 3. The third line fits the model to the Iris data. Fitting the model is the core part of the algorithm, where it will produce the three clusters with the given dataset and construct a mathematical function that describes the line or curve that best fits the data. To see the clusters that the algorithm produces, type the following code.

```
>>> kmeans.labels_
```

The output should look similar to this:

```
array([1, 1, 1, 1, 1, 1, 1, 1, 1, 1, 1, 1, 1, 1, 1, 1, 1,
       1, 1, 1, 1, 1, 1, 1, 1, 1, 1, 1, 1, 1, 1, 1, 1, 1,
       1, 1, 1, 1, 1, 1, 1, 1, 1, 1, 1, 1, 1, 1, 1, 1, 0,
       0, 2, 0, 0, 0, 0, 0, 0, 0, 0, 0, 0, 0, 0, 0, 0, 0,
       0, 0, 0, 0, 0, 0, 0, 0, 0, 2, 0, 0, 0, 0, 0, 0, 0,
       0, 0, 0, 0, 0, 0, 0, 0, 0, 0, 0, 0, 0, 0, 0, 2, 0,
       2, 2, 2, 2, 0, 2, 2, 2, 2, 2, 2, 0, 0, 2, 2, 2, 2,
       0, 2, 0, 2, 0, 2, 2, 0, 0, 2, 2, 2, 2, 2, 0, 2, 2,
       2, 2, 0, 2, 2, 2, 0, 2, 2, 2, 0, 2, 2, 0])
```

This is how the K-means algorithm labels the data as belonging to clusters, without input from the user about the target values. Here the only thing K-means knew was what we provided it: the number of clusters. This result shows how the algorithm viewed the data, and what it learned about the relationships of data items to each other — hence the term *unsupervised learning*.

You can see right away that some of the data points were mislabeled. You know, from the Iris dataset, what the target values should be:

✔ The first 50 observations should be labeled the same (as 1s in this case).

   This range is known as the *Setosa class.*

✔ Observations 51 to 100 should be labeled the same (as 0s in this case).

   This range is known as the *Versicolor class.*

✔ Observations 101 to 150 should be labeled the same (as 2s in this case).

   This range is known as the *Virginica class.*

It doesn't matter whether K-means labeled each set of 50 with a 0, 1, or 2. As long as each set of 50 has the same label, it accurately predicted the outcome. It's up to you to give each cluster a name and to find meaning in each cluster. If you run the K-means algorithm again, it may produce an entirely different number for each set of 50 — but the meaning would be the same for each set (class).

 You can create a K-means model that can generate the same output each time by passing the `random_state` parameter with a fixed seed value to the function that creates the model. The algorithm depends on randomness to initialize the cluster centers. Providing a fixed seed value takes away the randomness. Doing so essentially tells K-means to select the same initial data points to initialize the cluster centers, every time you run the algorithm. It is possible to get a different outcome by removing the `random_state` parameter from the function.

Visualizing the clusters

 As mentioned in the previous chapter, the Iris dataset is not easy to graph in its original form. Therefore you have to reduce the number of dimensions by applying a *dimensionality reduction algorithm* that operates on all four numbers and outputs two new numbers (that represent the original four numbers) that you can use to do the plot.

The following code will do the dimension reduction:

```
>>> from sklearn.decomposition import PCA
>>> from sklearn.datasets import load_iris
>>> iris = load_iris()
>>> pca = PCA(n_components=2).fit(iris.data)
>>> pca_2d = pca.transform(iris.data)
```

Lines 2 and 3 load the Iris dataset again. You can omit those two lines if you've been following along from the beginning of this chapter and have already loaded the Iris dataset.

After you run the code, you can type the pca_2d variable into the interpreter and it will output arrays (think of an *array* as a container of items in a list) with two items instead of four. Now that you have the reduced feature set, you can plot the results with the following code:

```
>>> import pylab as pl
>>> for i in range(0, pca_2d.shape[0]):
>>>    if iris.target[i] == 0:
>>>        c1 = pl.scatter(pca_2d[i,0],pca_2d[i,1],c='r',
                marker='+')
>>>    elif iris.target[i] == 1:
>>>        c2 = pl.scatter(pca_2d[i,0],pca_2d[i,1],c='g',
                marker='o')
>>>    elif iris.target[i] == 2:
>>>        c3 = pl.scatter(pca_2d[i,0],pca_2d[i,1],c='b',
                marker='*')
>>> pl.legend([c1, c2, c3], ['Setosa', 'Versicolor',
                'Virginica'])
>>> pl.title('Iris dataset with 3 clusters and known
                outcomes')
>>> pl.show()
```

The output of this code is a plot that should be similar to Figure 13-1. This is a plot representing how the known outcomes of the Iris dataset should look like. It is what you would like the K-means clustering to achieve. The figure shows a scatter plot, which is a graph of plotted points representing an observation on a graph, of all 150 observations. As indicated on the graph plots and legend:

- ✔ There are 50 pluses that represent the *Setosa class.*
- ✔ There are 50 circles that represent the *Versicolor class.*
- ✔ There are 50 stars that represent the *Virginica class.*

Figure 13-2 shows a visual representation of the data that we are asking K-means to cluster: a *scatter plot* with 150 data points that have not been labeled (hence all the data points are the same color and shape). The K-means algorithm doesn't know any target outcomes; the actual data that we're running through the algorithm hasn't had its dimensionality reduced yet.

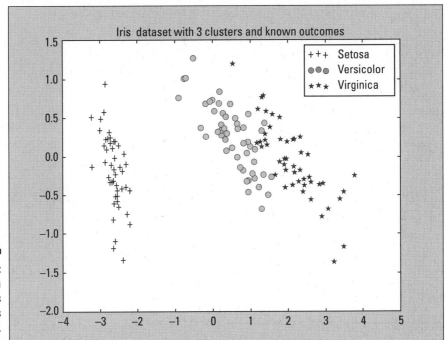

Figure 13-1:
Plotting data elements from the Iris dataset.

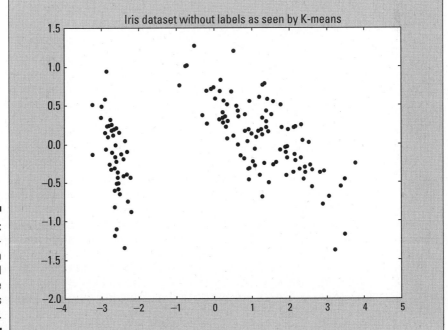

Figure 13-2:
Visual representation of data fed into the K-means algorithm.

242

The following line of code creates this scatter plot, using the X and Y values of `pca_2d` and coloring all the data points black (`c='black'` sets the color to black).

```
>>> pl.scatter(pca_2d[:,0],pca_2d[:,1],c='black')
>>> pl.show()
```

If you try fitting the two-dimensional data, that was reduced by PCA, the K-means algorithm will fail to cluster the Virginica and Versicolor classes correctly. Using PCA to preprocess the data will destroy too much information that K-means needs.

After K-means has fitted the Iris data, you can make a scatter plot of the clusters that the algorithm produced; just run the following code:

```
>>> for i in range(0, pca_2d.shape[0]):
>>>     if kmeans.labels_[i] == 1:
>>>         c1 = pl.scatter(pca_2d[i,0],pca_2d[i,1],c='r',
                marker='+')
>>>     elif kmeans.labels_[i] == 0:
>>>         c2 = pl.scatter(pca_2d[i,0],pca_2d[i,1],c='g',
                marker='o')
>>>     elif kmeans.labels_[i] == 2:
>>>         c3 = pl.scatter(pca_2d[i,0],pca_2d[i,1],c='b',
                marker='*')
>>> pl.legend([c1, c2, c3],['Cluster 1', 'Cluster 0',
            'Cluster 2'])
>>> pl.title('K-means clusters the Iris dataset into 3
            clusters')
>>> pl.show()
```

Recall that K-means labeled the first 50 observations with the label of 1, the second 50 with label of 0, and the last 50 with label of 2. In the code just given, the lines with the if, elif, and legend statements (lines 2, 5, 8, 11) reflects those labels. This change was made to make it easy to compare with the actual results.

The output of the scatter plot is shown in Figure 13-3.

Compare the K-means clustering output (shown in Figure 13-3) to the original scatter plot (refer to Figure 13-1) — which provides labels because the outcomes are known. You can see that the two plots resemble each other. The K-means algorithm did a pretty good job with the clustering. Although the predictions aren't perfect, they come close. That's a win for the algorithm.

In unsupervised learning, you rarely get an output that's 100 percent accurate because real-world data is rarely that simple. You won't know how many clusters to choose (or any initialization parameter for other clustering algorithms). You will have to handle outliers (data points that don't seem consistent with others) and complex datasets that are dense and not linearly separable.

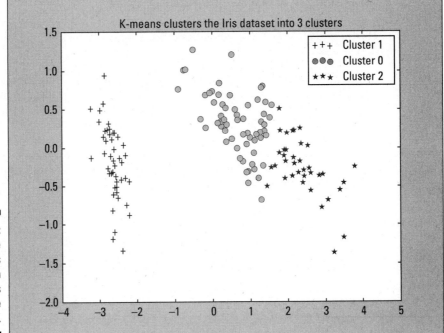

Figure 13-3:
The
K-means
algorithm
outputs
three
clusters.

You can only get to this point if you know how many clusters the dataset has. You don't need to worry about which features to use or reducing the dimensionality of a dataset that has so few features (in this case, four). We only reduced the dimensions for the sake of visualizing the data on a graph. We didn't fit the model with the dimensionality-reduced dataset.

Here's the full listing of the code that creates both scatter plots and color-codes the data points:

```
>>> from sklearn.decomposition import PCA
>>> from sklearn.cluster import KMeans
>>> from sklearn.datasets import load_iris
>>> import pylab as pl
>>> iris = load_iris()
>>> pca = PCA(n_components=2).fit(iris.data)
>>> pca_2d = pca.transform(iris.data)
>>> pl.figure('Reference Plot')
>>> pl.scatter(pca_2d[:, 0], pca_2d[:, 1], c=iris.target)
>>> kmeans = KMeans(n_clusters=3, random_state=111)
>>> kmeans.fit(iris.data)
>>> pl.figure('K-means with 3 clusters')
>>> pl.scatter(pca_2d[:, 0], pca_2d[:, 1], c=kmeans.labels_)
>>> pl.show()
```

Repeating the runs with a different K-value

A common outcome for clustering the Iris dataset is a two-cluster solution: one cluster contains the Setosa class and the other contains both the Versicolor and Virginica classes.

If you don't already know how many clusters you have in your dataset, you may have chosen to use two clusters with the K-means algorithm. With two clusters, K-means correctly clusters the Setosa class and combines the Virginica and the Versicolor classes into a single cluster.

The following code uses K-means to create two clusters, after which it displays a scatter plot of the results. Figure 13-4 shows the output of the K-means two-cluster solution.

```
>>> kmeans2 = KMeans(n_clusters=2, random_state=111)
>>> kmeans2.fit(iris.data)
>>> for i in range(0, pca_2d.shape[0]):
>>>     if kmeans2.labels_[i] == 1:
>>>         c1 = pl.scatter(pca_2d[i,0],pca_2d[i,1],c='r',
                marker='+')
>>>     elif kmeans2.labels_[i] == 0:
>>>         c2 = pl.scatter(pca_2d[i,0],pca_2d[i,1],c='g',
                marker='o')
>>> pl.legend([c1, c2], ['Cluster 1', 'Cluster 2'])
>>> pl.title('K-means clusters the Iris dataset into 2
            clusters')
>>> pl.show()
```

At first glance, the results seem to be within reason — and a potential candidate you might use to create your model. In fact, if you did use those results to make your predictive model, your success rate would be around 67 percent — not bad for a very basic model that uses unsupervised learning and a wrong guess for the number of clusters. You would have expected the accuracy to be around 67 percent because the algorithm is very accurate at clustering the linearly separable Setosa class (33.3 percent of the data). Clustering the remaining data into a single class would automatically give it an additional 33.3-percent accuracy because it only has two possibilities to choose from.

A four-cluster solution may yield a result that has one large cluster on the left (Setosa) and one on the right that's separated into three clusters (as shown in Figure 13-5). As you start increasing the value of K (the number of clusters), however, your results become less meaningful.

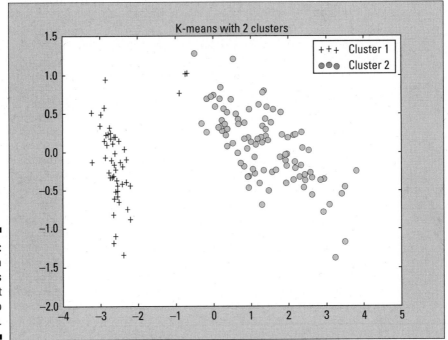

Figure 13-4:
Here's a K-means output of two clusters.

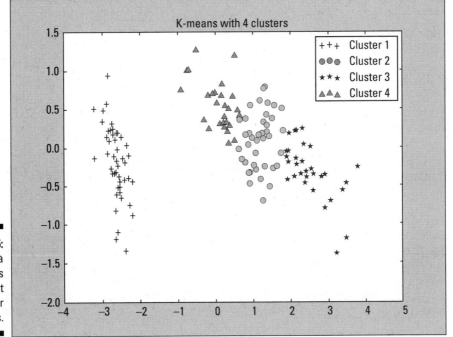

Figure 13-5:
Here's a K-means output of four clusters.

Evaluating the model

When you've chosen your number of clusters and have set up the algorithm to populate the clusters, you have a predictive model. You can make predictions based on new incoming data by calling the `predict` function of the K-means instance and passing in an array of observations. It looks like this:

```
>>> # to call the predict function with a single observation
>>> kmeans.predict([ 5.1,   3.5,   1.4,   0.2 ])
array([1])
```

When the `predict` function finds the cluster center that the observation is closest to, it outputs the index of that cluster center's array. Python arrays are indexed at 0 (that is, the first item starts at 0). Observations closest to a cluster center will be grouped into that cluster. In this example, the K-means algorithm predicts that the observation belongs to Cluster 1 (Setosa in this case) — an easy prediction because the Setosa class is linearly separable and far away from the other two classes. Also, we just selected the very first observation from the dataset to make the prediction verifiable and easy to explain. You can see that the attributes of the observation we're trying to predict are very close to the second cluster center (`kmeans.cluster_centers_[1]`).

To see the cluster centers, type the following code:

```
>>> kmeans.cluster_centers_
array([[ 5.9016129 ,   2.7483871 ,  4.39354839,   1.43387097],
       [ 5.006     ,   3.418     ,  1.464     ,   0.244     ],
       [ 6.85      ,   3.07368421,  5.74210526,   2.07105263]])
```

To see the cluster labels that the K-means algorithm produces, type the following code:

```
>>> kmeans.labels_
array([1, 1, 1, 1, 1, 1, 1, 1, 1, 1, 1, 1, 1, 1, 1, 1, 1,
       1, 1, 1, 1, 1, 1, 1, 1, 1, 1, 1, 1, 1, 1, 1, 1, 1, 1, 1,
       1, 1, 1, 1, 1, 1, 1, 1, 1, 1, 1, 1, 1, 1, 1, 1, 1, 0,
       0, 2, 0, 0, 0, 0, 0, 0, 0, 0, 0, 0, 0, 0, 0, 0, 0,
       0, 0, 0, 0, 0, 0, 0, 0, 0, 2, 0, 0, 0, 0, 0, 0, 0,
       0, 0, 0, 0, 0, 0, 0, 0, 0, 0, 0, 0, 0, 0, 0, 2, 0,
       2, 2, 2, 2, 0, 2, 2, 2, 2, 2, 2, 0, 0, 2, 2, 2, 2,
       0, 2, 0, 2, 0, 2, 2, 0, 0, 2, 2, 2, 2, 2, 0, 2, 2,
       2, 2, 0, 2, 2, 2, 0, 2, 2, 2, 0, 2, 2, 0])
```

You can also use the `predict` function to evaluate a set of observations, as shown here:

```
>>> # to call the predict method with a set of data points
>>> kmeans.predict([[ 5.1,   3.5,   1.4,   0.2 ],
                    [ 5.9,   3.0,   5.1,   1.8 ]])
array([1,0])
```

Although you know that the three-cluster solution is technically correct, don't be surprised if intuitively the two-cluster solution seems to look the best. If you increase the number of clusters beyond three, your predictions' success rate starts to break down. With a little bit of luck (and some educated guessing), you'll choose the best number of clusters. Consider the process as mixing a little bit of art with science. Even the algorithm itself uses randomness in its selection of the initial data points it uses to start each cluster. So even if you're guessing, you're in good company.

Evaluating the performance of an algorithm requires a label that represents the *expected* value and a *predicted* value to compare it with. Remember that when you apply a clustering algorithm to an unsupervised learning model, you don't know what the expected values are — and you don't give labels to the clustering algorithm. The algorithm puts data points into clusters on the basis of which data points are similar to one another; different data points end up in other clusters. For the Iris dataset, K-means has no concept of Setosa, Versicolor, or Virginica classes; it only knows it's supposed to cluster the data into three clusters and name them randomly from 0 to 2.

The purpose of unsupervised learning with clustering is to find meaningful relationships in the data, preferably where you could not have seen them otherwise. It's up to you to decide whether those relationships are a good basis for an actionable insight.

Creating an unsupervised learning model with DBSCAN

As mentioned earlier, DBSCAN is a popular clustering algorithm used as an alternative to K-means. It doesn't require that you input the number of clusters in order to run. But in exchange, you have to tune two other parameters. The scikit-learn implementation provides a default for the eps and min_ samples parameters, but you're generally expected to tune those. The eps parameter is the maximum distance between two data points to be considered in the same neighborhood. The min_samples parameter is the minimum amount of data points in a neighborhood to be considered a cluster.

One advantage that DBSCAN has over K-means is that DBSCAN is not restricted to a set number of clusters during initialization. The algorithm will determine a number of clusters based on the density of a region. Keep in mind, however, that the algorithm depends on the eps and min_samples parameters to figure out what the density of each cluster should be. The thinking is that these two parameters are much easier to choose for some clustering problems.

In practice, you should test with multiple clustering algorithms.

Because the DBSCAN algorithm has a built-in concept of noise, it's commonly used to detect outliers in the data — for example, fraudulent activity in credit cards, e-commerce, or insurance claims.

Running the full dataset

You'll need to load the Iris dataset into your Python session. If you're continuing from the previous section and already have it loaded, you can skip Steps 1 and 2. Here's the procedure:

1. **Open a new Python interactive shell session.**

   Use a new Python session so that memory is clear and you have a clean slate to work with.

2. **Paste the following code in the prompt and observe the output:**

   ```
   >>> from sklearn.datasets import load_iris
   >>> iris = load_iris()
   ```

   After running those two statements, you should not see any messages from the interpreter. The variable `iris` should contain all the data from the `iris.csv` file.

3. **Create an instance of DBSCAN. Type the following code into the interpreter:**

   ```
   >>> from sklearn.cluster import DBSCAN
   >>> dbscan = DBSCAN(random_state=111)
   ```

   The first line of code imports the `DBSCAN` library into the session for you to use. The second line creates an instance of DBSCAN with default values for `eps` and `min_samples`.

4. **Check what parameters were used by typing the following code into the interpreter:**

   ```
   >>> dbscan
   DBSCAN(eps=0.5, metric='euclidean', min_samples=5,
          random_state=111)
   ```

5. **Fit the Iris data into the DBSCAN clustering algorithm by typing the following code into the interpreter:**

   ```
   >>> dbscan.fit(iris.data)
   ```

6. **To check the outcome, type the following code into the interpreter:**

   ```
   >>> dbscan.labels_
   array([ 0.,  0.,  0.,  0.,  0.,  0.,  0.,  0.,  0.,  0.,
           0.,  0.,  0.,  0.,  0.,  0.,  0.,  0.,  0.,  0.,
           0.,  0.,  0.,  0.,  0.,  0.,  0.,  0.,  0.,  0.,
           0.,  0.,  0.,  0.,  0.,  0.,  0.,  0.,  0.,  0.,
           0., -1.,  0.,  0.,  0.,  0.,  0.,  0.,  0.,  0.,
           1.,  1.,  1.,  1.,  1.,  1.,  1., -1.,  1.,  1.,
          -1.,  1.,  1.,  1.,  1.,  1.,  1.,  1., -1.,  1.,
           1.,  1.,  1.,  1.,  1.,  1.,  1.,  1.,  1.,  1.,
           1.,  1.,  1.,  1.,  1.,  1.,  1., -1.,  1.,  1.,
           1.,  1.,  1., -1.,  1.,  1.,  1.,  1., -1.,  1.,
           1.,  1.,  1.,  1.,  1., -1., -1.,  1., -1., -1.,
           1.,  1.,  1.,  1.,  1.,  1.,  1., -1., -1.,  1.,
   ```

```
    1.,   1.,  -1.,   1.,   1.,   1.,   1.,   1.,   1.,   1.,
    1.,  -1.,   1.,   1.,  -1.,  -1.,   1.,   1.,   1.,   1.,
    1.,   1.,   1.,   1.,   1.,   1.,   1.,   1.,   1.,   1.])
```

If you look very closely, you'll see that DBSCAN produced three groups (−1, 0, and 1).

Visualizing the clusters

Let's get a scatter plot of the DBSCAN output. Type the following code:

```
>>> from sklearn.decomposition import PCA
>>> pca = PCA(n_components=2).fit(iris.data)
>>> pca_2d = pca.transform(iris.data)
>>> for i in range(0, pca_2d.shape[0]):
>>>    if dbscan.labels_[i] == 0:
>>>        c1 = pl.scatter(pca_2d[i,0],pca_2d[i,1],c='r',
            marker='+')
>>>    elif dbscan.labels_[i] == 1:
>>>        c2 = pl.scatter(pca_2d[i,0],pca_2d[i,1],c='g',
            marker='o')
>>>    elif dbscan.labels_[i] == -1:
>>>        c3 = pl.scatter(pca_2d[i,0],pca_2d[i,1],c='b',
            marker='*')

>>> pl.legend([c1, c2, c3], ['Cluster 1', 'Cluster 2',
            'Noise'])
>>> pl.title('DBSCAN finds 2 clusters and noise)
>>> pl.show()
```

The scatter plot that is the output of this code is shown in Figure 13-6.

You can see that DBSCAN produced three groups. Note, however, that the figure closely resembles a two-cluster solution: It shows only 17 instances of label −1. That's because it's a two-cluster solution; the third group (−1) is noise (outliers). You can increase the distance parameter (eps) from the default setting of 0.5 to 0.9, and it will become a two-cluster solution with no noise. The distance parameter is the maximum distance an observation is to the nearest cluster. The greater the value for the distance parameter, the fewer clusters are found because clusters eventually merge into other clusters. The −1 labels are scattered around Cluster 1 and Cluster 2 in a few locations:

✔ Near the edges of Cluster 2 (Versicolor and Virginica classes)

✔ Near the center of Cluster 2 (Versicolor and Virginica classes)

The graph only shows a two-dimensional representation of the data. The distance can also be measured in higher dimensions.

✔ One instance above Cluster 1 (the Setosa class)

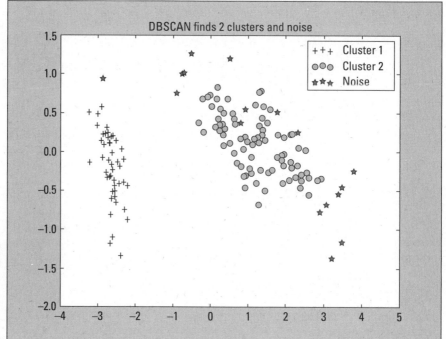

Figure 13-6:
DBSCAN
finds two
clusters and
noise.

Evaluating the model

In this example, DBSCAN did not produce the ideal outcome with the default parameters for the Iris dataset. Its performance was pretty consistent with other clustering algorithms that end up with a two-cluster solution.

The Iris dataset does not take advantage of DBSCAN's most powerful features — noise detection and the capability to discover clusters of arbitrary shapes. However, DBSCAN is a very popular clustering algorithm and research is still being done on improving its performance.

Chapter 14

Predictive Modeling with R

. . . .

. . . .

A book covering the major facets of predictive analysis is not complete unless it covers the R programming language. Our goal is to get you up and running as quick as possible. That goal entails getting you started making predictions and experimenting with predictive analysis, using standard tools such as R and the algorithms data scientists and statisticians use to make predictive models.

So do you have to know how to program to create predictive models? We would answer, "probably not, but it surely helps." Relax. We think you'll have fun learning R. Granted, this chapter is pretty high-level, so you may read it just to boost your understanding of how data scientists and statisticians use R.

In an enterprise environment, you'll most likely use commercial tools available from industry vendors. Getting familiar with a free, open-source, widely used, powerful tool like R prepares you to use the commercial tools with ease. By that point, you'll have gotten a big dose of the terminology, understand how to handle the data, and know all the steps of predictive modeling. After doing all those steps "by hand," you'll be well prepared to use the commercial tools.

Commercial tools aim to smooth out all the complexities of handling data; they even choose the algorithms for you. Learning some R helps you understand what the software tools are doing under the hood. That may give you the confidence to experiment even more by adjusting the default values and tweaking stuff here and there to see how it changes your predictive model.

R is an easy language with which to start learning programming. It has most, if not all, the same features you'll find in most of the programming languages commonly used for commercial software — Java, C++, Python, and such. So if you already have a programming language under your belt, this should be a cakewalk.

If R is the first programming language you've been exposed to, it'll still be easy, but it'll require some time spent playing around with it. But that's the beauty of the R language: You can play around with it and learn as you go. There is no boilerplate code that you have to remember to put in your code to make it work. You don't have to compile the program for it to work. It just works.

R is an *interpreted* language, which means you can run it interactively. You can run each line of code one by one and get an instant output (provided the code isn't for an intensive operation, and most operations in R shouldn't be intensive).

We also introduce you the RStudio integrated development environment (IDE). Using an IDE to write code will give you further help in learning R. IDEs have a vast number of features that even the most seasoned developers depend on. Using a commercial IDE for a software development class may seem over the top to seasoned programmers who prefer a plain text editor like vi or emacs with programming language support and syntax highlighting. Professional software development benefits from the use an IDE because the volume of production-level code is enormous. Even if you wrote the entire code base, there's no way to fully understand and navigate through all that code without an IDE. An IDE also lets you to do things much faster and easier.

Programming in R

R is a programming language originally written for statisticians to do statistical analysis. It's open-source software, used extensively in academia to teach such disciplines as statistics, bio-informatics, and economics. From its humble beginnings, it has since been extended to do data modeling, data mining, and predictive analysis.

R has a very active community; free code contributions are being made constantly and consistently. One of the benefits of using an open-source tool such as R is that most of the data analysis that you'll want to do has already been done by someone. Code samples are posted on many message boards and by universities. If you're stuck with some problematic code, simply post a question on a message board (such as stack-exchange or stack-overflow) and you'll have an answer in no time.

Because R is free to use, it's the perfect tool to use to build a rapid prototype to show management the benefits of predictive analytics. You don't have to ask management to buy anything in order to get started right away. Any one of your data scientists, business analysts, statisticians, or software engineers can do the prototype without any further investment in software.

Therefore R can be an inexpensive way to experiment with predictive analytics without having to purchase enterprise software. After you prove that predictive analytics can add (or is adding) value, you should be able to convince management to consider getting a commercial-grade tool for your newly minted data-science team.

Installing R

Installing R is an easy process that takes less than thirty minutes. Most of the default settings can be accepted during the installation process. You can install R by downloading the installation program for Windows and other operating systems from the R website at `http://cran.rstudio.com`. This chapter guides you through the installation process for the Windows operating system and the latest R release (version R-3.0.2). After you get to the R website, you can look for downloads link to get the file. After you've downloaded the file, just double-click it to begin the installation process.

Here is a direct link to the download for your convenience:

```
http://cran.rstudio.com/bin/windows/base/R-3.0.2-win.exe
```

Installing RStudio

After you've finished the R installation process, you may install RStudio. Installing the RStudio IDE is just as easy as installing R. You can download RStudio Desktop from their website at `http://www.rstudio.com`. You'll want to install the desktop version appropriate for your operating system (for example, RStudio version 0.97.551 for Windows). After you've downloaded the file, just double-click it to begin the installation process.

Here is a direct link for your convenience:

```
http://www.rstudio.com/ide/download/desktop
```

Getting familiar with the environment

RStudio is a graphical user interface for developing R programs. The default interface (the way it looks when you first start the program) has four window panes as shown in Figure 14-1. You'll use all four of them frequently; we describe what each one is used for and how to use it.

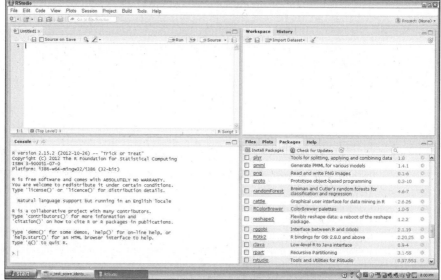

Figure 14-1:
RStudio in
the default
view of the
graphical
user
interface.

✓ **The top-left window is your script window.**

This is where you can copy and paste R code. You can run the code line-by-line or in chunks by highlighting the lines you want to execute. The script window is also where you can view the values of data frames. When you click a data frame from the workspace pane, it will open a new tab in the script pane with the data frame values.

✓ **The bottom-left window is your console window.**

This is where you type your R code one line at a time. The output (if there is any) is printed on the next line right after the command finishes execution.

✓ **The top-right window is your workspace and history window.**

It has two tabs:

- The History tab stores the history of all the code you've executed in the current session.

- The Workspace tab lists all the variables in the memory . Here you can click the variables to see their values and (if you so choose) load datasets interactively.

✓ **The bottom-right window is where you'll find four tabs of interest:**

- A Help tab offers documentation such as descriptions of functions.

- The Packages tab shows all the packages installed and available to load by your program. The checked packages are the ones that have been loaded for your program to use. You can search and install new packages here.

- The Plots tab is where the output of any plots will appear.

- The Files tab is your file explorer inside RStudio.

Learning just a bit of R

It doesn't take much to program something useful in R. The nice thing about R is that you can learn just what you need at the moment. And if you need something more, you can learn that, as you need it. So, at minimum, you'll need to know how to

✔ Assign values to variables

✔ Do operations on those variables

✔ Access and manipulate data types and structures

✔ Call a function to do something

The upcoming subsections detail these operations. Everything else you can learn as you go.

Assigning variables

Variables can be assigned in various ways in R. The convention for R is to use the less-than sign (<) and the minus sign (–) together, making an arrow-like sign (<–). Another way (standard for other programming languages) is to use just the equal sign (=). One other feature in R is that you may assign a variable in either direction using less-than and greater-than symbols with the minus sign to make the arrowlike sign (<– or –>).

The R interpreter has a leading > sign as the command prompt in the console window. You cannot copy and paste whole sections of code in that window. It will output an error if you do. You must use the script window of RStudio if you want to copy and paste sections of code. You can type the code that prints out the variable in one of three ways:

```
> x <- "hello there"
> x = "hello there"
> "hello there" -> x
```

The preceding three lines of code all do the same thing; knowing all the different ways will come in handy because you'll surely come across all of them when you start reading other people's code. As mentioned previously, the preferred way in R is the first one shown.

To print out the value of the variable, simply type the variable and then press Enter, like this:

```
> x
[1] "hello there"
```

In the RStudio pane, a line that has a number between [ ] symbols shows you the output from the execution of the previous line(s) of code.

Operating on variables

For most of its arithmetic and logical operators, R uses syntax that is standard to most other programming languages.

✔ Here are examples of the arithmetic operators in R:

```
> w <- 5 + 5    # addition
> x <- w * 5    # multiplication
> y <- x / 5    # division
> z <- y - 5    # subtraction
```

The # symbol is the start of a comment; the R interpreter ignores comments. You can print out the values by using the concatenate function, like this:

```
> c(w,x,y,z)
[1] 10 50 10 5
```

✔ Here are examples of the logical operators in R:

```
w == y       # is equal to
x > z        # is greater than
y >= 10      # is greater than or equal to
z < w        # is less than
10 <= y      # is less than or equal to
```

All these comparisons evaluate to TRUE values; you can see the results by executing them:

```
> w == y
[1]  TRUE
> x > z
[1]  TRUE
> y >= 10
[1]  TRUE
> z < w
[1]  TRUE
> 10 <= y
[1]  TRUE
```

Working with data types and structures

Data *types* are sometimes confused with data *structures*. Each variable in the program memory has a data type. Sure, you can get away with having several variables in your program and still be manageable. But that probably won't work so well if you have hundreds (or thousands) of variables; you have to give every variable a name so you can access it. It's more efficient to store all those variables in a logical collection.

For instance, if you have a million customers, you can use the vector data structure (see the "Data structures" section later in this chapter) to store the names of all your customers and give the vector a name of *customer*. That's one variable (`customer`) with a data type of `character` that stores all million customer names. You can use array notation to access each customer. (For more about array notation, flip to the upcoming subsection's discussion of data structures.)

Data types

Like other full-fledged programming languages, R offers many data types and data structures. You'll only be working with just a handful of them in this chapter. There is no need to specify the type that you're assigning to a variable; the interpreter will do that for you. However, you can specify or convert the type if the need arises; this is called *casting*. You'll see examples of casting when you load the dataset in a later section of this chapter. The data types that we'll be dealing with in this chapter are as follows:

- ✔ **Numerical:** These are your typical decimal numbers. These are called *floats* (short for *floating-point numbers*) or *doubles* in other languages.

- ✔ **Characters:** These are your strings formed with combinations of letters, characters, and numbers. They are not meant to have any numerical meaning. These are called *strings* in other languages.

- ✔ **Logical:** TRUE or FALSE. Always capitalize these values in R. These values are called *Booleans* in other languages.

Comparing a string of numbers to a numerical number results in the interpreter converting the string of numbers into a numerical and then doing a numerical comparison.

Examples of data types are as follows:

```
> i <- 10        # numeric
> j <- 10.0      # numeric
> k <- "10"      # character
> m <- i == j    # logical
> n <- i == k    # logical
```

After you execute those lines of code, you can find out their values and types by using the `str()` function. That operation looks like this:

```
> str(i)
 num 10
> str(j)
 num 10
> str(k)
 chr "10"
> str(m)
 logi TRUE
> str(n)
 logi TRUE
```

The expression in the n assignment is an example of the interpreter temporarily converting the data type of k into a numeric to do the evaluation between numeric i and character k.

Data structures

R will need a place to store groups of data types in order to work with it efficiently. These are called *data structures*. A real-life example of this concept is a parking garage: It's a structure that stores automobiles efficiently. It's designed to park as many automobiles as possible, and allows for automobiles to efficiently enter and exit the structure (in theory, at least). Also, no other objects besides automobiles should be parked in a parking structure. The data structures we use in this chapter are as follows:

- **Vectors:** Vectors store a set of values of a single data type. Think of it as a weekly pillbox. Each compartment in the pillbox can only store a certain type of object. After you put some pills in one of the compartments, all the other compartments must also be filled with either zero pills or more pills. You can't put coins in that same box; you have to use a different "pill box" (vector) for that. Likewise, once you store a number in a vector, all future values should also be numbers. Otherwise the interpreter converts all your numbers to characters.

- **Matrices:** A *matrix* looks like an Excel spreadsheet: Essentially it's a table consisting of rows and columns. The data populates the empty cells by row or column order, in which you specify when you create the matrix.

  All columns must have the same data type.

- **Data frames:** A data frame is similar to a matrix, except a data frame's columns can contain different data types. The datasets used in predictive modeling are loaded into data frames and stored there for use in the model.

- **Factors:** A *factor* is like a vector with a limited number of distinct values. The number of distinct values is referred to as its *level*. You can use factors to treat a column that has a limited and known number of values as categorical values. By default, character data is loaded into data frames as factors.

You access vectors, matrices, and data frames by using *array notation*. For example, you would type **v[5]** to access the fifth element of vector *v*. For a two-dimensional matrix and data frame, you put in the row number and column number, separated by a comma, inside the square brackets. For example, you type **m[2,3]** to access the second row, third column value for matrix *m*.

Data structures are an advanced subject in computer science. For now, we're sticking to the practical. Just remember that data structures were built to store specific types of data and they have functions for data insertion, deletion, and retrieval.

Calling a function

Functions are lines of code that do something useful and concrete. Because these operations are often repeated, they are usually saved with a name so you can *call* (use) them again. Typically a function takes an input parameter, does something with it, and outputs a value. You save functions in your own programs or libraries for future use.

There are many built-in functions in the R programming language for developers to use. You've already used the str() function to find out the structure of a variable.

Calling a function will always be in the same form: the function name followed by parentheses. (Inside the parentheses is the parameter list that may or may not be empty).

Whenever you start to suspect that the operation you're doing must be common, check to see whether a function exists that does it for you. Getting to know all the built-in functions in R will greatly improve your productivity and your code. Having a cheat sheet or reference card of all the built-in functions is handy when you're learning a new language. Here is a link to an R reference card:

http://cran.r-project.org/doc/contrib/Short-refcard.pdf

Making Predictions Using R

We use R to make two predictive models in this chapter. All the R commands are entered into the RStudio console (the bottom-left pane onscreen) for execution. The first predictive model uses a regression algorithm to predict an automobile's fuel economy as miles per gallon. The second predictive model uses a classification algorithm to predict which category of wheat a particular seed belongs to.

Predicting using regression

A crucial task in predictive analytics is to predict the *future* value of something — such as the value of a house, the price of a stock at a future date, or sales you want to forecast for a product. You can do such tasks by using *regression analysis* — a statistical method that investigates the relationship between variables.

Introducing the data

The dataset we use to make a prediction on is the Auto-MPG dataset. This
dataset has 398 observations and 8 attributes plus the label. The *label* is the
expected outcome; it's used to train and evaluate the accuracy of the predictive model. The outcome that we're trying to predict is the expected mpg
(attribute 1) of an automobile when given the values of the eight attributes.

Here are the attributes in the column order in which they are provided:

1. mpg

2. cylinders

3. displacement

4. horsepower

5. weight

6. acceleration

7. model year

8. origin

9. car name

You can get the dataset from the UCI machine-learning repository at

http://archive.ics.uci.edu/ml/datasets/Auto+MPG

To get the dataset from the UCI repository and load it into memory, type the
following command into the console:

```
> autos <-
      read.csv("http://archive.ics.uci.edu/ml/machine-
      learning-databases/auto-mpg/auto-mpg.data",
      header=FALSE, sep="", as.is=TRUE)
```

You'll see that the dataset was loaded into memory as the data frame variable
autos, by looking at your workspace pane (the top-right pane). Click the
autos variable to see the data values in the source pane (the top-left pane).
Figure 14-2 shows how the data looks in the source pane.

	V1	V2	V3	V4	V5	V6	V7	V8	V9
									398 observations of 9 variables
1	18.0	8	307.0	130.0	3504	12.0	70	1	chevrolet chevelle malibu
2	15.0	8	350.0	165.0	3693	11.5	70	1	buick skylark 320
3	18.0	8	318.0	150.0	3436	11.0	70	1	plymouth satellite
4	16.0	8	304.0	150.0	3433	12.0	70	1	amc rebel sst
5	17.0	8	302.0	140.0	3449	10.5	70	1	ford torino
6	15.0	8	429.0	198.0	4341	10.0	70	1	ford galaxie 500
7	14.0	8	454.0	220.0	4354	9.0	70	1	chevrolet impala
8	14.0	8	440.0	215.0	4312	8.5	70	1	plymouth fury iii
9	14.0	8	455.0	225.0	4425	10.0	70	1	pontiac catalina
10	15.0	8	390.0	190.0	3850	8.5	70	1	amc ambassador dpl
11	15.0	8	383.0	170.0	3563	10.0	70	1	dodge challenger se

Figure 14-2:
View of the
autos data
loaded into
memory.

Bache, K. & Lichman, M. (2013). UCI Machine Learning Repository [`http://archive.ics.uci.edu/ml`]. Irvine, CA: University of California, School of Information and Computer Science.

Using the `head` and `tail` functions can come in handy sometimes if you just want to see the first and last five rows of the data. This is also a quick way to verify that you actually loaded the correct file and it was read correctly. The `summary` function can give you basic statistics on each column of the data. You can copy and paste the following three lines of code into the source pane and have the output shown in the console:

```
head(autos,5)
tail(autos,5)
summary(autos)
```

Preparing the data

You have to get the data into a form that the algorithm can use to build a model. To do so, you have to take some time to understand the data and to know the structure of the data. Type in the `str` function to find out the structure of the `autos` data. The command and its output look like this:

```
> str(autos)

'data.frame':    398 obs. of  9 variables:
 $ V1: num  18 15 18 16 17 15 14 14 14 15 ...
 $ V2: int  8 8 8 8 8 8 8 8 8 8 ...
 $ V3: num  307 350 318 304 302 429 454 440 455 390 ...
 $ V4: chr  "130.0" "165.0" "150.0" "150.0" ...
 $ V5: num  3504 3693 3436 3433 3449 ...
 $ V6: num  12 11.5 11 12 10.5 10 9 8.5 10 8.5 ...
 $ V7: int  70 70 70 70 70 70 70 70 70 70 ...
 $ V8: int  1 1 1 1 1 1 1 1 1 1 ...
 $ V9: Factor w/ 305 levels "amc ambassador brougham",..:
                50 37 232 15 162 142 55 224 242 2 ...
```

From looking at the structure, we can tell that there is some data preparation and cleanup to do. Here's a list of the needed tasks:

✔ **Rename the column names.**

This is not strictly necessary, but for the purposes of this example, it's better to use column names we can understand and remember.

✔ **Change the data type of V4 (`horsepower`) to a `numeric` data type.**

In this example, `horsepower` is a continuous numerical value and not a `character` data type.

✔ **Handle missing values.**

Here `horsepower` has six missing values.

✔ **Change the attributes that have discrete values to factors.**

Here `cylinders`, `model year`, and `origin` have discrete values.

✔ Discard the V9 (`car name`) attribute.

Here `car name` doesn't add value to the model that we're creating. If the `origin` attribute weren't given, we could have derived the origin from the `car name` attribute.

To rename the columns type in the following code:

```
> colnames(autos) <-
        c("mpg","cylinders","displacement","horsepower",
        "weight","acceleration","modelYear","origin",
        "carName")
```

Next, we change the data type of `horsepower` to `numeric` with the following code:

```
> autos$horsepower <- as.numeric(autos$horsepower)
```

The program will complain because not all the values in horsepower were string representations of numbers. There were some missing values that were represented as the "?" character. That's fine for now because R converts each instance of ? into NA. A common way to handle the missing values of continuous variables is to replace each missing value with the mean of the entire column. The following line of code does that:

```
> autos$horsepower[is.na(autos$horsepower)] <-
        mean(autos$horsepower,na.rm=TRUE)
```

It's important to have `na.rm=TRUE` in the `mean` function. It tells the function not to use columns with null values in its computation. Without it, the function will return NA.

Next, we change the attributes with discrete values to factors. We have identified three attributes as discrete. The following three lines of code change the attributes.

```
> autos$origin <- factor(autos$origin)
> autos$modelYear <- factor(autos$modelYear)
> autos$cylinders <- factor(autos$cylinders)
```

Finally, we remove the `car name` attribute from the data frame with this line of code:

```
> autos$carName <- NULL
```

At this point, we've finished preparing the data for the modeling process. The following is a view of the structure after the data-preparation process:

```
> str(autos)

'data.frame':  398 obs. of  8 variables:
 $ mpg         : num  18 15 18 16 17 15 14 14 14 15 ...
 $ cylinders   : Factor w/ 5 levels "3","4","5","6",..:
               5 5 5 5 5 5 5 5 5 ...
 $ displacement: num  307 350 318 304 302 429 454 440 455
               390 ...
 $ horsepower  : num  130 165 150 150 140 198 220 215 225
               190 ...
 $ weight      : num  3504 3693 3436 3433 3449 . . .
 $ acceleration: num  12 11.5 11 12 10.5 10 9 8.5 10 8.5
               ...
 $ modelYear   : Factor w/ 13 levels "70","71","72",..:
               1 1 1 1 1 1 1 1 1 1 ...
 $ origin      : Factor w/ 3 levels "1","2","3":
               1 1 1 1 1 1 1 1 1 1 ...
```

Creating the model

We want to create a model that we can evaluate by using known outcomes. To do that, we're going to split our `autos` dataset into two sets: one for training the model and one for testing the model. A 70/30 split between training and testing datasets will suffice. The next two lines of code calculate and store the sizes of each set:

```
> trainSize <- round(nrow(autos) * 0.7)
> testSize <- nrow(autos) - trainSize
```

To output the values, type in the name of the variable used to store the value and press Enter. Here is the output:

```
> trainSize
[1] 279
> testSize
[1] 119
```

This code determines the sizes of the datasets that we intend to make our training and test datasets. We still haven't actually created those sets. Also, we don't want simply to call the first 279 observations the training set and call the last 119 observations the test set. That would create a bad model because the `autos` dataset appears ordered. Specifically, the `modelYear` column is ordered from smallest to biggest.

From examining the data, you can see that most of the heavier, eight-cylinder, larger-displacement, greater-horsepower autos reside on the top of the dataset. From this observation, without having to run any algorithms on the data, you can already tell that (in general for this dataset) older cars compared to newer cars as follows:

- Are heavier
- Have eight cylinders
- Have larger displacement
- Have greater horsepower

Okay, obviously many people know something about automobiles, so a guess as to what the correlations are won't be too farfetched after you see the data. Someone with a lot of automobile knowledge may have already known this without even looking at the data. This is just a simple example of a domain (cars) that many people can relate to. If this was data about cancer, however, most people would not immediately understand what each attribute means.

This is where a domain expert and a data modeler are vital to the modeling process. Domain experts may have the best knowledge of which attributes may be the most (or least) important — and how attributes correlate with each other. They can suggest to the data modeler which variables to experiment with. They can give bigger weights to more important attributes and/or smaller weights to attributes of least importance (or remove them altogether).

So we have to make a training dataset and a test dataset that are truly representative of the entire set. One way to do so is to create the training set from a random selection of the entire dataset. Additionally, we want to make this test reproducible so we can learn from the same example. Thus we set the seed for the random generator so we'll have the same "random" training set. The following code does that task:

```
> set.seed(123)
> training_indices <- sample(seq_len(nrow(autos)),
        size=trainSize)
> trainSet <- autos[training_indices, ]
> testSet <- autos[-training_indices, ]
```

The training set contains 279 observations, along with the outcome (`mpg`) of each observation. The regression algorithm uses the outcome to train the model by looking at the relationships between the predictor variables (any of the seven attributes) and the response variable (`mpg`).

The test set contains the rest of the data (that is, the portion not included in the training set). You should notice that the test set also includes the response (mpg) variable. When you use the `predict` function (from the model) with the test set, it ignores the response variable and only uses the predictor variables as long as the column names are the same as those in the training set.

To create a linear regression model that uses the mpg attribute as the response variable and all the other variables as predictor variables, type in the following line of code:

```
> model <- lm(formula=trainSet$mpg ~ . , data=trainSet)
```

Explaining the results

To see some useful information about the model you just created, type in the following code:

```
> summary(model)
```

The output provides information that you can explore if you want to tweak your model further. For now, we'll leave the model as it is. Here are the last two lines of the output:

```
Multiple R-squared: 0.8741, Adjusted R-squared: 0.8633
F-statistic: 80.82 on 22 and 256 DF,   p-value: < 2.2e-16
```

A couple of data points stand out here:

- ✔ The `Multiple R-squared` value tells you how well the regression line fits the data (goodness of fit). A value of 1 means that it's a perfect fit. So an `r-squared` value of 0.874 is good; it says that 87.4 percent of the variability in mpg is explained by the model.

- ✔ The `p-value` tells you how significant the predictor variables affect the response variable. A `p-value` of less than (typically) 0.05 means that we can reject the null hypothesis that the predictor variables collectively have no effect on the response variable (mpg). The `p-value` of 2.2e-16 (that is, 2.2 with 16 zeroes in front of it) is much smaller than 0.05, so the predictors clearly have an effect on the response.

With the model created, we can make predictions against it with the test data we partitioned from the full dataset. To use this model to predict the mpg for each row in the test set, you issue the following command:

```
> predictions <- predict(model, testSet,
        interval="predict", level=.95)
```

This is the code and output of the first six predictions:

```
> head(predictions)

    fit       lwr       upr
2 16.48993 10.530223 22.44964
4 18.16543 12.204615 24.12625
5 18.39992 12.402524 24.39732
6 12.09295  6.023341 18.16257
7 11.37966  5.186428 17.57289
8 11.66368  5.527497 17.79985
```

The output is a matrix that shows the predicted values in the `fit` column and the prediction interval in the `lwr` and `upr` columns — with a confidence level of 95 percent. The higher the confidence level, the wider the range, and vice versa. The predicted value is in the middle of the range; so changing the confidence level doesn't change the predicted value. The first column is the row number of the full dataset.

To see the actual and predicted values side by side so we can easily compare them, you can type in the following lines of code:

```
> comparison <- cbind(testSet$mpg, predictions[,1])
> colnames(comparison) <- c("actual", "predicted")
```

The first line creates a two-column matrix with the actual and predicted values. The second line changes the column names to actual and predicted. Type in the first line of code to get the output of the first six lines of `comparison`, as follows:

```
> head(comparison)

   actual predicted
2      15  16.48993
4      16  18.16543
5      17  18.39992
6      15  12.09295
7      14  11.37966
8      14  11.66368
```

We also want to see a summary of the two columns to compare their means. This is the code and output of the summary:

```
> summary(comparison)

     actual           predicted
 Min.   :10.00    Min.   : 8.849
 1st Qu.:16.00    1st Qu.:17.070
 Median :21.50    Median :22.912
 Mean   :22.79    Mean   :23.048
 3rd Qu.:28.00    3rd Qu.:29.519
 Max.   :44.30    Max.   :37.643
```

Next we use the *mean absolute percent error* (mape), to measure the accuracy of our regression model. The formula for mean absolute percent error is

$$(\Sigma(|Y-Y'|/|Y|)/N)*100$$

where Y is the actual score ,Y' is the predicted score, and N is the number of predicted scores. After plugging the values into the formula, we get an error of only 10.94 percent. Here is the code and the output from the R console:

```
> mape <- (sum(abs(comparison[,1]-comparison[,2]) /
        abs(comparison[,1]))/nrow(comparison))*100
> mape
[1] 10.93689
```

The following code enables you to view the results and errors in a table view:

```
> mapeTable <- cbind(comparison, abs(comparison[,1]-
        comparison[,2])/comparison[,1]*100)
> colnames(mapeTable)[3] <- "absolute percent error"
> head(mapeTable)

  actual predicted     absolute percent error
2     15  16.48993                   9.932889
4     16  18.16543                  13.533952
5     17  18.39992                   8.234840
6     15  12.09295                  19.380309
7     14  11.37966                  18.716708
8     14  11.66368                  16.688031
```

Here's the code that enables you to see the percent error again:

```
> sum(mapeTable[,3])/nrow(comparison)
                    [1]  10.93689
```

Making new predictions

To make predictions with new data, you simply use the predict function with a list of the seven attribute values. The following code does that job:

```
> newPrediction <- predict(model,
        list(cylinders=factor(4), displacement=370,
        horsepower=150, weight=3904, acceleration=12,
        modelYear=factor(70), origin=factor(1)),
        interval="predict", level=.95)
```

This is the code and output of the new prediction value:

```
> newPrediction
    fit      lwr      upr
1 14.90128 8.12795 21.67462
```

What you have here is your first real prediction from the regression model. Because it's from unseen data and you don't know the outcome, you can't compare it against anything else to find out whether it was correct. After you've evaluated the model with the testing dataset, and you're happy with its accuracy, you can have confidence that you built a good predictive model. You'll have to wait for business results to measure the effectiveness of your predictive model.

There may be optimizations you can make to build a better and more efficient predictive model. By experimenting, you may find the best combination of predictors to create a faster and more accurate model. One way to construct a subset of the features is to find the correlation between the variables and remove the highly correlated variables. Removing the redundant variables that add nothing (or add very little information) to the fit, you can increase the speed of the model. This is especially true when you're dealing with many observations (rows of data) where processing power or speed might be an issue. For a big dataset, more attributes in a row of data will slow down the processing. So you should try to eliminate as much redundant information as possible.

Using classification to predict

Another task in predictive analytics is to classify new data by predicting what class a target item of data belongs to, given a set of independent variables. You can, for example, classify a customer by type — say, as a high-value customer, a regular customer, or a customer who is ready to switch to a competitor — by using a decision tree.

Introducing the data

The dataset we use to make a prediction on is the Seeds dataset. This dataset has 210 observations and 7 attributes plus the label. The label is the expected outcome and is used to train and evaluate the accuracy of the predictive model. The outcome that we're trying to predict is the type of seed it is (attribute 8), given the values of the seven attributes. The three possible values for the seed type are labeled 1, 2, and 3, and represent the Kama, Rosa, and Canadian varieties of wheat.

The attributes in the column order they are provided:

1. `area`

2. `perimeter`

3. compactness

4. length of kernel

5. width of kernel

6. asymmetry coefficient

7. length of kernel groove

8. class of wheat

You can get the dataset from the UCI machine-learning repository at

```
http://archive.ics.uci.edu/ml/datasets/seeds
```

To get the dataset from the UCI repository and load it into memory, type the following command into the console:

```
> seeds <-
        read.csv("http://archive.ics.uci.edu/ml/machine
        -learning-databases/00236/seeds_dataset.txt",
        header=FALSE, sep="", as.is=TRUE)
```

You see that the dataset was loaded into memory as the data frame variable *seeds,* by looking at your workspace pane (the top-right). Click the *seeds* variable to see the data values in the source pane (the top-left). Figure 14-3 shows how the data looks in the source pane.

	V1	V2	V3	V4	V5	V6	V7	V8
1	15.26	14.84	0.8710	5.763	3.312	2.2210	5.220	1
2	14.88	14.57	0.8811	5.554	3.333	1.0180	4.956	1
3	14.29	14.09	0.9050	5.291	3.337	2.6990	4.825	1
4	13.84	13.94	0.8955	5.324	3.379	2.2590	4.805	1
5	16.14	14.99	0.9034	5.658	3.562	1.3550	5.175	1
6	14.38	14.21	0.8951	5.386	3.312	2.4620	4.956	1
7	14.69	14.49	0.8799	5.563	3.259	3.5860	5.219	1
8	14.11	14.10	0.8911	5.420	3.302	2.7000	5.000	1
9	16.63	15.46	0.8747	6.053	3.465	2.0400	5.877	1
10	16.44	15.25	0.8880	5.884	3.505	1.9690	5.533	1
11	15 26	14 85	0 8696	5 714	3 242	4 5430	5 314	1

210 observations of 8 variables

Figure 14-3:
View of the seeds data loaded into memory.

You can find more information about the data you just loaded by using the summary() function.

```
> summary(seeds)

        V1                V2                V3
 Min.    :10.59    Min.    :12.41    Min.    :0.8081
 1st Qu.:12.27    1st Qu.:13.45    1st Qu.:0.8569
 Median :14.36    Median :14.32    Median :0.8734
 Mean    :14.85    Mean    :14.56    Mean    :0.8710
 3rd Qu.:17.30    3rd Qu.:15.71    3rd Qu.:0.8878
 Max.    :21.18    Max.    :17.25    Max.    :0.9183

...
```

Preparing the data

You have to get the data into a form that the algorithm can use to build a model. To do that, you have to take some time to understand the data and to know its structure. Type in the `str` function to find out the structure of the seeds data. Here's what it looks like:

```
> str(seeds)

'data.frame':    210 obs. of  8 variables:
 $ V1: num   15.3 14.9 14.3 13.8 16.1 ...
 $ V2: num   14.8 14.6 14.1 13.9 15 ...
 $ V3: num   0.871 0.881 0.905 0.895 0.903 ...
 $ V4: num   5.76 5.55 5.29 5.32 5.66 ...
 $ V5: num   3.31 3.33 3.34 3.38 3.56 ...
 $ V6: num   2.22 1.02 2.7 2.26 1.35 ...
 $ V7: num   5.22 4.96 4.83 4.8 5.17 ...
 $ V8: int   1 1 1 1 1 1 1 1 1 1 ...
```

From looking at the structure, we can tell that the data needs one pre-processing step and one convenience step:

- ✔ **Rename the column names.** This is not strictly necessary, but for the purposes of this example, it's more convenient to use column names we can understand and remember.

- ✔ **Change the attribute with categorical values to a factor.** The label has three possible categories.

To rename the columns, type in the following code:

```
> colnames(seeds) <-
        c("area","perimeter","compactness","length",
          "width","asymmetry","length2","seedType")
```

Next, we change the attribute that has categorical values to a factor. (We've identified the label as categorical.) The following code changes the data type to a factor:

```
> seeds$seedType <- factor(seeds$seedType)
```

This command finishes the preparation of the data for the modeling process. The following is a view of the structure after the data-preparation process:

```
> str(weeds)

'data.frame':  210 obs. of  8 variables:
 $ area       : num  15.3 14.9 14.3 13.8 16.1 ...
 $ perimeter  : num  14.8 14.6 14.1 13.9 15 ...
 $ compactness: num  0.871 0.881 0.905 0.895 0.903 ...
 $ length     : num  5.76 5.55 5.29 5.32 5.66 ...
 $ width      : num  3.31 3.33 3.34 3.38 3.56 ...
 $ asymmetry  : num  2.22 1.02 2.7 2.26 1.35 ...
 $ length2    : num  5.22 4.96 4.83 4.8 5.17 ...
 $ seedType   : Factor w/ 3 levels "1","2","3":
               1 1 1 1 1 1 1 1 1 ...
```

Creating the model

We want to create a model that we can evaluate using known outcomes. To do that, we're going to split our seeds dataset into two sets: one for training the model and one for testing the model. A 70/30 split between training and testing datasets will suffice. The next two lines of code calculate and store the sizes of each dataset:

```
> trainSize <- round(nrow(seeds) * 0.7)
> testSize <- nrow(seeds) - trainSize
```

To output the values, type in the name of the variable that we used to store the value and press Enter. Here is the output:

```
> trainSize
[1] 147
> testSize
[1] 63
```

This code determines the sizes for the training and testing datasets. We haven't actually created the sets yet. Also, we don't just want the first 147 observations to be the training set and the last 63 observations to be the test set. That would create a bad model because the seeds dataset is ordered in the label column.

Thus we have to make both the training set and the test set representative of the entire dataset. One way to do that is create the training set from a random selection of the entire dataset. Additionally, we want to make this test reproducible so we can learn from the same example. We can do that by setting the `seed` dataset for the random generator so we have the same "random" training set, like this:

```
> set.seed(123)
> training_indices <- sample(seq_len(nrow(seeds)),
        size=trainSize)
> trainSet <- seeds[training_indices, ]
> testSet <- seeds[-training_indices, ]
```

The training set we get from this code contains 147 observations along with an outcome (`seedType`) of each observation. When we create the model, we'll tell the algorithm which variable is the outcome. The classification algorithm uses those outcomes to train the model by looking at the relationships between the predictor variables (any of the seven attributes) and the label (`seedType`).

The test set contains the rest of the data, that is, all data not included in the training set. Notice that the test set also includes the label (`seedType`). When you use the `predict` function (from the model) with the test set, it ignores the label and only uses the predictor variables, as long as the column names are the same as they are in the training set.

The `party` package is one of several packages in R that create decision trees. (Other common decision-tree packages include `rpart`, `tree`, and `randomForest`.) Our next step is to use the `party` package to create a decision-tree model, using `seedType` as the target variable and all the other variables as predictor variables. The first step in that process is to install the `party` package and load it into our R session.

Type in the following lines of code to install and load the `party` package:

```
> install.packages("party")
> library(party)
```

We're now ready to train the model. Type in the following line of code:

```
> model <- ctree(seedType~., data=trainSet)
```

Explaining the results

To see some useful information about the model you just created, type in the following code:

```
> summary(model)
     Length        Class        Mode
          1 BinaryTree          S4
```

The `Class` column tells you that you've created a decision tree. To see how the splits are being determined, you can simply type in the name of the variable in which you assigned the model, in this case `model`, like this:

```
> model

Conditional inference tree with 6 terminal nodes

Response:   seedType
Inputs:   area, perimeter, compactness, length, width,
          asymmetry, length2
Number of observations:   147

1) area <= 16.2; criterion = 1, statistic = 123.423
   2) area <= 13.37; criterion = 1, statistic = 63.549
      3) length2 <= 4.914; criterion = 1, statistic = 22.251
         4)*  weights = 11
      3) length2 > 4.914
         5)*  weights = 45
   2) area > 13.37
      6) length2 <= 5.396; criterion = 1, statistic = 16.31
         7)*  weights = 33
      6) length2 > 5.396
         8)*  weights = 8
1) area > 16.2
   9) length2 <= 5.877; criterion = 0.979, statistic =
            8.764
      10)*  weights = 10
   9) length2 > 5.877
      11)*  weights = 40
```

Even better, you can visualize the model by creating a plot of the decision tree with this code:

```
> plot(model)
```

Figure 14-4 shows a graphical representation of a decision tree. You can see that the overall shape mimics that of a real tree. It's made of *nodes* (the circles and rectangles) and *links* or *edges* (the connecting lines). The very first node (starting at the top) is called the *root node* and the nodes at the bottom of the tree (rectangles) are called *terminal nodes*. There are five decision nodes and six terminal nodes.

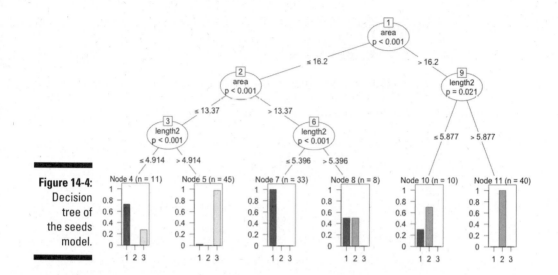

Figure 14-4:
Decision
tree of
the seeds
model.

At each node, the model makes a decision based on the criteria in the circle and the links, and chooses a way to go. When the model reaches a terminal node, a verdict or a final decision is reached. In this particular case, two attributes, the length2 and the area, are used to decide whether a given seed type is in class 1, 2 or 3.

For example, take observation #2 from the seeds dataset. It has a length2 of 4.956 and an area of 14.88. We can use the tree we just built to decide which particular seed type this observation belongs to. Here's the sequence of steps:

1. We start at the root node, which is node 1 (the number is shown in the small square at the top of the circle). We decide based on the area attribute: Is the area of observation #2 less than or equal to (denoted by <=) 16.2? The answer is yes, so we move along the path to node 2.

2. At node 2, the model asks: Is the area <= 13.37? The answer is no, so we try the next link which asks: Is the area > 13.37? The answer is yes, so we move along the path to node 6. At this node the model asks: Is the length2 <= 5.396? It is, and we move to terminal node 7 and the verdict is that observation #2 is of seed type 1. And it is, in fact, seed type 1.

   The model does that process for all other observations to predict their classes.

3. To find out whether we trained a good model, we check it against the training data. We can view the results in a table with the following code:

```
> table(predict(model),trainSet$seedType)

       1   2   3
   1  45   4   3
   2   3  47   0
   3   1   0  44
```

The results show that the error (or misclassification rate) is 11 out of 147, or 7.48 percent.

4. With the results calculated, the next step is to read the table.

   The correct predictions are the ones that show the column and row numbers as the same. Those results show up as a diagonal line from top-left to bottom-right; for example, [1,1], [2,2], [3,3] are the number of correct predictions for that class. So for seed type 1, the model correctly predicted it 45 times, while misclassifying the seed 7 times (4 times as seed type 2, and 3 times as type 3). For seed type 2, the model correctly predicted it 47 times, while misclassifying it 3 times. For seed type 3, the model correctly predicted it 44 times, while misclassifying it only once.

We find that this is a good model. So now we evaluate it with the test data. Here is the code that uses the test data to predict and store it in a variable (testPrediction) for later use:

```
> testPrediction <- predict(model, newdata=testSet)
```

To evaluate how the model performed with the test data, we view it in a table and calculate the error, for which the code looks like this:

```
> table(testPrediction, testSet$seedType)

testPrediction   1   2   3
            1  23   2   1
            2   1  19   0
            3   1   0  17
```

The results show that the error is 5 out of 64, or 7.81 percent. This is consistent with the training data.

Making new predictions

To make predictions with new data, you simply use the predict function ith a list of the seven attribute values. The following code does that:

```
> newPrediction <- predict(model, list(area=11,
        perimeter=13, compactness=0.855, length=5,
        width=2.8, asymmetry=6.5, length2=5),
        interval="predict", level=.95)
```

This is the code and output of the new prediction value.

```
> newPrediction
```

```
   [1]  3
Levels:  1 2 3
```

The prediction was seed type 3, which is not surprising because values were deliberately chosen that were close to observation #165.

Chapter 15

Avoiding Analysis Traps

*I*n the quest for building a predictive model, you'll need to make decisions every step of the way — and some decisions are harder than others. Informed decisions — and an awareness of the common mistakes that most analysts make while building their predictive models — give you your best shot at success.

This chapter offers insights on the issues that could arise when you embark on a journey toward the effective use of predictive analytics. At the outset, consider this general definition:

> A *predictive model* is a system that can predict the next possible out-come, and assign a realistic probability to that outcome.

As you build your predictive model, you're likely to run into problems in two areas — (1) the data and (2) the analysis. This chapter delves into both types of problems to help you strengthen your safeguards, and allow you to stay on top of your project.

How well you handle both the data and the analysis at the core of your predictive model defines the success of your predictive analytics project. Data issues are more prominent now because *big data* (massive amounts of analyzable data generated online) is all the rage — and only getting bigger, thanks to explosive growth of data in the digital and social media worlds.

The more data you have, however, the more diverse the cases that generate it. Your job as a modeler can be harder if the data you're using contains *outliers* (extreme cases): Then your model must take into account

✔ How rare those outliers are

✔ How much complexity they add to your model

✔ Whether to create risk management components to deal with them

Modeling requires that you choose which variables to report on — and that you understand not only the variables but also their impact on the business (for example, how an unusually active storm season might affect a fishery). Right off the bat, you need to consult someone with *domain knowledge* (expertise in the business) so you can identify those variables accurately. After all, the model should reflect the real world in which the business is operating. The model's predictions should be accurate enough to improve return on investment for the business — by helping its decision-makers answer tough questions and make bold decisions.

People with expert-level domain knowledge are best qualified to analyze the data in a comprehensive and meaningful way. *Hint:* You'll want to make sure your analysis has appropriate degrees of data validity, variety, *velocity* (the speed at which the data changes), and volume — all addressed at length in Chapter 4.

Data Challenges

Data mining is more than just gathering, generating, or retrieving data. It's a first step in treating data as a resource for your business, and it raises more issues:

✔ What type of analysis or analyses to adopt

✔ What algorithms to employ

✔ What data points to include and exclude and why

✔ How to prepare your data for use in your model

✔ How to select your variables for building your model

✔ What data to use for training and testing your model

Data is at the center of predictive analytics. Data quality is crucial to the effectiveness of the predictions. As a data analyst, you have to get familiar enough with the data to examine its limitations (if any). Here's a quick list of questions to ask about the data:

✔ Is it well documented?

✔ Does it contain errors?

✔ Are there any missing values?

✔ Does it need to be *cleaned* of corrupt or inaccurate records?

✔ Does it contain outliers?

✔ Does it need *smoothing* to have individual aberrations minimized?

✔ Does it require any kind of preprocessing before use in the model?

When the data is collected from multiple sources, potential problems — such as formatting issues, data duplication, and consolidation of similar data — become more likely. In view of all these questions and uncertainties, don't be surprised if your incoming data requires some preprocessing before you can run it through your model and use it in a meaningful analysis. Data preparation can be tedious and time-consuming, so at this stage of developing your predictive model, experts in data preparation can be essential to the success of your project.

Outlining the limitations of the data

As with many aspects of any business system, data is a human creation — so it's apt to have some limits on its usability when you first obtain it. Here's an overview of some limitations you're likely to encounter:

✔ **The data could be incomplete.** Missing values, even the lack of a section or a substantial part of the data, could limit its usability. For example, your data might cover only one or two conditions of a larger set that you're trying to model — as when a model built to analyze stock market performance only has data available from the past 5 years, which skews both the data and the model toward the assumption of a bull market. The moment the market undergoes any correction that leads to a bear market, the model fails to adapt — simply because it wasn't trained and tested with data representing a bear market.

Make sure you're looking at a timeframe that gives you a complete picture of the natural fluctuations of your data; your data shouldn't be limited by *seasonality*.

✔ **If you're using data from surveys, keep in mind that people don't always provide accurate information.** Not everyone will answer truthfully about (say) how many times they exercise — or how many alcoholic beverages they consume — per week. People may not be dishonest so much as self-conscious, but the data is still skewed.

✔ **Data collected from different sources can vary in quality and format.** Data collected from such diverse sources as surveys, e-mails, data-entry forms, and the company website will have different attributes and structures. Data from various sources may not have much compatibility among data fields. Such data requires major preprocessing before it's analysis-ready. The accompanying sidebar provides an example.

What's the date where you are?

Different sources format data differently — and many fields may have different weights. A date collected from an American website (for example) could have the format mm/dd/yyyy — while the same company, collecting that same data in Europe, uses the dd/mm/yyyy format.

Thus, in source documents from the American and European branch offices of the same company, the numerical date 05/11/2014 would mean (respectively) May 11, 2014 or 5 November 2014.

Data collected from multiple sources may have differences in formatting, duplicate records, and inconsistencies across merged data fields. Expect to spend a long time cleaning such data — and even longer validating its reliability.

To determine the limitations of your data, be sure to:

- ✔ Verify all the variables you'll use in your model.

- ✔ Assess the scope of the data, especially over time, so your model can avoid the seasonality trap.

- ✔ Check for missing values, identify them, and assess their impact on the overall analysis.

- ✔ Watch out for extreme values (outliers) and decide on whether to include them in the analysis.

- ✔ Confirm that the pool of training and test data is large enough.

- ✔ Make sure *data type* (integers, decimal values, or characters, and so forth) is correct and set the upper and lower bounds of possible values.

- ✔ Pay extra attention to data integration when your data comes from multiple sources.

Be sure you understand your data sources and their impact on the overall quality of your data.

- ✔ Choose a relevant dataset that is representative of the whole population.

- ✔ Choose the right parameters for your analysis.

Even after all this care and attention, don't be surprised if your data still needs preprocessing before you can analyze it accurately. Preprocessing often takes a long time and significant effort because it has to address several issues related to the original data — these issues include:

- ✔ Any values missing from the data.

- ✔ Any inconsistencies and/or errors existing in the data.

- ✔ Any duplicates or outliers in the data.

- ✔ Any normalization or other transformation of the data.

- ✔ Any derived data needed for the analysis.

Dealing with extreme cases (outliers)

Your data may contain *outliers* — extreme values that are often significant but atypical. You'll have to deal with these outliers — maintaining data integrity without affecting your predictive model negatively. It's a key challenge.

Part of your data preparation is to determine whether the values and data types of your data are what you expected. Check for

- ✔ The expected minimum and maximum values

- ✔ The data types and the expected values for a given field

- ✔ Any anomaly in the values and/or data types

Outliers caused by outside forces

Be sure you check carefully for outliers *before* they influence your analysis. Outliers can distort both the data and data analysis. For example, any statistical analysis done with data that leaves outliers in place ends up skewing the means and variances. Unchecked or misinterpreted outliers may lead to false conclusions. Say your data that shows that a stock that was traded for a whole year at a price above $50 — but for only a few minutes out of that whole year the stock was traded at $20. The $20 price — an obvious exception — is the outlier in this dataset.

Now you have to decide whether to include the $20 stock price in your analysis; if you do, it has ramifications for the overall model. But what do you consider normal? Was the "flash crash" that took the stock market by surprise on May 6, 2010 a normal event or an exception? During that brief time, the stock market experienced a sharp decline in prices across the board — which knocked the sample stock price down from $50 to $20, but had less to do with the stock than with wider market conditions. Does your model need to take the larger fluctuations of the stock market into account?

Anyone who's lost money on brief moments of free-fall market considers those few minutes real and normal (even if they felt like an eternity to go through). A portfolio that diminishes in milliseconds due to a rapid decline, albeit short-lived, is clearly real. Yet the flash crash is an anomaly, an outlier that poses a problem for the model.

Regardless of what's considered normal (which can change anyway), data sometimes contains values that don't fit the expected values. This is especially true in the stock market, where virtually any event may send the market flying or plunging. You don't want your model to fail when the reality changes suddenly — but a model and a reality are two different things.

Outliers caused by errors in the system

When we rely on technology or instrumentation to conduct a task, a glitch here or there can cause these instruments to register extreme or unusual values. If sensors register observational values that fail to meet basic quality-control standards, they can produce real disruptions that are reflected in data.

Someone performing data entry, for example, can easily add an extra 0 at the end of a value by mistake, taking the entry out of range and producing an outlier. If you're looking at observational data collected by a water sensor installed in Baltimore Harbor — and it reports a water depth of 20 feet above mean sea level — you've got an outlier. The sensor is obviously wrong unless Baltimore is completely covered by water.

Data can end up having outliers because of external events or an error by a person or an instrument. If a real event such as a flash crash is traced to an error in the system, its consequences are still real — but if you know the source of the problem, you may conclude that a flaw in the data, not your model, was to blame if your model didn't predict the event.

Knowing the source of the outlier will guide your decision on how to deal with it. Outliers that were the result of data-entry errors can easily be corrected after consulting the data source. Outliers that reflect a change reality may prompt you to change your model.

There's no one-size-fits-all answer when you're deciding whether to include or disregard extreme data that isn't an error or glitch. Your response depends on the nature of the analysis you're doing — and on the type of the model you're building. In a few cases, the way to deal with those outliers is straightforward:

> ✔ If you trace your outlier to a data-entry error when you consult the data source, you can easily correct the data and (probably) keep the model intact.

✔ If that water sensor in Baltimore Harbor reports water to a depth of 20 feet above mean sea level, and you're in Baltimore, look out your window:

- If Baltimore isn't completely covered by water, the sensor is obviously wrong.

- If you see a fish looking in at you, the reality has changed; you may have to revise your model.

✔ The flash crash may have been a one-time event (over the short term, anyway), but its effects were real — and if you've studied the market over the longer term, you know that something similar may happen again. If your business is in finance and you deal with the stock market all the time, you want your model to account for such aberrations.

In general, if the outcome of an event normally considered an outlier can have a significant impact on your business, consider how to deal with those events in your analysis. Keep these general points in mind about outliers:

✔ The smaller dataset is, the more significant the impact outliers can have on the analysis.

✔ As you develop your model, be sure you also develop techniques to find outliers and to systematically understand their impact on your business.

✔ Detecting outliers can be a complex process; there is no simple way of identifying them.

✔ A *domain expert* (someone who knows the field you're modeling) is your best go-to person to verify whether a data point is valid, an outlier you can disregard, or an outlier you have to take into account. The domain expert should be able to explain what factors created the outlier, what its range of variability is, and its impact on the business.

✔ Visualization tools can help you spot outliers in the data. Also, if you know the expected range of values you can easily query for data that falls outside that range.

Keeping the outliers in the analysis — or not

Deciding to include outliers in the analysis — or to exclude them — will have implications for your model.

Keeping outliers as part of the data in your analysis may lead to a model that's not applicable — either to the outliers or to the rest of the data. If you decide to keep an outlier, you'll need to choose techniques and statistical methods that excel at handling outliers without influencing the analysis. One such technique is to use mathematical functions such as natural algorithms and square root to reduce the gap between the outliers and the rest of the data. These functions, however, only work for numerical data that is greater than zero — and other issues may arise. For example, transforming the data may require interpretations of the relationship between variables in the newly transformed data that differ from the interpretation that governs those variables in the original data.

The mere presence of outliers in your data can provide insights into your business that can be very helpful in generating a robust model. Outliers may draw attention to a valid business case that illustrates an unusual bit significant event.

Looking for outliers, identifying them, and assessing their impact should be part of data analysis and preprocessing. Business domain experts can provide insight and help you decide what to do with unusual cases in your analysis. Although sometimes common sense is all you need to deal with outliers, often it's helpful to ask someone who knows the ropes.

If you're in a business that benefits from rare events — say, an astronomical observatory with a grant to study Earth-orbit-crossing asteroids — you're more interested in the outliers than in the bulk of the data.

Outliers can be a great source of information. Deviating from the norm could be a signal of suspicious activity, breaking news, or an opportunistic or catastrophic event. You may need to develop models that help you identify outliers and asses the risks they signify.

It's prudent to conduct two analyses: one that includes outliers, and another that omits them. Then examine the differences, try to understand the implications of each method, and assess how adopting one method over the other would influence your business goals.

Data smoothing

Data smoothing is, essentially, trying to find the "signal" in the "noise" by discarding data points that are considered "noisy". The idea is to sharpen the patterns in the data and highlight trends the data is pointing to.

Figure 15-1 shows a typical graph that results from data smoothing.

The implication behind data smoothing is that the data consists of two parts: one part (consisting of the *core data points*) that signifies overall trends or real trends, and another part that consists mostly of deviations (*noise*) — some fluctuating points that result from some volatility in the data. Data smoothing seeks to eliminate that second part.

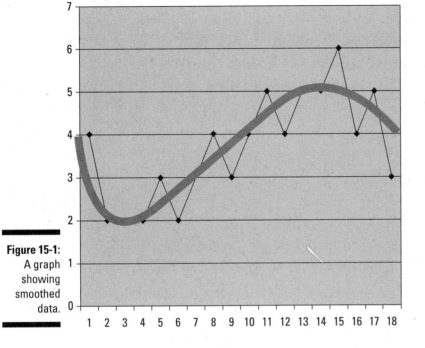

Figure 15-1:
A graph
showing
smoothed
data.

Turning down the noise

Data smoothing operates on several assumptions:

✔ That fluctuation in data is likeliest to be noise.

✔ That the noisy part of the data is of short duration.

✔ That the data's fluctuation, regardless of how varied it may be, won't affect the underlying trends represented by the core data points.

Noise in data tends to be random; its fluctuations should not affect the overall trends drawn from examining the rest of the data. So reducing or eliminating noisy data points can clarify real trends and patterns in the data — in effect, improving the data's "signal-to-noise ratio."

Provided you've identified the noise correctly and then reduced it, data smoothing can help you predict the next observed data point simply by following the major trends you've detected within the data. Data smoothing concerns itself with the majority of the data points, their positions in a graph, and what the resulting patterns predict about the general trend of (say) a stock price, whether its general direction is up, down, or sideways. This technique won't accurately predict the exact price of the next trade for a given stock — but predicting a general trend can yield more powerful insights than knowing the actual price or its fluctuations.

A forecast based on a general trend deduced from smoothed data assumes that whatever direction the data has followed thus far will continue into the future in a way consistent with the trend. In the stock market, for example, past performance is no definite indication of future performance, but it certainly can be a general guide to future movement of the stock price.

Methods, advantages, and downsides of data smoothing

Data smoothing is not to be confused with *fitting a model,* which is part of the data analysis consisting of two steps:

1. Find a suitable model that represents the data.

2. Make sure that the model fits the data effectively.

   For details of the model-fitting process, see Chapter 12.

Data smoothing focuses on establishing a fundamental direction for the core data points by (1) ignoring any noisy data points and (2) drawing a smoother curve through the data points that skips the wriggling ones and emphasizes primary patterns — trends — in the data, no matter how slow their emergence. Accordingly, in a numerical time series, data smoothing serves as a form of filtering.

Data smoothing can use any of the following methods:

- **Random walk** is based on the idea that the next outcome, or future data point, is a random deviation from the last known, or present, data point.

- **Moving average** is a running average of consecutive, equally spaced periods. An example would the calculation of a 200-day moving average of a stock price.

- **Exponential smoothing** assigns exponentially more weight, or importance, to recent data points than to older data points.

  - **Simple:** This method should be used when the time series data has no trend and no seasonality.

  - **Linear:** This method should be used when the time series data has a trend line.

  - **Seasonal:** This method should be used when the time series data has no trend but seasonality.

What these smoothing methods all have in common is that they carry out some kind of averaging process on several data points. Such averaging of adjacent data points is the essential way to zero in on underlying trends or patterns.

The advantages of data smoothing are

- ✔ It's easy to implement.
- ✔ It helps identify trends.
- ✔ It helps expose patterns in the data.
- ✔ It eliminates data points that you've decided are not of interest.
- ✔ It helps predict the general direction of the next observed data points.
- ✔ It generates nice smooth graphs.

But everything has a downside. The disadvantages of data smoothing are

- ✔ It may eliminate valid data points that result from extreme events.
- ✔ It may lead to inaccurate predictions if the test data is only seasonal and not fully representative of the reality that generated the data points.
- ✔ It may shift or skew the data, especially the peaks, resulting in a distorted picture of what's going on.
- ✔ It may be vulnerable to significant disruption from outliers within the data.
- ✔ It may result in a major deviation from the original data.

If data smoothing does no more than give the data a mere facelift, it can draw a fundamentally wrong in the following ways:

- ✔ It can introduce errors through distortions that treat the smoothed data as if it were identical to the original data.
- ✔ It can skew interpretation by ignoring — and hiding — risks embedded within the data.
- ✔ It can lead to a loss of detail within your data — which is one way that a smoothed curve may deviate greatly from that of the original data.

How seriously data smoothing may affect your data depends on the nature of the data at hand, and which smoothing technique was implemented on that data. For example, if the original data has more peaks in it, then data smoothing will lead to major shifting of those peaks in the smoothed graphs — most likely a distortion.

Here are some cautionary points to keep in mind as you approach data smoothing:

- ✔ It's a good idea to compare smoothed graphs to untouched graphs that plot the original data.

✔ Data points removed during data smoothing may not be noise; they could be valid, real data points that are result from rare-but-real events.

✔ Data smoothing can be helpful in moderation, but its overuse can lead to a misrepresentation of your data.

By applying your professional judgment and your business knowledge expertise, you can use data smoothing effectively. Removing noise from your data — without negatively affecting the accuracy and usefulness of the original data — is at least as much an art as a science.

Curve fitting

Curve fitting, as mentioned earlier, is a process distinct from data smoothing: Here the goal is to create a curve that depicts the mathematical function that best fits the actual (original) data points in a data series.

The curve can either pass through every data point or stay within the bulk of the data, ignoring some data points in hopes of drawing trends from the data. In either case, one single mathematical function is assigned to the entire body of data, with the goal of fitting all data points into a curve that delineates trends and aids prediction.

Figure 15-2 shows a typical graph that results from curve-fitting a body of data.

Curve fitting can be achieved in one of three ways:

✔ By finding an exact fit for every data point (a process called *interpolation*)

✔ By staying within the bulk of the data while ignoring some of data points in hopes of drawing trends out of the data

✔ By employing data smoothing to come up with a function that represents the smoothed graph

Curve fitting can be used to fill in possible data points to replace missing values or help analysts visualize the data.

When you're working to generate a predictive analytics model, avoid tailoring your model to fit your data sample perfectly. Such a model will fail — miserably — to predict similar yet varying datasets outside the data sample. Fitting a model too closely to a particular data sample is a classic mistake called *overfitting*.

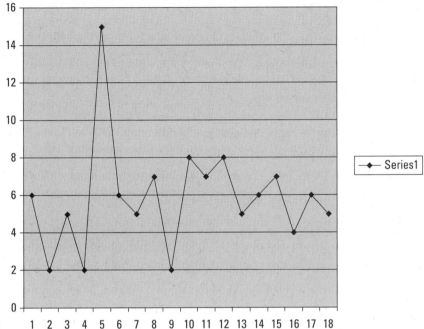

The woes of overfitting

In essence, overfitting a model is what happens when you overtrain the model to represent only your sample data — which isn't a good representation of the data as a whole. Without a more realistic dataset to go on, the model can then be plagued with errors and risks when it goes operational — and the consequences to your business can be serious.

Overfitting a model is a common trap because people want to create models that work — and so are tempted to keep tweaking variables and parameters until the model performs perfectly — on too little data. To err is human. Fortunately, it's also human to create realistic solutions.

To avoid overfitting your model to your sample dataset, be sure to have a body of test data available that's separate from your sample data. Then you can measure the performance of your model independently before making the model operational. Thus one general safeguard against overfitting is to divide your data to two parts: training data and test data. The model's performance against the test data will tell you a lot about whether the model is ready for the real world.

Another best practice is to make sure that your data represents the larger population of the domain you're modeling for. All an overtrained model knows is the specific features of the sample dataset it's trained for. If you train the model only on (say) snowshoe sales in winter, don't be surprised if it fails miserably when it's run again on data from any other season.

Avoiding overfitting

It's worth repeating: Too much tweaking of the model is apt to result in overfitting. One such tweak is including too many variables in the analysis. Keep those variables to a minimum. Only include variables that you see as absolutely necessary — those you believe will make a significant difference to the outcome. This insight only comes from intimate knowledge of the business domain you're in. That's where the expertise of domain experts can help keep you from falling into the trap of overfitting.

Here's a checklist of best practices to help you avoid overfitting your model:

- ✔ Chose a dataset to work with that is representative of the population as a whole.
- ✔ Divide your dataset to two parts: training data and test data.
- ✔ Keep the variables analyzed to a healthy minimum for the task at hand.
- ✔ Enlist the help of domain knowledge experts.

In the stock market, for example, a classic analytical technique is *back-testing* — running a model against historical data to look for the best trading strategy. Suppose that, after running his new model against data generated by a recent bull market, and tweaking the number of variables used in his analysis, the analyst creates what looks like an optimal trading strategy — one that would yield the highest returns *if* he could go back and trade only during the year that produced the test data. Unfortunately, he can't. If he tries to apply that model in a current bear market, look out below: He'll incur losses by applying a model too optimized for a narrow period of time and set of conditions that don't fit current realities. (So much for hypothetical profits.) The model worked only for that vanished bull market because it was overtrained, bearing the earmarks of the context that produced the sample data — complete with its specifics, outliers, and shortcomings. All the circumstances surrounding that dataset probably won't be repeated in the future, or in a true representation of the whole population — but they all showed up in the overfitted model.

If a model's output is too accurate, consider that a hint to take a closer look. Enlist the help of domain knowledge experts to see whether your results really are too good to be true, and run that model on more test data for further comparisons.

Keeping the assumptions to a minimum

In spite of everything we've all been told about assumptions causing trouble, a few assumptions remain at the core of any predictive analytics model. Those assumptions show up in the variables selected and considered in the analysis — and those variables directly affect the accuracy of the final model's output. Therefore your wisest precaution at the outset is to identify which assumptions matter most to your model — and to keep them at an absolute minimum.

Creating a predictive model that works well in the real world requires an intimate knowledge of the business. Your model starts out knowing only the sample data — in practical terms, almost nothing. So start small and keep on enhancing the model as necessary. Probing possible questions and scenarios can lead to key discoveries and/or can shed more light on the factors at play in the real world. This process can identify the core variables that could affect the outcome of the analysis. In a systematic approach to predictive analysis, this phase — exploring "what-if" scenarios — is especially interesting and useful. Here's where you change the model inputs to measure the effects of one variable or another on the output of the model; what you're really testing is its forecasting capability.

Improving the model's assumptions — by testing how they affect the model's output, probing to see how sensitive the model is to them, and paring them down to the minimum — will help you guide the model toward a more reliable predictive capability. Before you can optimize your model, you have to know the *predictive variables* — features that have a direct impact on its output.

You can derive those decision variables by running multiple simulations of your model — while changing a few parameters with each run — and recording the results, especially the accuracy of the model's forecasts. Usually you can trace variations in accuracy back to the specific parameters you changed.

At this point, the twenty-first century can turn to the fourteenth for help. William of Ockham, an English Franciscan friar and scholastic philosopher who lived in the 1300s, developed the research principle we know as Occam's Razor: You should cut away unnecessary assumptions until your theory has as few of them as possible. Then it's likeliest to be true.

Too many assumptions weigh down your model's forecasts with uncertainties and inaccuracies. Eliminating unnecessary variables leads to a more robust model, but it's not easy to decide which variables to include in the analysis — and those decisions directly affect the performance of the model.

But here's where the analyst can run into a dilemma: Including unnecessary factors can skew or distort the output of the model, but excluding a relevant variable leaves the model incomplete. So when it comes time to select those all-important decision variables, call in your domain knowledge experts. When you have an accurate, reality-based set of decision variables, you don't have to make too many assumptions — and the result can be fewer errors in your predictive model.

Analysis Challenges

Predictive modeling is gaining popularity as a tool for managing many aspects of business. Ensuring that data analysis is done right will boost confidence in the models employed — which, in turn, can generate the needed buy-in for predictive analytics to become part of your organization's standard toolkit.

Perhaps this increased popularity comes from the ways in which a predictive analytics project can support decision-making by creating models that describe datasets, discover possible new patterns and trends (as indicated by the data), and predict outcomes with greater reliability.

To accomplish this goal, a predictive analytics project must deliver a model that best fits the data by selecting the decision variables correctly and efficiently. Some vital questions must be answered en route to that goal:

- What are the minimum assumptions and decision variables that enable the model to best fit the data?
- How does the model under construction compare to other applicable models?
- What criteria are best for evaluating and scoring this model?

Once again, you can call the voice of experience to the rescue: Domain knowledge experts can discuss these questions, interpret any results that show hidden patterns in the data, and help verify and validate the model's output. Their can also help you navigate the tricky aspects of predictive analytics described in the upcoming sections of this chapter.

Supervised analytics

In *supervised analytics,* both input and preferred output are part of the training data. The model is presented with the correct results as part of its learning process. Such supervised learning assumes pre-classified examples: The goal is to get the model learn from the previously known classification so it can correctly label the next unknown data point based on what it has learned.

When the model's training is complete, a mathematical function is inferred by examining the training data. That function will be used to label new data points.

For this approach to work correctly, the training data — along with the test data — must be carefully selected. The trained model should be able to predict the correct label for a new data point quickly and precisely, based on the data type(s) the model has seen in the training data.

Supervised analytics offer some distinct advantages:

✔ The analyst is in charge of the process.

✔ Labeling is based on known classifications.

✔ Labeling errors can be easily resolved.

The flip side of these advantages is an equally distinct set of potential disadvantages:

✔ Any mistakes at the training phase will be reinforced later on.

✔ The classification provided by the analyst may not describe the whole population adequately.

✔ The model may be unable to detect classes that deviate from the original training set.

✔ The assumption that the clusters within the data don't overlap — and that they can easily be separated — may not prove valid.

Relying on only one analysis

As you probably guessed, predictive analytics is not a one-size-fits-all activity — nor are its results once-and-for-all. For the technique to work correctly, you have to apply it again and again over time — so you'll need an overall approach that fits your business well. The success of your predictive analytics project depends on multiple factors:

✔ The nature of your data

✔ The nature of your business and its culture

✔ The availability of the in-house expertise

✔ Access to appropriate analytical tools

The approach you choose will influence the model's output, the process of analyzing its results, and the interpretation of its forecasts. And choosing an approach is no walk in the park. There are many things that can go wrong, many traps that you can fall into, and misleading paths you can take.

Happily, you can defend against these pitfalls by adopting a couple of wise practices early on:

- ✔ **Continuously test the results of your predictive analytics model.** Don't rely on the results of one single analysis; instead, run multiple analyses in parallel — and compare their outcome.

- ✔ **Run, test, compare, and evaluate multiple models and their outcomes.** Use as many simulations as you can, and check as many permutations as you can. Some limitations in your data can only come to light when you compare the results you get from your model to those you get from other models. Then you can assess the impact of each model's results vis-à-vis your business objectives.

Use multiple models to identify as many relevant patterns as possible in your data.

Describing the limitations of the model

Any predictive analytic model has certain limitations based on the algorithms it employs and the dataset it runs on. You should be aware of those limitations and make them work to your advantage; those related to the algorithms include

- ✔ Whether the data has nonlinear patterns (does not form a line)
- ✔ How highly correlated the variables are (statistical relationships between features)
- ✔ Whether the variables are independent (no relationships between features)
- ✔ Whether the scope of the sample data makes the model prone to overfitting (as described earlier in this chapter)

To overcome the limitations of your model, use sound *cross-validation* techniques to test your models. Start by dividing your data into training and test datasets, and run the model against each of those datasets separately to evaluate and score the predictions of the model.

Testing and evaluating your model

No model can produce 100-percent accurate forecasts; any model has the potential to produce inaccurate results. Be on the lookout for any significant variation between the forecasts your model produces and the observed data — especially if the model's outputs contradict common sense. If it looks too good, bad, or extreme to be true, then it probably isn't true (to reality, anyway).

In the evaluation process, thoroughly examine the outputs of the models you're testing and compare them to the input variables. Your model's forecast capability should answer all stated business goals that drove its creation in the first place.

If errors or biases crop up in your model's output, try tracing them back to

✔ The validity, reliability, and relative seasonality of the data

✔ Assumptions used in the model

✔ Variables that were included or excluded in the analysis

Work with business users to evaluate every step of your model's process; make sure that the model outputs can be easily interpreted and used in a real-world business situation. Balance the accuracy and reliability of the model with how easily the model's outputs can be interpreted and put to practical use.

Avoiding non-scalable models

When you're building a model, always keep scalability in mind. Always check the performance, accuracy, and reliability of the model at various scales. Your model should be able to change its scale — and scale up as big as necessary — without falling apart or outputting bad predictions.

Scalability was quite a challenge in the past. Predictive models took a long time to build and to run. The datasets the models ran on were small, and the data was expensive to collect, store, and search. But that was all in the "pre-big data" era.

Today big data is cheap, plentiful, and growing. In fact, another potential problem looms: The formidable data volume currently available may negatively affect the model and degrade its performance, outdating the model in a relatively short period of time. Properly implemented, scalability can help "future-proof" your model.

The future isn't the only threat. Even in the present online era, streamed data can overwhelm a model — especially if the streams of data increase to a flood.

Data volume alone can cause the decision variables and predicting factors to grow to giant numbers that require continuous updating to the model. So yes, your model had better be scalable — rapidly scalable.

Scoring your predictions accurately

When analyzing the quality of a predictive model, you'll want to measure its accuracy. The more accurate a forecast the model makes, the more useful it is to the business, which is an indication of its quality. This is all good — except for when the predicted event is rare. In such case, the high accuracy of the predictive model may be meaningless.

For example if the probably of rare event to occur is 5 percent, a model that simply answers "no" all the time when asked whether the rare event has occurred would be right 95 percent of the time. But how useful would such a model be? Thus, if your business must deal routinely with rare events (if such a thing is possible), don't rely on accuracy alone as a measure of your model's reliability.

In such a case, you can evaluate the efficacy and the quality of a predictive model in the light of the how likely the rare event is to take place. A useful metric to follow is to specify which types of errors you can accept from the model and which you cannot.

Here's a quick list of other ways to evaluate your model:

- ✔ Check to see whether the model's output meets your evaluation criteria.
- ✔ Devise a testing strategy so you can test your model repeatedly and consistently.
- ✔ Measure how well the model meets the business goals for which it was built.
- ✔ Assess the risks of deploying the model live.

Help stamp out overfitting. When building a predictive model, keep in mind that your dataset is only a sample of the whole population. There will always be unknown factors that your data cannot account for, no matter what.

- ✔ Approach the analysis of your predictive model with care, starting with this quick checklist:
- ✔ Prepare your data with the utmost diligence before using it to train your model.
- ✔ Carefully consider outliers before including or excluding them.
- ✔ Remain vigilant in repeated testing and evaluation.
- ✔ Cross-check sample data and test data to steer away from overfitting.
- ✔ Consult your domain knowledge experts often and appropriately.

Chapter 16

Targeting Big Data

· ·

· ·

A t a broad level, *big data* is the mass of data generated on the Internet at every moment. It includes — for openers — data emerging in real time from

✔ Online social networks such as Facebook

✔ Micro-blogs such as Twitter

✔ Online customer-transaction data

✔ Climate data gathered from sensors

✔ GPS locations for every device equipped with GPS

✔ User queries on search engines such as Google

And that list barely scratches the surface; think of big data as a growing worldwide layer of data. What to do with it all? Answer: Start by using predictive analytics as a means to extract valuable information from the mass of big data, find patterns in the data, and predict future outcomes.

Here's a familiar example: You might have noticed ads appearing on websites while you're browsing that "just happen" to mention products that you already intended to buy. No magic at work here; the sites that show such ads are utilizing predictive analytics to *data-mine* (dig up insights from) big data: Your buying patterns leave a trail of valuable data online; the well-targeted ad shows that someone is using that data.

This chapter shows you how predictive analytics can crack the big-data nut and extract the nutmeat. First we guide you through a number of trends in the predictive analytics market — in particular, predictive analytics as a service — that offer significant applications for businesses. You're also introduced to some aspects of predictive analytics and how it can be used to tame big data:

✔ Utilize big data to predict future outcomes

✔ Explore predictive analytics as a service

✔ Apply free, open-source tools to fuse, and make use of data from different sources

✔ Prepare for building a predictive analytics model

✔ Build and test a proof-of-concept predictive analytics model

Major Technological Trends in Predictive Analytics

Traditional analytical techniques can only provide insights on the basis of historical data. Your data — both past and incoming — can provide you with a reliable predictor that can help you make better decisions to achieve your business goals. The tool for accomplishing that goal is predictive analytics.

Companies that adopt and apply this tool extensively are looking not only for insights, but also for usable *forward-looking insights* from multiple sources of data. Using a wide range of data, companies want to predict their customer's next action before it occurs, to predict marketing failures, detect fraud, or predict the likelihood that future business decisions will succeed.

Exploring predictive analytics as a service

As the use of predictive analytics has become more common and widespread, an emerging trend is (understandably) toward greater ease of use. Arguably the easiest way to use predictive analytics is as software — whether as a standalone product or as a cloud-based service provided by a company whose business is providing predictive analytics solutions for other companies.

If your company's business is to offer predictive analytics, you can provide that capability in two major ways:

✔ **As a standalone software application with an easy-to-use graphical user interface:** The customer buys the predictive analytics product and uses it to build customized predictive models.

✔ **As a cloud-based set of software tools that help the user choose a predictive model to use:** The customer applies the tools to fulfill the requirements and specifications of the project at hand, and the type of data that the model will be applied to. The tools can offer predictions quickly, without involving the client in the workings of the algorithms in use or the data management involved. These services don't require that the user have prior knowledge of the inner workings of the provided models and services. Cloud-based services allow for third-party integration with no need for client interaction, and also offer a marketplace for other services.

A simple example can be as straightforward as these three steps:

1. A client uploads data to your servers, or chooses data that already resides in the cloud.

2. The customer applies some of the available predictive model to that data.

3. The customer reviews visualized insights and predictions from the results of the analysis or service.

Aggregating distributed data for analysis

A growing trend is to apply predictive analytics to data gathered from diverse sources. Deploying a typical predictive analytics solution in a distributed environment requires collecting data — sometimes big data — from different sources; an approach that must rely on data management capabilities. Data needs to be collected, pre-processed, and managed *before* it can be considered usable for generating actionable predictions.

The architects of predictive analytics solutions must always face the problem of how to collect and process data from different data sources. Consider, for example, a company that wants to predict the success of a business decision that affects one of its products by evaluating one of the following options:

✔ To put company resources into increasing the sales volume

✔ To terminate manufacture of the product

✔ To change the current sales strategy for the product

The predictive analytics architect must engineer a model that helps the company make this decision, using data about the product from different departments (as illustrated in Figure 16-1):

✔ **Technical data:** The engineering department has data about the product's specifications, its lifecycle, and the resources and time needed to produce it.

✔ **Sales data:** The sales department has information about the product's sales volume, the number of sales per region, and profits generated by those sales.

✔ **Customer data from surveys, reviews, and posts:** The company may have no dedicated department that analyzes how customers feel about the product. Tools exist, however, that can automatically analyze data posted online and extract the attitudes of authors, speakers, or customers toward a topic, a phenomenon, or (in this case) a product. The process is known as *sentiment analysis* or *opinion mining*.

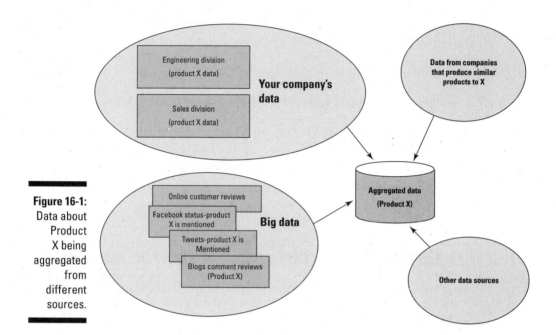

Figure 16-1:
Data about
Product
X being
aggregated
from
different
sources.

For instance, if a user posts a review about Product X that says, "I really like Product X and I'm happy with the price," a *sentiment extractor* automatically labels this comment as positive. Such tools can classify responses as "happy," "sad," "angry," and so on, basing the classification on the words that an author uses in text posted online. In the case of Product X, the predictive analytics solution would need to aggregate customer reviews from external sources (such as social networks and micro-blogs) with data derived from internal company sources.

Figure 16-1 shows such an aggregation of data from multiple sources, both internal and external — from the engineering and sales divisions (internal), and from customer reviews gleaned from social networks (external) — which is also an instance of using big data in predictive analytics. A standard tool that can be used for such aggregation is Hadoop — a big-data framework that enables building predictive analytics solutions from different sources. (More about Hadoop in the next section.)

Real-time data-driven analytics

Delivering insights as new events occur in real time is a challenging task because so much is happening so fast. Modern high-speed processing has shifted the quest for business insight away from traditional data warehousing and toward real-time processing. But the volume of data is also high — a tremendous amount of varied data, from multiple sources, generated constantly and at different speeds. Companies are eager for scalable predictive analytics solutions that can derive real-time insights from a flood of data that seems to carry "the world and all it contains."

The demand is intensifying for analyzing data in real time *and* generating predictions quickly. Consider the real-life example (mentioned earlier in this chapter) of encountering an online ad placement that corresponds to a purchase you were already about to make. Companies are interested in predictive analytics solutions that can provide such capabilities as the following:

✔ Predict — in real time — the specific ad that a site visitor would most likely click (an approach called *real-time ad placement*).

✔ Speculate accurately on which customers are about to quit a service or product in order to target those customers with a retention campaign (*customer retention and churn modeling*).

✔ Identify voters who can be influenced through a specific communication strategy such as a home visit, TV ad, phone call, or e-mail. (You can imagine the impact on political campaigning.)

In addition to encouraging buying and voting along desired lines, real-time predictive analytics can serve as a critical tool for the automatic detection of cyber-attacks. For example, RSA — a well-known American computer and network security company — has recently adopted predictive analytics and big-data visualization as part of a web-threat detection solution. The tool analyzes a large number of websites and web users' activities to predict, detect, visualize, and score (rate) cyber-threats such as denial-of-service attacks and malicious web activities such as online banking fraud.

Applying Open-Source Tools to Big Data

This section highlights two Apache projects that are important and relevant to big data. The most important one of all is Apache Hadoop, a framework that allows storing and processing various datasets using parallel processing on a cluster of computers bundled together. The other project is Mahout, which consists of a set of libraries that provide implementations of important data-mining and machine-learning algorithms.

Apache Hadoop

Apache Hadoop is a free, open-source software platform for writing and running applications that process a large amount of data. It enables a distributed parallel processing of large datasets generated from different sources. Essentially, it's a powerful tool for storing and processing big data.

Hadoop stores any type of data, structured or unstructured, from different sources — and then aggregates that data in nearly any way you want. Hadoop handles heterogeneous data using distributed parallel processing — which makes it a very efficient framework to use in analytic software dealing with big data. No wonder some large companies are adopting Hadoop, including Facebook, Yahoo!, Google, IBM, Twitter, and LinkedIn.

Before Hadoop, companies were unable to take advantage of big data, which was not analyzed and almost unusable. The cost to store that data in a proprietary relational database and create a structured format around it did not justify the benefits of analyzing that data and making use of it. Hadoop, on the other hand, is making that task seamless — at a fraction of the cost — allowing companies to find valuable insights in the abundant data they have acquired and are accumulating.

The power of Hadoop lies in handling different types — in fact, any type — of data: text, speech, e-mails, photos, posts, tweets, you name it. Hadoop takes care of aggregating this data, in all its variety, and provides you with the ability to query all of the data at your convenience. You don't have to build a schema before you can make sense of your data; Hadoop allows you to query that data in its original format.

In addition to handling large amounts of varied data, Hadoop is fault-tolerant, using simple programs that handle the scheduling of the processing distributed over multiple machines. These programs can detect hardware failure and divert a task to another running machine. This arrangement enables Hadoop to deliver high availability, regardless of hardware failure.

Hadoop uses two main components (subprojects) to do its job: MapReduce and Hadoop Distributed File System. The two components work co-operatively:

- **MapReduce:** Hadoop's implementation of MapReduce is based on Google's research on programming models to process large datasets by dividing them into small blocks of tasks. MapReduce uses distributed algorithms, on a group of computers in a cluster, to process large datasets. It consists of two functions:

  - **The** `Map ( )` **function** which resides on the master *node* (networked computer). It divides the input query or task into smaller subtasks, which it then distributes to *worker nodes* that process the smaller tasks and pass the answers back to the master node. The subtasks are run in parallel on multiple computers.

  - **The** `Reduce ( )` **function** collects the results of all the subtasks and combines them to produce an aggregated final result — which it returns as the answer to the original big query.

- **Hadoop Distributed File System (HDFS):** HDFS replicates the data blocks that reside on other computers in your data center (to ensure reliability) and manages the transfer of data to the various parts of your distributed system.

Consider a database of two billion people, and assume you want to compute the number of social friends of Mr. X and arrange them according to their geographical locations. That's a tall order. The data for two billion people could originate in widely different sources such as social networks, e-mail contact address lists, posts, tweets, browsing histories — and that's just for openers. Hadoop can aggregate this huge, diverse mass of data so you can investigate it with a simple query.

You would use MapReduce programming capabilities to solve this query. Defining Map and Reduce procedures makes even this large dataset manageable. Using the tools that the Hadoop framework offers, you would create a MapReduce implementation that would do the computation as two subtasks:

✔ Compute the average number of social friends of Mr. X.

✔ Arrange Mr. X's friends by geographical location.

Your MapReduce implementation program would run these subtasks in parallel, manage communication between the subtasks, and assemble the results. Out of two billion people, you would know who Mr. X's online friends are.

Hadoop provides a range of Map processors; which one(s) you select will depend on your infrastructure. Each of your processors will handle a certain number of records. Suppose, for example, that each processor handles one million data records. Each processor executes a Map procedure that produces multiple records of key-value pairs <G, N> where G (key) is the geographical location a person (country) and N (value) is the number of contacts the person has.

Suppose each Map processor produces many pairs of the form `<key, value>`, such as the following:

Processor Map#1: `<France, 45>`

Processor Map#2: `<Morocco, 23>`

Processor Map#3: `<USA, 334>`

Processor Map#4: `<Morocco, 443>`

Processor Map#5: `<France, 8>`

Processor Map#6: `<Morocco, 44>`

In the Reduce phase, Hadoop assigns a task to a certain number of processors: Execute the Reduce procedure that aggregates the values of the same keys to produce a final result. For this example the Reduce implementation sums up the count of values for each key — geographical location. So, after the Map phase, the Reduce phase produces the following:

`<Morocco, 23+44+443=510>` ------→ `<Morocco, 510>`

`<France, 8+45=53>`----→ `<France, 53>`

Clearly, Mr. X is a popular guy — but this was a very simple example of how MapReduce can be used. Imagine you're dealing with a large dataset where you want to perform complex operations such as clustering billions of documents as mentioned in Chapter 6 where the operation and the data is just too big for a single machine to handle. Hadoop is the tool to consider.

Apache Mahout

Another open-source tool that is uniquely useful in predictive analytics is Apache Mahout. This machine-learning library includes large-scale versions of the clustering, classification, collaborative filtering, and other data-mining algorithms that can support a large-scale predictive analytics model. A highly recommended way to process the data needed for such a model is to run Mahout in a system that's already running Hadoop (see the previous section). Hadoop designates a master machine that orchestrates the other machines (such as Map machines and Reduce machines) employed in its distributed processing. Mahout should be installed on that master machine.

Imagine you have a large amount of streamed data — Google news articles — and you would like to cluster by topic, using one of the clustering algorithms mentioned in Chapter 6. After you install Hadoop and Mahout, you can execute one of the algorithms — such as K-means — on your data.

The implementation of K-means under Mahout uses a MapReduce approach, which makes it different from the normal implementation of K-means (described earlier in Chapter 6). Mahout subdivides the K-means algorithm into these sub-procedures:

- **KmeansMapper** reads the input dataset and will assign each input point to its nearest initially selected means (cluster representatives).

- **KmeansCombiner** procedure will take all the records — <key, value> pairs — produced by KmeansMapper and produces partial sums to ease the calculation of the subsequent cluster representatives.

- **KmeansReducer** receives the values produced by all the subtasks (combiners) to calculate the actual centroids of the clusters which is the final output of K-means.

- **KmeansDriver** handles the iterations of the process until all clusters have converged. The output of a given iteration, a partial clustering output, is used as the input for the next iteration. The process of mapping and reducing the dataset until the assignment of records and clusters show no further changes. (For more about K-means, see Chapter 6.)

Apache Mahout is a recently developed project; its functionality still has a lot of space to accommodate extensions. In the meantime, Mahout already uses MapReduce to implement classification, clustering, and other machine-learning techniques — and can do so on a large scale.

Building a Rapid Prototype of Your Predictive Analytics Model

This section addresses briefly the steps needed to build a prototype for a proof-of-concept predictive model. (For more details on how to build a predictive model, refer to Chapters 8 to 11.)

Prototyping for predictive analytics

A good model needs a prototype as proof of concept. To build a prototype for your predictive analytics model, start by defining a potential *use case* (a scenario drawn from the typical operations of your business) that illustrates the need for predictive analytics.

Fitting the model to the type of decision

Business decisions take diverse forms. As you undertake to build a predictive analytics model, you're concerned with two main types of decision:

- ✔ **Strategic decisions** are often not well defined, and focus only on the big picture. Strategic decisions have an impact on the long-term performance of your company — and correlate directly with your company's mission and objectives. Senior managers are usually the ones who make strategic decisions.

- ✔ **Operational decisions** focus on specific answers to existing problems and define specific future actions. Operational decisions usually don't require a manager's approval, although they generally have a standard set of guidelines for the decision-makers to reference.

The two classes of decisions require different predictive analytics models. For instance, the chief financial officer of a bank might use predictive analytics to gauge broad trends in the banking industry that require a company-wide response (strategic). A clerk in the same bank might use a predictive analytic model to determine credit-worthiness of a particular customer who is requesting a loan (operational).

With these two major types of decisions in mind, you can identify colleagues at your company who make either operational or strategic decisions. Then you can determine which type of decision is most in need of predictive analytics — and design an appropriate prototype for your model.

Defining the problem for the model to address

The basic objective of a predictive analytics model is make your business do better. You may find that a prototype of your model will work best if you apply it to operational examples and then link those results to solving broad, high-level business issues. Here is a list of general steps to follow next:

1. Focus on the operational decisions at your company that can have a major impact on a business process.

2. Select those processes that have a direct effect on overall profitability and efficiency.

3. Conduct one-to-one interviews with the decision-makers whose support you want to cultivate for your project. Ask about

    • The process they go through to make decisions.

    • The data they use to make decisions.

    • How predictive analytics would help them make the right decisions.

4. Analyze the stories you gathered from the interviews, looking for insights that clearly define the problem you're trying to solve.

5. Pick one story that defines a problem of a small enough scope that your prototype model should be able to address it.

    For instance, suppose you interviewed a marketing specialist who is struggling to decide which customers to send a specific product ad. He or she has a limited budget for the ad campaign, and needs to have high confidence in the decision. If predictive analytics could help focus the campaign and generate the needed confidence, then you have an appropriate problem for your prototype to address.

Defining your objectives

An effective way to state your business objectives clearly is as a bulleted list of user decisions. Then run your prototype to generate predictions and scores for each possible decision. For instance, in the earlier example of Product X, you could list your objectives as a range of possible business decisions to be assessed:

✔ Increase the sales volume of Product X

✔ Terminate manufacture of Product X

✔ Change the marketing strategy behind Product X

    • Increase ads in a specific geographical location

    • Increase ads for specific customers

The predictive model will evaluate these decisions according to their future likelihood of successful profitability. The output might indicate, for example, that the company has an 80-percent chance of increasing profit by increasing the sales volume of Product X.

Find the right data

After you've clearly stated the business objective and the problem you're willing to tackle, the next step is to collect the data that your predictive model will use. In this phase, you have to identify your data source(s).

For instance, if you're developing a prototype for predicting the right decision on a specific product, then you need to gather both internal and external data for that product. You should not restrict the type or source of data, as long as it's relevant to the business goal.

If (say) your company is considering the introduction of a new hybrid sports car, you can contact the sales department and gather information about the sales data generated by similar products. You can contact the engineering department to find out how much the components cost (how about those longer-lasting batteries?), as well as the resources and time needed to produce the product (any retooling needed?). You might also include data about previous decisions made about a similar product (say, an overpowered convertible introduced some years ago), and their outcome (market conditions and fuel prices depressed sales).

You might want to consider using big data related to the product in question. For instance, download customer reviews about company products, tweets or Facebook posts where the products are mentioned. One way to do that is to use application programming interfaces (APIs) provided by those companies. For instance, if you want to gather tweets that contain a specific word, Twitter provides a set of APIs that you could use to download such tweets. There's a limit to how much data you can capture free of charge; in some cases, you might have to pay to keep downloading the needed data from Twitter.

When you've determined the most relevant data and the most useful source from which to get it, start storing the data you intend to use for your predictive model. Data may need to undergo some preprocessing, for which you'd use techniques mentioned in Chapter 9.

Design your model

For a prototype, your input could be a data matrix (see Chapter 6) that represents known factors derived from historical data.

Such a data matrix, when analyzed, can produce output that looks something like this:

> 57.6 percent of customers stated they were unhappy with the product.
>
> The product requires three hours on average to produce.
>
> Positive sentiment on the product is 80 percent.

Inputs to the prototype model could include historical data about similar products, the corresponding decisions made about them, and the impact of those decisions on your business processes. The prototype's output would be predictions and their corresponding scores as possible actions toward attaining the objectives you've set.

To get a usable prototype, you have to employ a mixture of techniques to build the model. For instance, you could use K-means algorithm as one of the clustering algorithms; you could use it to build clusters like these:

✔ Products that were terminated — and that decision's impact on profit

✔ Products that were increased in volume and that decision's impact on profit

✔ Products whose marketing strategy was changed and that decision's impact profit

Then you could use classification algorithms such as a decision tree or Naïve Bayes (see Chapter 7) that would classify or predict missing values (such as sales profit value) for the product in question (Product X).

Testing your predictive analytics model

This section introduces testing your model by using a test dataset that's similar to your training dataset. (See Chapter 10 for more on testing and evaluating your model.)

Identify your test data

To evaluate your predictive analytics model, you have to run the model over some test data that it hasn't seen yet. You could run the model over several historical datasets as input and record how many of the model's predictions turn out correct.

Run the model on test data

Evaluating your predictive model is an iterative process — essentially trial and error. Effective models rarely result from a mere first test. If your predictive model produces 100-percent accuracy, consider that result too good to be true; suspect something wrong with your data or your algorithms. For instance, if the first algorithm you use to build your prototype is the Naïve Bayes classifier and you're not satisfied with the predictions it gives you when you run the test data, try another algorithm such as the Nearest Neighbor classifier (see Chapter 6). Keep running other algorithms until you find the one that's most consistently and reliably predictive.

During the testing, you might find out that you need to revisit the initial data that you used to build the prototype model. You might need to find more relevant data for your analysis.

As a precaution, always verify that the steps involved in building the model are correct. In addition, comparing the output of the model on the test dataset to the actual results will help you evaluate the accuracy of your model.

The higher the confidence in the results of your predictive model, the easier it is for the stakeholders to approve its deployment.

To make sure that your model is accurate, you need to evaluate whether the model meets its business objectives. Domain experts can help you interpret the results of your model.

Part V
The Part of Tens

In this part . . .

- ✔ Important selling features
- ✔ Simple steps
- ✔ Visit `www.dummies.com` for great Dummies content online.

Chapter 17

Ten Reasons to Implement Predictive Analytics

*B*usiness competition is fierce and global, which leads companies to employ everything in their power to survive and thrive. In such an environment, companies are seeking to increase their revenues while keeping the operating cost to a minimum.

Predictive analytics is a business enabler that helps accomplish the very essence of increasing companies' return on investments. If implemented successfully, it will drive your company's profits higher. It will help you turn your data into valuable information you can capitalize on, and it will give you the competitive edge you need to outperform your competition.

Predictive analytics enables companies to use the massive data they've accumulated from their operations as refined resource to advance their businesses. Financial institutions, for example, were early adopters of predictive analytics, using it to boost their odds in successfully outperforming the market and market-participants. Other sectors of business are catching up by adopting predictive analytics programs to make industry-specific improvements in operations and strategy.

Outlining Business Goals

Predictive analytics can help you solve many business problems more effectively, but the crucial step toward that advantage is to identify specific business goals so you can choose the appropriate analytical tools to achieve them.

The process is twofold: The business goals you define help you build your predictive analytics project, and the completed model helps you measure how successfully your company is moving toward the goals. At the heart of this process is the development of your predictive model by running real data — both historical and incoming — against it.

Predictive analytics can effectively align the wealth of information acquired through business operations and data mining with business goals. Once the business goals are defined, the next step is to formulate a clear mission statement that fits the predictive model into the broader company vision.

Set project goals that you can accomplish in a relatively short timeframe and can measure — concrete steps toward the company's general vision and overall mission. Depending on your current strategies and which phase of market development your business is in, your business goals may change — which is why it's important to evaluate your project goals periodically and adjust them accordingly. Here are examples:

- ✔ If you're after increasing your customer base, then your predictive analytics model should help you run targeted marketing campaigns to acquire new customers.

- ✔ If you want to reduce the operational costs of your business, your predictive analytics model should help you balance the workload across departments, efficiently distribute resources, skills, and raw material, and accurately predict product demand.

- ✔ If you seek to identify fraud, then the model should be designed to rapidly and accurately evaluate whether a transaction is fraudulent — and react accordingly.

Industries that already use predictive analytics to detect fraud include healthcare, finance, and insurance.

Knowing Your Data

The quality of your predictive models is dependent on the quality and relevance of your data. Predictive analytics explores your data through well-defined algorithms and techniques, mines the data, searches for hidden patterns or trends you were unaware of, and uncovers valuable facts about your business. But you have to feed good data to the model to make that happen.

Data can be a big driver of predictive analytics. To ensure that your data is the best resource possible, your organization needs to know

- ✔ What data is needed for a given analysis
- ✔ Where the data resides
- ✔ How to put the data to use in the analytic model
- ✔ How the model's predictions can empower the business

Volume of data is no substitute for relevance; you want your data to have ample history. It should span enough of an extended period of time that you can track changes and spot any marked seasonality in your business.

Poor data quality — generally incomplete or irrelevant data — can skew your predictions' results and lead to much wasted energy and work by your experts to distinguish between real patterns and false signals and noise in the data.

Knowing your data will lead to better predictive analytics. Fortunately, establishing a predictive analytics project will lead to better knowledge of your data; one feeds into the other. The model helps you improve the quality of the data; the better the data, the more useful the predictions. The better the predictions, the better you know your data. In the course of that process, the output of your model helps you uncover relationships within your data that you were unaware of — giving you a much firmer foundation from which to embark on the predictive analytics journey.

Organizing Your Data

Transforming your data into knowledge — and transforming that knowledge into actionable decisions — is the core promise of predictive analytics.

Consider your data as a resource to be refined. Data residing in your databases, text documents, and other data sources is not yet ready for use in a predictive analytics project. Raw data will need to undergo extraction, cleaning, and transformation before the model can use it to create useful predictions.

It's important to clean your data of any errors, inconsistencies, and missing values. And ensure it has enough records, spans an extended period of time, and comprises all the necessary fields required by the analysis.

In addition to historical data, however, your predictive model needs some up-to-date input, and you may need to derive data from existing data points. To analyze and evaluate a stock's performance, for example, you might calculate a 200-day moving average of the stock price.

Preprocessing your data is a prerequisite for modeling data analytics; so is sampling your datasets. You'll need at least two datasets:

- ✔ A *training dataset* on which to run your experiments while you're building your model. This dataset usually comprises historical data with known inputs and outputs.

- ✔ A *testing dataset* consisting of data that the model has not seen before. This dataset helps you avoid overfitting the model to the training dataset. (See Chapter 15 for more about overfitting.)

Organizing your data is more of a challenge when the data comes from multiple sources. It's essential to closely examine each data source for quality and relevance. If you've reached the point at which clearly stated business goals drive a decision to create a predictive model to accomplish the goals, a close look into all data sources is mandatory. You have to evaluate how (even whether) those data sources can contribute to the success of your analytics project.

When data is coming in from multiple sources, data integration and consolidation is crucial to the success of your model. Modelers need one pooled, cleansed dataset that is ready to be used in their modeling project.

Satisfying Your Customers

Global competition drives companies to lower prices to attract new customers. Companies strive to please their customers and gain new ones; customers increasingly demand high-quality products at cheaper prices. In response to these pressures, businesses strive to deliver the right balance of quality and price, at the right time, through the right medium, to the people most likely to buy.

Customers' experience of a product, if publicized through the power of the Internet — essentially a vast medium of communications — can make or break a business. Businesses that use predictive analytics can take advantage of the data they have to better understand their customers — to increase positive customer experiences while reaching out to attract new customers.

The Internet is a two-way street; companies have been gathering valuable information about their customers through transactional data that includes

- ✔ Counting the number of items bought by customers

- ✔ Tracking methods of payment used

- ✔ Identifying customers' demographics

- ✔ Collecting customers' responses to filled-out surveys

To complete the picture, other sources of information come from business operations — for example, the amount of time customers spend on the company websites and the customers' browsing histories.

All that data can be combined and analyzed to answer some important questions:

- ✔ What are the demographics of your customers?
- ✔ What drives the sales of your products?
- ✔ How can your business improve the customer experience?
- ✔ How can you retain existing customers and attract new customers?
- ✔ What would your customers like to buy next?
- ✔ What can you recommend to a particular customer?

Any information that can shed light about how customers think and feel can bring insight to understanding them and anticipating their needs. Such insight has a direct impact on creating marketing campaigns. It helps shape the message of those campaigns and keeps them on target. Analyzing that data, businesses can provide their customers with personalized experiences, serve them better, and attract prospective new customers.

Such are the practical goals of predictive analytics. Guiding the pursuit of these goals with the company mission in mind will help your business and guide you every step of the way — from data collection about customers to data analysis, providing you with insights about your customers allowing you to make relevant recommendations to them, and identify potentially wayward customers whom your company will have to make a special effort to retain.

Predictive analytics can also help improve your customers' experience by enhancing such processes as these:

- ✔ Creating successful marketing campaigns
- ✔ Building programs to reward customers' loyalty
- ✔ Building recommender systems
- ✔ Reducing operational costs
- ✔ Delivering relevant service and products to your customers

Predictive analytics can also help you focus on identifying significant segments within your customer base — and make accurate predictions about their future behaviors. It can allow you to offer relevant products to them with competitive prices, build targeted marketing campaigns, and enable you develop strategies to retain your customers and attract new ones.

Many online businesses use predictive analytics to manage customer relations. They harvest information about their customers, identify attributes that are the best predictors of customer behaviors, and use that information to make recommendations in real time. The result is that their customers get specialized and personalized service and attention, from marketing and cross-selling to customer retention.

Reducing Operational Costs

Predictive analytics is an effective tool for more than customer management. It can help you reduce cost in many ways and at different levels of the organization — planning resources, increasing customer retention, managing inventories, and that's just for openers.

Predictive analytics is especially useful for reducing operational costs in these areas:

- ✔ Balancing the workload across departments

- ✔ Waging only targeted marketing campaigns

- ✔ Effectively allocating available skills and raw materials

- ✔ Accurately estimating demand for your products

- ✔ Positioning your products correctly in the pricing war waged by the competition

- ✔ Purchasing raw materials and hedging against market fluctuations

- ✔ Producing better forecasts of your inventory needs and efficiently managing resources

There is a dollar value associated with every task performed in a company. If you can save here and there, you'll end up substantially reducing your operational costs — which can have dramatic effect on the bottom line.

Predictive models can reduce operational costs by helping you decide when to make new orders, when to increase your marketing campaigns, as well as how to correctly price your products, manage inventories, and obtain a clear view (and a solid grasp) of your supply-and-demand chains.

By making more accurate decisions that correctly anticipate your business needs, you gain an advantage over businesses that manage their operations as a guessing game.

Increasing Returns on Investments (ROI)

Predictive analytics can help you increase return on investment (ROI) through

- ✔ Targeted marketing campaigns

- ✔ Improved risk assessment and management

- ✔ Reducing operational costs

- ✔ Making actionable decisions

By implementing predictive analytics, companies can accurately assess the present state of the business, optimize their operations, and compete more effectively in gaining market share. By scoring the predictive outcomes of future events, and using that information to their advantage, companies can improve their revenue and enhance the business performance as a whole. Deploying successful predictive models can help companies minimize risk and increase revenue across the board.

When embarking on your predictive analytics projects, be sure to document everything meticulously and methodically. It's equally important to establish a baseline before launching so you can accurately measure the ROI after the launch. You can calculate the improvement in ROI by measuring the enhancements of business processes and the improvement to the overall production as a result of implementing predictive analytics.

Automating predictive analytics and extending it to all areas of business are two important and strategic ways to increase ROI. Sharing and co-ordinating the results of predictive analytics conducted by any one department with results obtained by other departments increases the benefits of those analytical projects. Among the different departments, synergies emerge that you can capitalize on.

Increasing the number of successful business decisions always leads to better performance. Informed decisions — backed up with accurate predictive scores — increase the confidence of management in decisions that resulted from deploying predictive analytics models. Better decision-making, on the basis of more accurate information, is the core of predictive analytics.

The more those models are deployed and used, the more relevant they become — and the more they contribute to the success of the business. Successful models, run long and often, can provide a consistent increase in longer-term ROI.

Increasing Confidence

Predictive analytics enables businesses to make smarter decisions, some of which take place in real time. It allows businesses to improve all aspects of decision-making — including confidence in decisions based on insights derived from the in-depth analysis of trusted information.

Predictive analytics helps your organization predict future events with confidence and make optimal decisions to improve business outcomes. It automatically gives your organization an edge over competitors who are still using guesswork to manage their operations.

Predictive analytics models can evaluate complex scenarios and make real-time decisions quickly — and more accurately — in anticipating your business needs. The more such results accumulate, the more you boost confidence in the model and its predictive capability.

Real-time systems that employ predictive models can now make trades on your behalf, offer or deny credits, detect intrusions and threats, flag fraudulent transactions, identify adverse events, and recommend the products most relevant to specific groups of consumers. Any and all such operations can become not only more accurate, but automatic.

The automation of this decision-making, backed by thorough testing and refined by feedback from operational deployment, allows for greater consistency of those decisions that require precision. The effect is to avoid the subjective analysis or emotional attachment that can often lead to biased decisions.

Deriving actionable information from the use of analytics promotes faster response to rapidly changing business environments and external conditions. This process empowers your business with the agility to better position itself, taking advantage of emergent business opportunities while managing risks and reducing costs.

Companies that adopt predictive analytics undergo a cultural change that affects every area of the business. Making more informed decisions provides them with the confidence necessary to adopt those decisions and develop better strategic plans. The larger result is that they become more efficient, increase their profitability, and position themselves to play a more competitive role in the marketplace.

Making Informed Decisions

Predictive analytics, properly developed and applied, turns your data into key insights, and enables you to take action by making informed decisions about many areas of your business — based on extensive data. Greater accuracy in predicting future events is an advantage unto itself — in part because it can be applied to so many areas.

Sometimes the ultimate objective of a predictive model is the automation of certain business decisions. An example is an automated trading system that places real-time trades on your behalf, manages your portfolio (money and assets) and any financial leverage you may have. The goal is to make the best decision as quickly as possible — automatically — taking into consideration the many complex factors that affect money management in response to existing market dynamics.

Business can also use predictive analytics to build a model that analyzes various aspects of not only a particular decision, but also its aftermath and possible scenarios — and then suggest the optimal decision for the circumstances.

Models' outputs can help a company make decisions affecting many aspects of the business, from supply-chain management to identifying opportunities and budgeting.

Companies use predictive analytics models to identify effective strategies that are effective and optimized to handle future events automatically, their actions guided by strategies based on knowledge acquired from thorough and exhaustive analysis.

A functioning predictive model can lead to making informed decisions guided by data analysis. If the model does its job well, its results are reinforced through testing — and validated by the feedback generated in response to its deployment. Then, when faced with new events, the business can rely on models that were built to handle them — especially if the events are unprecedented and unfolding in real time.

Gaining Competitive Edge

Making decisions with confidence based on predictive analytics models can provide your business with an edge over the competition by enabling you to

- ✔ Exploit new opportunities
- ✔ Navigate hidden risks
- ✔ Create a better customer experience
- ✔ Recommend best choices for your customers
- ✔ Quickly adapt to a changing business environment
- ✔ Reduce operational costs

Accumulating data is not enough in itself. Mining that data to extract insightful information, uncover hidden patterns and relationships in that data and making informed decisions will enable you create competitive advantages for your business.

With real-time predictive analytics, businesses can take full advantage of opportunities as they arise and steer away from any unforeseen risks. It's about acting correctly, quickly, and seamlessly.

Predictive analytics can also play an important role in your planning, giving you the agility you need to stay ahead of your competitors. You can no longer afford to rely only on past experience and executives' intuitions to run your business. Instead, predictive analytics can help you turn your wealth of data into a wealth of actionable insights and informed decisions (some of them made in real time).

Improving the Business

Predictive analytics can free your company from taking a scattershot approach to improving performance by boosting various areas of the business:

- Targeted marketing campaigns
- Increased cross-selling
- Retention and acquisition of customers
- Agility in the planning process
- Inventory management
- Accurate risk calculation
- Effective resource allocation

Companies use analytical models at various scales that range from better understanding customers' needs — and anticipating their actions — to automating their business processes and forging better strategic predictions of future opportunities.

Because predictive analytics models can also improve the reliability of business data and the agility of responses to emergent conditions, companies see a range of improvements:

- Better, more accurate business decisions
- Better understanding of internal business processes and external market conditions
- Better management of customer relations
- Better, faster response to real-time windows of opportunity

Chapter 18

Ten Steps to Build a Predictive Analytic Model

*T*his chapter discusses best practices in building predictive analytics models. You'll get a handle on the importance of defining the business objectives early on — and on getting the leaders of your business to champion your project.

We cover the importance of preparing the data that will be used for the project, highlight some tips to follow, and help you refine your data to avoid that old bugbear of business computing, "garbage in, garbage out." We address how to build deployable models, outline how to test and evaluate them, and offer guidance on how to monitor them once they go operational — as well as retrain them if necessary.

We also lay out these vital principles for building a successful predictive model:

✔ Put the right analytical team in place.

✔ Provide your team with relevant and accurate data.

✔ Let your team build the model iteratively, establishing quick victories early in the process.

Lastly, we address organizational support: To get your predictive analytics model up and running, you have to ensure that the business leaders will take actionable decisions based on the insights they can get from the model. To this end, we offer hints on fostering an organizational culture that embraces the value of predictive analytics and understands the advantage of turning data patterns into actionable decisions.

Building a Predictive Analytics Team

To assemble your predictive analytics team, you'll need to recruit business analysts, data scientists, and information technologists. Regardless of their particular areas of expertise, your team members should be curious, engaged, motivated, and excited to dig as deep as necessary to make the project — and the business — succeed.

Getting business expertise on board

Business analysts serve as your domain experts (see Chapter 15): They provide the business-based perspective on which problems to solve — and give valuable insight on all business-related questions. Their experience and domain knowledge give them an intuitive savvy about what approaches might or might not work, on where to start and what to look at to get something going.

A model is only as relevant as the questions you use it to answer. Solid knowledge of your specific business can start you off in the right direction; use your experts' perspectives to determine:

- ✔ What are the right questions? (Which aspects of your business do you want predictive analytics to improve?)

- ✔ What is the right data to include in the analysis? (Should your focus be on the efficiency of your business processes? The demographics of your customers? Which body of data stands out as the most critical?)

- ✔ Who are the business stakeholders and how can they benefit from the insights gained from your predictive analytics project?

The success of a predictive analytics project requires clear understanding of the business objectives you're trying to address. They also require a broader perspective and analysis from different angles and point of views that can affect the business objective. Accordingly, your team should be inclusive and broad in its nature; it should have members from key departments and across business lines.

Hiring analytical team members who understand your line of business will help you focus the building of your predictive analytics solutions on the desired business outcomes.

Firing up IT and math expertise

Data scientists can play an important role linking together the worlds of business and data to the technology and algorithms while following well-established methodologies that are proven to be successful. They have a big say in developing the actual models and their views will affect the outcome of your whole project. This role will require expertise in statistics such as knowledge of regression/non-regression analysis and cluster analysis. (*Regression analysis* is a statistical method that investigates the relationships between variables.) The role also requires the ability to correctly choose the right technical solutions for the business problem and the ability to articulate the business value of the outcome to the stakeholders.

Your data scientists should possess knowledge of advanced algorithms and techniques such as machine learning, data mining, and natural language processing.

Then you need IT experts to apply technical expertise to the implementation, monitoring, maintenance, and administration of the needed IT systems. Their job is to make sure the actual computer network and database work smoothly together.

When data scientists have selected the appropriate techniques, then (together with IT experts) they can oversee the overall design of the system's architecture, and improve its performance in response to different environments and different volumes of data.

Problem-solving and creativity are essential skills to look for when you're doing the hiring. Hire talents with different backgrounds and complementary skills — and then give them the freedom to explore possibilities and create solutions for you.

In addition to the usual suspects — business experts, math and statistical modelers, and computer scientists — you may want to spice up your team with specialists from other disciplines such as physics, psychology, philosophy, or liberal arts to generate fresh ideas and new perspectives.

Setting the Business Objectives

To give your predictive analytics project its best shot at success, be sure to set out specific business goals right from the start. Is the company adding to its product line? Targeting new customers? Changing its overall business model? Whatever the major focus is, pay particular attention to how your project will make a positive impact on the bottom line. This practical perspective will help you get your stakeholders to champion your project — which in turn generates the confidence you need to go forward.

When embarking on a predictive analytical project, getting business stakeholders involved from the outset is wise: They'll help you define the business goals at the beginning, and having this early stake in your project will encourage them to collaborate with you on the later stages of the project as well.

In the early phase of the project, your analytics team should gather relevant business information by meeting with the stakeholders to understand and record their business needs — and their take on the issues that the project is expected to solve. The stakeholders' domain knowledge and firsthand insights can

- ✔ Help the team evaluate possible solutions
- ✔ Identify attainable, quantifiable business objectives
- ✔ Provide a practical perspective for prioritizing the project's goals

A successful planning phase boosts the overall success of the project — and helps the team develop a coherent predictive analytics strategy to implement later.

Preparing Your Data

This step in building your predictive analytics project is as crucial as it is unavoidably time-consuming and tedious: data preparation. The actual needed steps vary from one project to the other; they depend on the initial state of your data and the requirements for your project.

You'll need to outline a strategy on how to handle these common data issues:

- ✔ What variables do you need to include in the analysis?
- ✔ How will you check the correctness of certain field values?
- ✔ How do you handle missing values in your data?

✔ Will you include or exclude outliers?

✔ Will you normalize some fields? Which ones?

✔ Will you need to derive new variables from the existing data?

✔ Will you need to include third-party data?

✔ Does your data comprise enough records and variables?

After you examine your data thoroughly in light of these questions, you can begin the process of transforming the data so the model can use it in the expected format. This process involves sampling the data, checking it for consistent quality, and refining that quality by using the data to test a series of project iterations.

Sampling Your Data

To ensure that you can accurately measure the performance of the predictive analytics model you're building, separate your historical business data into training and test datasets:

✔ **The training dataset:** This dataset comprises the majority (about 70 percent) of the data. You'll use it to train the predictive model.

✔ **The test dataset:** This is a smaller percentage (about 30 percent) of the data, used to test and measure the model's performance. It's an independent set of data that the model has not yet seen.

The goal is to make the performance of the model on your test data serve as a preview of how the model will perform when it goes live.

Splitting historical data into training and test datasets helps protect against overfitting the model to the training data. (See Chapter 15 for more about overfitting.) You want your model to identify true signals, patterns, and relationships, and to avoid any false ones that could be attributed to the noise within the data. The essence of overfitting is as follows: When a model is tuned to a specific dataset, there is a higher chance that any uncovered patterns are only true for that dataset; the same model may not perform as well on other datasets. Use your testing dataset to help eliminate these dataset-specific patterns (which are considered mostly noise), and your predictive model will become more accurate.

For better model development, make sure your training and test datasets are similar enough to each other to minimize inconsistencies in data quality, relevance, and time coverage. One common way to get a true representation of similar data in both datasets is to choose these data samples at random.

Use your test data to evaluate your model and measure the accuracy of its predictions. Your test dataset should provide a preview of how your model will actually perform in the production environment. A model that performs well against a test dataset will probably produce good results when it goes live.

Avoiding "Garbage In, Garbage Out"

More data does not necessarily mean better data. A successful predictive analytics project requires, first and foremost, relevant and accurate data.

Keeping it simple isn't stupid

If you're trying to address a complex business decision, you may have to develop equally complex models. Keep in mind, however, that an overly complex model may degrade the quality of those precious predictions you're after, making them more ambiguous. The simpler you keep your model, the more control you have over the quality of the model's outputs.

Limiting the complexity of the model depends on knowing what variables to select before you even start building it — and that consideration leads right back to the people with domain knowledge. Your business experts are your best source for insights into what variables have direct impact on the business problem you're trying to solve.

Use those insights to ensure that your training dataset includes most (if not all) the possible data that you expect the model to encounter in practice.

Data preparation puts the good stuff in

To ensure high data quality as a factor in the success of the model you're building, data preparation and cleaning can be of enormous help. When you're examining your data, pay special attention to

- Data that was automatically collected (for example, from web forms)
- Data that did not undergo thorough screening
- Data collected via a controlled process
- Data that may have out-of-range values, data-entry errors, and/or incorrect values

Common mistakes that lead to the dreaded "garbage in, garbage out" scenario include these classic goofs:

✔ Including more data than necessary

✔ Building more complex models than necessary

✔ Selecting bad predictor variables or features in your analysis

✔ Using data that lacks sufficient quality and relevance

Creating Quick Victories

Because building a predictive analytics model can be time-consuming and labor-intensive, your best chance is to start small and expand as you go, using an agile methodology. This means using an iterative approach: train, test, validate, and repeat. With each iteration, you incrementally increase scope. As you go, you apply what you learn to the project, and communicate your findings to stakeholders with each step.

An *iterative* approach to building the model — trying a version of the model, fine-tuning it in light of your results, and then trying the improved version — will allow you to evaluate the variables and algorithms used in your model, and choose those best suited to your final solution. Building your model iteratively may help you make some decisions and choices:

✔ Determining whether to include other data types

✔ Determining whether to aggregate some of the data fields

✔ Clearly identifying a rollout plan

✔ Identifying any data gaps early enough to improve the processes involved

✔ Evaluating your model's scalability for bigger transactions and larger volume of data

In general, starting small can allow you to tackle many challenges and address many issues early on — which can lead to a smoother rollout later on.

You can show the value of the analytics for your business by implementing a small pilot project and showing quick victories. Delivering a specific solution can bring you the buy-in necessary to build larger-scale solutions and more powerful models. Creating quick victories early in the process will allow you to understand pressing business questions, and when you provide solutions to those questions, you can reinforce the buy-in from the business stakeholders. Success breeds success — and it doesn't have to be overnight. By establishing a track record of success for your model, you can help foster the cultural change needed for a widespread adoption of predictive analytics within your organization.

Fostering Change in Your Organization

Impressive past performance does not guarantee an equally impressive future for an organization. It's not enough to look at how the business has been done thus far. Instead, organizations should look at how predictive analytics can transform the way they're doing business in response to a rapidly changing present environment. For that to happen, business leaders need a major shift in the way they think and operate the business.

Your predictive analytics project is a good place for them to start that shift.

Granted, the old guard — traditional business leaders who have been operating their businesses on gut feelings — may be close-minded at first, reluctant to adopt new technologies and trust the predictions and recommendations that come from them. This is especially true if an analytical system detects a major shift in trends — or a bigger crisis than anticipated — prompting the business leaders to distrust the system's recommendations and rely on historical analysis. If the business managers aren't willing to act on the recommendations of the predictive model, the project will fail.

Thus the iterative development of your model — and a clear demonstration of the pilot project — are vital to the wider success of predictive analytics in your company. Questioning old ways of doing business is the first step of critical and analytical work. The team may look at different experiences and lessons from competitors and other industries and evaluate the impact of adopting such measures in their line of business.

Creating cultural changes that promote the use of predictive analytics to drive business decisions is not only essential to the success of your project, but also — if you've built the model well — to the success of your business. You have to build not only a working model, but also an in-house culture that champions the use of predictive analytics as an aspect of business intelligence.

When you've demonstrated that your analytics program can guide the organization effectively toward achieving its business goals, be sure you clearly communicate — and widely publicize — those results within the organization. The idea is to increase awareness and buy-in for the program.

Educating stakeholders about the benefits of predictive analytics entails emphasizing the possible loss of both opportunities and competitive edge if this tool isn't developed and deployed. Maintaining focus on such business values can have a direct and positive impact on creating a cultural change that favors predictive analytics.

By highlighting the impact on the business and expressing the outcome of the analytical program in a language familiar to the business leaders, you're making predictive analytics more appealing to them — and (from their point of view) more transparent. Training analysts on the tools and techniques used with the analytical programs also facilitates the needed cultural change.

The process of educating and training may take time to bear fruit; most organizational changes require time to implement and to be adopted. Be sure you recruit business team members who have both an understanding of and experience in managing organizational change and developing internal communications strategy.

Building Deployable Models

Building a predictive model does not translate automatically into deploying that model into production. A model may successfully and accurately predict the next business outcome and still not be deployable. (An example would be a model that makes the right prediction, but takes longer to do so than the window of opportunity allows.) This limitation could be because of operational constraints such as complex processes, large datasets, or heterogeneous data environments that require tremendous effort to integrate. Other obstacles could include performance issues, or the sheer amount of time and data needed to make particular decisions.

In order to ensure a successful deployment of the predictive model you're building, you'll need to think about deployment very early on. The business stakeholders should have a say in what the final model looks like. Thus, at the beginning of the project, be sure your team discusses the required accuracy of the intended model and how best to interpret its results.

Data modelers should understand the business objectives the model is trying to achieve, and all team members should be familiar with the metrics against which the model will be judged. The idea is to make sure everyone is on the same page, working to achieve the same goals, and using the same metrics to evaluate the benefits of the model.

Keep in mind that the model's operational environment will undoubtedly be different from the development environment. The modelers have to know all the requirements needed for a successful deployment in production before they can build a model that will actually work on the production systems. Implementation constraints can become obstacles that come between the model and its deployment.

Understanding the limitations of your model is also critical to ensuring its success. Pay particular attention to these typical limitations:

- ✔ The time the model takes to run
- ✔ The data the model needs; sources, types, and volume
- ✔ The platform on which the model resides

Communication is an ongoing aspect of developing and deploying a predictive analytical model: You must ensure that the model's outputs are not only provided, but also correctly interpreted and clearly explained to the business stakeholders; the buy-in needed for operational deployment depends on it.

Ideally, the model has a higher chance of getting deployed if

- ✔ It uncovers some patterns within the data that were previously unknown.
- ✔ It can be easily interpreted by the business stakeholders.
- ✔ The newly uncovered patterns actually make sense businesswise and offer an operational advantage.

Evaluating Your Model

Your goal, of course, is to build an analytical model that can actually solve the business objectives it was built for. Expect to spend some time evaluating the accuracy of your model's predictions so as to prove its value to the decision-making process — and to the bottom line.

Evaluate your model from these two distinct angles:

- ✔ **Business:** The business analyst should evaluate the model's performance and the accuracy of its predictions in terms of how well they address business objectives. Are the insights derived from the model making it easier for you to make decisions? Are you spending more time or less time in meetings because of these new insights?

- ✔ **Technical:** The data scientists and IT professionals should evaluate the algorithms used and the statistical techniques and methods applied. Are the algorithms chosen optimal for the model's purpose? Are the insights being generated fast enough to produce actionable advantages?

Evaluating the model is essentially an ongoing process of re-examining the algorithms used, the data included, and the features selected for analysis — as well as by constantly monitoring the accuracy of the model's performance in a live systems and a real business environment.

In addition to closely examining the data used, selecting variables with the most predictive power, and the algorithms applied, the most critical test is to evaluate whether the model meets business needs and whether it adds value to the business.

Creating an actionable decision is the foremost criterion against which to judge the success of the model. If your organization can act on the output of the model and come out ahead, your model is a success.

Test your model in a test environment that closely resembles the production environment. Set the metrics to evaluate the success of the model at the beginning of the project. Specifying the metrics early makes the model easier to validate later on.

Updating Your Model

Successful deployment of the model in production is no time to relax. You'll need to closely monitor its accuracy and performance over time. A model tends to degrade over time; and a new infusion of energy is required from time to time to keep that model up and running. To stay successful, a model must be revisited and re-evaluated in light of new data and changing circumstances.

If conditions change so they no longer fit the model's original training, then you'll have to retrain the model to meet the new conditions. Such demanding new conditions include

- ✔ An overall change in the business objective
- ✔ The adoption of — and migration to — new and more powerful technology
- ✔ The emergence of new trends in the marketplace
- ✔ Evidence that the competition is catching up

Your strategic plan should include staying alert for any such emergent need to refresh your model and take it to the next level, but updating your model should be an ongoing process anyway. You'll keep on tweaking inputs and outputs, incorporating new data streams, retraining the model for the new conditions and continuously refining its outputs. Keep these goals in mind:

- ✔ Stay on top of changing conditions by retraining and testing the model regularly; enhance it whenever necessary.

- ✔ Monitor your model's accuracy to catch any degradation in its performance over time.

- ✔ Automate the monitoring of your model by developing customized applications that report and track the model's performance.

  Automated monitoring saves time and helps you avoid errors in tracking the model's performance.

Index

• *C* •

About the Authors

Dr. Anasse Bari holds a Ph.D. in computer science, with a focus on data mining, from the George Washington University. Dr. Bari is a Fulbright Scholar and is currently a visiting assistant professor of computer science at the School of Engineering and Applied Science of the George Washington University. Students voted him Computer Science Professor of the Year 2014.

Anasse has over eight years' of experience in large-scale software architecture and in designing and implementing software systems under different platforms for both the public and private sectors. Anasse recently worked at the World Bank Group Headquarters at the Poverty Reduction Group, and then at the Information Technology Solutions division where he was involved in a data analytics project. He was the recipient of the World Bank Spot award for his extraordinary efforts in service of the organization. While at the World Bank, he attended an executive program at Stanford University d.school — the Hasso Plattner Institute of Design.

His research has been focused on predictive analytics, data mining, biologically inspired knowledge discovery, and information retrieval. He is the author of several research publications published at peer-reviewed IEEE venues on data mining with practical applications in social network analytics, bioinformatics and text mining.

Anasse lives in Georgetown,Washington DC.

Mohamed Chaouchi has a master's degree in computer science from the George Washington University. He has over 14 years of experience in software development and project management in the public and private sectors.

He is an application architect and technical lead, responsible for building software applications with high business impact and visibility. His technical expertise includes service-oriented architecture, web services, and application security.

Mohamed has extensive experience working with management and IT leadership, participates in information technology governing boards, and represents his division at inter-organizational conferences.

Mohamed has conducted extensive research using predictive analytics and data mining in both the health and financial domains. He has published several papers in peer-reviewed journals in cancer research and ocean-data integration.

He is also an inventor of an issued patent for a data-mining platform to analyze cancer development.

Mohamed currently lives in Kensington, MD with his wife Jennifer and his son Zacharia.

Tommy Jung holds a bachelor's degree in computer science. He is an entrepreneur, investor, and consultant. He spends most of his time building software and analyzing data.

Tommy has over 14 years of professional experience in technology. In his previous job, he was the head of operations at UmeVoice, a company specializing in speech recognition and noise cancellation. He has played various roles inside the organization, including operations, engineering, and marketing. His expertise encompasses predictive analytics, data mining, natural language processing, web development, database marketing, search engine optimization, and search engine marketing.

While not working, Tommy enjoys playing chess face-to-face with his daughters, online with his friends, and sometimes elsewhere (he may pick up a game or two on a downtown bench). He currently lives in Silicon Valley with his wife and two young daughters.

Dedication

Dr. Anasse Bari: I dedicate this book to my parents Rachida Bargach and Ali Bari, and to my siblings Nima and Mounir Bari.

Mohamed Chaouchi: This book is dedicated to my wife, Jennifer, my son Zacharia, and my parents, Fatima El Bote and Mohamed Chaouchi.

Tommy Jung: This book is dedicated to my daughters, Tiffany and Victoria. To Tiffany, thanks for keeping me on track with my chapters and always thinking about me. To Victoria, thanks for keeping me company late at night (way past your bedtime!) and making me laugh.

Authors' Acknowledgments

We were able to write this book thanks to the help and support of the great people at John Wiley & Sons. Thank you to Susan Spilka for getting the conversation started. Thank you to our acquisition editor Amy Fandrei, whose idea it was to write this book, and for her guidance, support, and encouragement. We greatly appreciate the support and advice of our project editor, Pat O'Brien, who kept us on target throughout the writing of the book.

Thank you to Barry Childs-Helton for his valuable edits and for blending three writing styles into one voice, and to Dr. Smita Rajpal Kachroo for her technical review. We are grateful to Steve Hayes for helping us whenever we needed it. And thanks to all the other members of the Wiley team that we did not have direct contact with and who have helped produce this book.

Dr. Anasse Bari: My thanks and deepest appreciation goes to Professor Abdelghani Bellaachia of the George Washington University who introduced me to, and sparked my interest in, data mining since day one of my doctoral degree. His guidance and ingenuity has profoundly influenced me as a scientist. I would also like to thank Jennifer Fulton for providing invaluable insights and extensive revisions, and my friend Usayd Casewit for his helpful reviews. I would like to thank my dear friends, Elvina Kamalova, the Casewit family, Adil Abaz, and Amine Chergui, for their support.

I would also like to thank my co-authors (and friends) for their dedication and hard work that enabled us to meet all deadlines.

Mohamed Chaouchi: I would like to thank my beloved wife, Jennifer Fulton, for being my first sounding board, asking me great questions and providing invaluable suggestions. And my amazing son, Zacharia: you are my source of joy and my inspiration for everything!

I would like to also thank my co-authors (and friends) for their effort and commitment to this project.

Tommy Jung: I would like to thank my beautiful wife Jenine, and kids Tiffany and Victoria, for always making each day special. Without sharing each chapter of the book with you girls, the joy of writing would not be any fun. Without writing each chapter of our lives together as a family, life would not be as meaningful. Thank you for always being by my side and encouraging me to write, even when you didn't get to see much of me on some occasions.

I would like to thank my parents, Michael and Holly Jung, for always encouraging me to make a difference, to work hard, and to take on new challenges with open arms. I would like to thank my father and mother in-law, Jerry and Joellyn Gor, for always being there for us when we needed something — like spending time with my kids when I needed some extra time to do some writing. It's the greatest joy to see them bonding with my kids, their first grandkids.

I would like to thank my brother Jimmy Jung for his ideas and feedback. If he can understand what I wrote, then any dummy can (of course, we brothers *never* tease each other).

I'd like also to thank my co-authors (and friends) for being so easy to work with. It's always a pleasure to work with you guys in every capacity.

Publisher's Acknowledgments

Acquisitions Editor: Amy Fandrei

Project Editor: Pat O'Brien

Senior Copy Editor: Barry Childs-Helton

Technical Editor: Dr. Smita Rajpal Kachroo, Post Doctorate Fellow, University of Waterloo

Editorial Assistant: Anne Sullivan

Sr. Editorial Assistant: Cherie Case

Project Coordinator: Phillip Midkiff

Cover Image: ©iStockphoto.com/adventtr